A CRITICAL INTRODUCTION TO LAW

Second Edition

Wade Mansell, BA, LLB, LLM

Belinda Meteyard, MPhil

Alan Thomson, BA, LLB

of the University of Kent Law School

Cavendish
Publishing
Limited

London • Sydney

First published in Great Britain 1995 by Cavendish Publishing Limited, The Glass House, Wharton Street, London WC1X 9PX
Telephone: +44 (0) 20 7278 8000   Facsimile: +44 (0) 120 7278 8080
E-mail: info@cavendishpublishing.com
Visit our Home Page on http://www.cavendish publishing.com

First edition   1995
Reprinted   1995, 1997 and 1998
Second edition   1999

British Library Cataloguing in Publication Data

Mansell, Wade
A critical introduction to law. - 2nd ed.
1. Critical legal studies 2. Jurisprudence
I. Title II. Meteyard, Belinda III. Thomson, Alan
340.1'15

ISBN 1 85941 533 4

Printed and bound in Great Britain

Acknowledgments

The first edition of this book contained the following acknowledgments:

> 'This book is very much a product of the Kent Law School. That it fell to us to write it has both advantages and disadvantages. The advantage is that we have been able to resolve all intellectual disputes in our favour. The disadvantage is that the substantial contribution of many of our colleagues is less explicit than it should ideally have been. Because the book has been so long in gestation, it is difficult to remember with precision exactly who thought of what, when. To Paddy Ireland, Ian Grigg-Spall and Richard de Friend we offer our thanks and acknowledge their substantial and continuing contribution to the Introduction to Law course, out of which this book has emerged.
>
> We are very grateful to our colleagues in the Kent Law School and to students, past and present on the Introduction to Law course, who have contributed their ideas and given us their support, whilst the project of writing this book was in progress. Particular thanks to Anne Bottomley, Chad Broughton, Husam Hourani, Myra Loughney, Kendal Loughney, Rory Mates, Sue Mohan-Das, Sally Sheldon, Julia Sohrab and Paul Street for their help and encouragement. Thanks too to William Shaw, and especially to Joanne Scott who has provided vital help at crucial times.
>
> Derek Meteyard has been a constant source of reason and calmness regardless of the condition of the Whitstable sea which washes upon his shores. Sara Mansell has done so much more than her share of child care for her to doubt the good faith of Chapters 6, 7 and 8. She remains firmly of the view that parity ought to begin at home! Irene Thomson has given invaluable support when, over the years, some of the ideas in this book proved controversial and unpopular.
>
> Obviously, no three authors are ever agreed about everything but, in the interests of coherence, we have each suppressed our individual disagreements whilst hoping that enough of our differences remain visible to stimulate the argument and debate which are the very stuff of a critical approach.
>
> Credit for errors unfortunately remains with the authors.'

Since that was written, several people have moved, but our gratitude remains.

We are also grateful to our publishers who have elevated 'gentle badgering' to an art form.

Finally, and unfortunately, we must acknowledge a debt to Tony Blair's New Labour government. We had expected (hoped) that much of the critique in this book might become redundant with the defeat of the Conservatives. Instead, it seems to have received reinforcement.

Preface

Many law degrees offer a second or third year course in which students are encouraged to analyse the philosophical or political underpinnings of the law. Such a course will usually be optional and will attract only a small proportion of law students and those students who take the course will already have been immersed in, and possibly seduced by, the intricacies of legal reasoning. They will have grappled with the problem of reconciling cases and of accounting for the splitting of legal hairs. They may well have become adept at playing the legal game of chess. At that stage in their legal education, it may even be too late to introduce them to the idea that the rules of the game are not neutral and that groups of people are likely to be differentially affected by the outcome. Hence, the argument for an introductory law book which attempts to question common sense assumptions (or authoritative pronouncements) about law and about the relationship between law and society, even before the student has begun to 'think like a lawyer'.

One prevalent view amongst those contemplating a legal education is that law is a discrete object of study, clearly defined and labelled, with distinct boundaries and categories comprising a recognisable body of knowledge. Such a view has been strengthened by the setting up of Law Schools within the Universities and by the law's own claim to a distinctive logic and mode of reasoning and decision making. But, such a view takes for granted, and therefore leaves unanalysed, the ways in which law presents this discrete appearance.

The orthodoxy as to what must necessarily be in an introductory law book has traditionally included a description of the institutions of the law, an explanation of the methods of the law and some consideration of legal principles and rules. Such a format takes as real that which it describes, believes the objects of study to be obvious and unproblematic and, although various jurisprudential questions may be raised, most commonly about law and justice or law and morality, the true focus is upon law as an essentially discrete subject. Upon reflection, it can be argued that such an approach fundamentally misrepresents the very object of description. The legal system and all that it includes has only very limited meaning in terms such as these because, critically, a legal system has no function in itself but only as it plays a role in the society in which it exists.

Furthermore, there is a considerable danger that this approach may be not only limited but positively misleading because, in its assumptions about legal reality, it not only fails to discuss the role of law but actually colludes in the perpetuation of the legal myth of legal objectivity and political neutrality. Paradoxically, the apparent neutrality of the approach is in itself political because it reinforces ideas which are functional to a continuing uncritical acceptance of the apparently unproblematic need for, and role of, law. This is a likely result of any study of law which attempts to divorce the topic from questions of power and politics, and ignores the role of law in creating and maintaining a world in which liberal capitalism dictates the fortunes and misfortunes (and, perhaps, even the very ideology) of citizens. Unless the objective of legal study for the student is merely the ability to obtain financial reward, the objectives of the legal system are assumed rather than considered in much legal education. Most obviously, the implicitly accepted objectives of the legal system are order and perhaps social engineering. But, neither of these objectives is either unproblematic or apolitical and that they may appear to be so is significantly misleading. If these objectives are simply accepted, then this certainly reinforces one of the greatest strengths (the term is used neutrally) of the law; viz its ability to assert some sort of political neutrality which enables it to achieve political goals without political opposition. While it is trite to observe that statutes are merely policy in legal form, it is significant that policy may be resisted but the obligation to obey the law is generally accepted as being very nearly absolute.

An alternative approach to the study of law must begin by attempting to understand the role of law – and the role of the 'Rule of Law' – in the wider world rather than simply in its own terms. This requires consideration both of law as ideology and law as politics. Such an holistic approach carries within it considerable problems and is itself open to criticism in that what is revealed, it might be argued, is merely another, but not inherently superior, perspective on law and the legal system. Nevertheless, it does seem to provide some explanation of otherwise inexplicable phenomena and, most importantly, it carries within it a political critique of law's role in facilitating a capitalist world. Demystification is no longer seen by many as either as possible or as significant as it was once assumed to be, but it does have the considerable merit of addressing issues which, if regarded as unproblematic, reinforce a power structure to the considerable advantage of the already advantaged. Obviously, the premiss which underlies this approach in an introductory law book is no less political than that which underlies the more orthodox approach but, whereas the politics are hidden in one, they are manifest and explicit in the other. Furthermore, these revelations are not themselves prescriptive. Even if critique is accepted, political decisions remain to be made.

The crucial starting point for any study of law might not at first sight look like a study of law at all. This is, in itself, instructive because it reveals that the common sense of law is that it is about institutions, procedures and rules and many law students, actual and potential, will initially (and significantly) want to argue that any attempt at a sociological understanding of law is not 'real law' nor yet real legal study. Others will wish to argue that, without an understanding of those institutions, it is not possible to consider the role of law as politics or ideology. The second point is at least arguable, but here one is faced with a dilemma in that the more students internalise the reality of the law as institutions, procedures and rules, the more difficult it becomes to see these things not simply as social facts (which they are) but as contingent and socially constructed phenomena which have no natural role or even existence, but which have a function related both to the economic structure and the division of wealth within society and to the ideology of those with power within that society.

We would argue that the existence of this common sense about law is not the result of naivety but is an indication of law's capacity to present itself as neutral, at any rate to those who are relatively privileged in our society. And, it is this capacity which is one of the objects of analysis in this book. Feminist perspectives and anthropological and historical materials are all relevant in trying to pinpoint what is peculiar about law in our society, and the particular kind of order which law appears to reinforce and replicate. By looking at other societies and other periods in our own history, it is possible to see more clearly the ways in which law operates at the present time in western capitalist societies and the particular class and gender interests which it tends to prioritise.

This book therefore begins with a consideration of what the common sense of law is, proceeds to consider how this is constructed, and compares and contrasts the rule of law way of understanding the world with other systems of dispute resolution. We consider how it is that some interpretations are accepted as authoritative. This, in turn, leads to a consideration of gender and the law and the role of law in perpetuating sexual differences. In Chapters 9 and 10, we examine some implications of the 'rule of law organising principle' in an international setting and focus upon the problems posed by some fundamental legal concepts such as freedom and sanctity of contract, individual legal personality and private property, which have a deleterious effect when transported into the world of international finance where they have contributed to the situation in which, in the servicing of massive debts, the poorer populations of many countries are actually providing financial support for the richer nations. The penultimate chapter reassesses the notion of formal equality which underlies the rule of law.

The book has been written with the primary aim of making accessible to non-lawyers (including those starting out on a law degree) some of the crucial issues about law which we think should remain important throughout any course of legal study and which will also be relevant to anyone who wants an understanding of law. As a book written for students, and primarily for those beginning their study of law, it is designed simply to stimulate interest and discussion; to open up possibilities and in no sense to provide theoretical 'truths'. In keeping with this aim, it is at times deliberately provocative. The most obvious criticism which could be made is that we have oversimplified complex matters. If the result is that we have nevertheless provided ways of beginning to think about law, then simple clarity at the expense of complex opacity will have been a price worth paying.

Contents

1   The Common Sense of Law

The intention of this book is to persuade the reader to reconsider what is usually taken for granted and to question common sense assumptions about the law. There is an apocryphal story which well illustrates the central theme. A very new and very small sovereign state was admitted as a member of the United Nations in the 1970s. Within the United Nations, the formal position is that each sovereign state is equal and has one vote in the United Nations General Assembly, even though, beneath that technical equality, the usual hierarchy exists with the richest and most powerful states exerting the most influence. The newly appointed representative from the newly independent state did not initially grasp that the equality was supposed only to be formal. Consequently, he (or she) spoke at length on every topic which fell for debate to the obvious chagrin of the representatives of larger and greater states. At last, in considerable frustration, he was taken into the office of a delegate of one of the great states, upon the wall of which hung a large map of the world. The 'Important Delegate' explained to the unimportant new representative his position by showing the vast area of the map covered by such states as the US, Canada, Ghana, and even New Zealand, when compared with the tiny dots which represented the new delegate's country. The new delegate's immediate response was to ask a question – 'Who drew that map?'.

What we will try to do in this book is to keep asking that apparently naive question with reference to law. Hopefully, the law map we consequently construct will have as little in common with the orthodox map drafted by an endless stream of orthodox texts which purport to introduce the legal system as objective and as sensible, as the map which the new delegate might have designed. And, although that story might seem trite, we should at least be in a better position than before to recognise that it is the projection which inevitably distorts the image.

In this introductory chapter, we will consider briefly some of the themes and ideas which will be taken up later. If you are standing in a book shop skimming and trying to decide whether or not to buy the book, this chapter is for you. It should at least suggest why the approach we will follow is distinguishable from other introductory law texts you may already have perused.

Before doing that, however, there are two underlying premises of the book which should be made quite explicit. The premises are value judgments – that is, they are fundamental assumptions not capable of proof through reason. The first premiss is that knowledge has value even if it cannot be instantly (or ever) translated into earning capacity. This is a traditional assumption in education,

1

particularly in Universities at least in the Arts and Humanities and in Pure Mathematics, but it is not necessarily an assumption shared by those with power in governments, nor yet by law (or accounting) students. It is, however, a non-negotiable premiss for the book and, if it is not shared, there is little point in reading on. This book is promised not to make you rich. Even though it will do little for wealth, we hope, however, to show that such knowledge is not useless and its uses will appear in due course.

The second premiss of the book is that it continues to be better to be an unhappy Socrates than a happy pig. The clichéd old saying to the effect that if ignorance is bliss it is folly to be wise has no place in real education, even though it may be acceptable in training courses. Much of what we will be discussing is, at least in some senses, disturbing and even perhaps a little destabilising simply because much of what we will be discussing should challenge both preconceived ideas and common sense. What is required to enjoy this book is the ability to be surprised by the ordinary, and the ability to reassess what has been taken for granted. Not everybody will either want or be able to do this, and for those this book will probably be an irrelevance.

If, however, these premisses are acceptable, then the book does have the advantage of providing ways of thinking about the law. There is nothing which need be 'learnt' as opposed to understood. Those who respond to the ideas will make them their own.

Traditional introductory law texts do not always find these premisses necessary. Most such books begin with the assumption that the reader knows nothing of law and proceed to provide an introduction to the intricacies of statute law and common law; public law and private law; to the institutions of the law such as parliament, the courts, the professions, the police force, and prisons; and to the procedures, that is, the processes, by which law is made and cases handled. The reader is expected, at least apparently, to learn about these things looking neither to right nor to left because the introduction is intended to be the first stage in a process leading to the legal profession by which time the new recruit will be able to deal with the law and legal problems in an efficient and objective way. But, while the necessary knowledge has *apparently* been acquired looking neither to right nor to left, the argument we shall pursue is that nothing in law is without politics nor is apolitical. This does not of course mean 'political' in the sense of party politics (although that is often relevant) but rather political in the dictionary definition of 'being characterised by policy'. Indeed, one of the central questions we will in due course discuss is how it is that law comes to be seen as politically neutral law when so much of it begins life as party political policy. The first significant point of this chapter is that law is political.

We do not share the view that people who have not studied law know little about it. Almost every adult knows a great deal about law and is well equipped to talk about it and read about it, if not about its procedures and methods.

Actually (and this might seem paradoxical), it might be more possible to analyse law and the role of law at the very beginning of legal study, before becoming a part of the legal institution. It is not coincidental that many of the best novels and plays about law (that is, those which reveal things about law and lawyers) are written not by legal practitioners but by legal observers. Very often, the people least able to evaluate an institution, whether it be a family, a school, the police force, or even a university are the members of the institution itself. This is simply because (and this is a point which will be developed later) the members do in fact become institutionalised. They come to see through the eyes of the institution and lose distance and perspective in their vision.

This book will attempt to build upon the knowledge of the lay person in order to provide an 'external' description of the legal system and of the role of law in society generally, and in contemporary 'Rule of Law' societies particularly. In a sense, the intention is to provide an anthropological study of law in such societies.

The appreciation of law which it is anticipated lay readers will have is very briefly as follows. Many 'law consumers', as opposed to people directly involved in legal institutions, tend to think of law as something which maintains order in society and without which we would have massive disorder or anarchy, with no individual safe from violence or from threats to his or her own property. Without law, many people think Thomas Hobbes's famous 17th century quotation, 'In a state of nature man's life is nasty, brutish and short', would quickly prove to be true. It is difficult to get away from this common sense view simply because, from an early age, we become aware that this is common sense. The newspapers confirm it, the police confirm it, the government confirms it, *Lord of the Flies* confirms it. Law, we are taught, is what protects and preserves civilisation from chaos. We know what a state of lawlessness is; it is the antithesis of a society governed by law. And, if we think of situations of lawlessness, most of us tend to think of places such as Somalia, Kosovo, Angola, Sierra Leone, or perhaps even, until recently, Northern Ireland, in which, at least from the outside, no one seems secure in their person or their property.

Nevertheless, parenthetically, but importantly, one should observe that something more than law and laws are required to prevent lawlessness. This is a point well made by reference to the US where despite probably having more people per capita involved in legal institutions than anywhere else the crime figures and the imprisonment rate are much higher than in any comparable state. Thus, it is clearly not laws alone, or even law enforcement agencies, which ensure a peaceable kingdom. Nevertheless, a common assumption remains as a piece of common sense that without law we could not have order.

A second feature of law which most people would observe is that law also seems to be about coercion and force. Law means we *have* to do things. The police, the courts and the prisons may be used in order to deal with those people who disobey the rules. But, this notion of the law being about coercion, if necessary by the exercise of force, is only a partial feature of the law. It is not all force used by the 'forces of law and order' which we see as lawful force. Rather, though force seems to be an obvious aspect of law, only force which can be justified according to the rules is acceptable as 'legal'. The arbitrary use of force by the tyrant seems fundamentally different from the use of just, or legal, force. What must be shown is that the use of force was within the rules. If it was not, it was not legal force.

This feature of force justified by rules leads to the next prominent aspect of law in the common sense world; that of rules. We think of rules which are to be found in books and which tell us what we may or may not do. Many lay people characterise the job of lawyers as one of applying rules which they know, in order to determine legality and to ensure that actions conform to the rules. Although the rules may be slightly malleable, one of the great benefits of the Rule of Law is believed to be that the rules are always discoverable.

The idea of law as a body of rules discoverable in books points to a further feature of our legal system, and that is the separation of law from everyday life or social situations. The rules, or the laws, exist separately from the social situations they are called upon to resolve. Resolving disputes using the law is utterly different from resolving disputes without the law. Without using the law, a social dispute remains simply that, and all the social aspects of the dispute are arguable; or are 'at large' as a lawyer might say. In our own society, we see this clearly in many family disputes where there is no limit upon subjects open to discussion in a dispute. The law way of resolving disputes is very different. Many social facts become irrelevant because the law determines and circumscribes what is at issue. The selection of relevant facts is often a task for a lawyer and what is deemed relevant is not determined by the parties but by the law. Many clients express surprise when their solicitors explain to them what their dispute is 'really about'.

We have then a separation of law from society. While the law is in books, the problem is in the social world, and the law seems to exist already for disputes which appear in the social world. The implications of this will be explored further in due course but the point here is that for a dispute to become legal the social problem must be transformed into a legal problem.

Furthermore, the law takes on an existence of its own. Just as Muslims refer to the Quran and Hadith for rules, and the Jewish people use the Torah to find social rules with their sources claiming to reflect the will of God, so our laws found in books seem to have an authority of their own and seem to be more than simply person-made rules. Law has the appearance of having an independent existence; a life of its own apart from the world of politics and the social world and an established existence which is never more obvious than when one visits a law library.

Later, we will consider how it is that this separation arises and discuss its significance. It is the separation which also gives law one of its greatest

4

strengths. Often, if one asks why a law must be obeyed it is thought to be a sufficient answer to simply reply 'Because it is the law' without further justification. 'The law is the law' is not the tautology it might at first seem. As WH Auden puts it (1966):

'Law is as I've told you before
Law is as you know I suppose
Law is, but let me explain it once more
Law is the Law.'

To say 'The law is the law' conveys well the notion of the impropriety of not accepting and obeying law. The significance is brought out by a consideration of the way in which debates are changed when policy is transformed into law. (And, for those who believe that reason, not magic, governs our lives it is worth mentioning in passing how it *is* that policy becomes law. Explicit party political policy, subject to debate and opposition, transforms into law which must be obeyed, 'because it is the law', upon the signature of the Sovereign upon a piece of paper! This is a particularly powerful piece of magic. It is able to alter people's behaviour by a ritual culminating in the signed paper of the Sovereign!)

When policy becomes law, the possibility of opposition changes dramatically. Policy may be opposed. Law must be obeyed. There are a myriad of examples of this phenomenon. In the UK, the introduction of the poll tax (or the community charge as the government wished it to be euphemistically called) in the 1980s is a prime example. Although its introduction was bitterly opposed, according to the polls by a large majority of voters, nevertheless, once it became law, in spite of vehement argument, even those representatives in Parliament who had opposed it overwhelmingly took the view that the tax should be paid and not withheld.

Later in this book, we will analyse how and why it is that 'The law is the law' seems such obvious common sense. And, before the reader decides that it is so obviously right that law be obeyed that it is foolish to question it, it is worth remembering the case of South Africa where we have a state which, until the ending of apartheid, was utterly preoccupied with legality and absolutely blind to the suffering its laws perpetuated. Should the obligation to obey the law remain a value in such a situation?

The point about South Africa brings us to the final aspect of the common sense of law we will consider. In many ways, it is the most difficult, but most people would not be satisfied with a description of law which did not contain some mention of justice. Quite what justice is, however, is not easy. At one level, there is the personification of Justice as a blindfolded woman holding in one hand the scales of justice, and in the other the sword of justice, with the blindfold representing the suggestion that justice is blind to individuals. All are equal before the law. The sword represents the force which is available to enforce any judgment.

Much of our notion of justice depends upon this idea of equality and fairness between individuals but obviously, important though it is, formal equality cannot always be equated with substantive equality. To quote Judge Sturgess (1928), 'Justice is open to everybody in the same way as the Ritz Hotel'. This too we will consider further but the significant point here is that the justice inherent in the law as rules seems to derive from the fact that laws are *generalised*. They apply to all relevant individuals equally.

Thus, to summarise, we have, perhaps presumptuously, suggested that, as elements in our common sense description of law, we have first the idea that law is necessary for order; secondly, that law is about force and coercion, defining things which must and must not be done with the possible application of force in the event of disobedience (but not simply force but only lawful or legitimate force); thirdly, that law is about rules, and is a body of rules where the rules are discoverable and known and which are separate from, stand outside, and in some respects are superior to our ordinary social world (that is, legal rules are different from social rules and they have some independent existence irrespective of the will of individuals); fourthly, we have seen that there is a value in law itself which means that there is an obligation to obey some rules *because* they are law; and, finally, it has been suggested that law has something to do with justice in the sense of treating different individuals impartially.

We come now to the first difficult point. These notions of what law might be are not simply common sense. They are also ideological. By ideological we mean, at its narrowest in dictionary terms, 'the manner of thinking characteristic of a society a class or an individual', or rather more explicitly the suggestion is that our common sense of what law is about does not merely reflect the reality that is law but affects that reality too. Our common sense about what law is, is not common sense to many peoples in other societies as we shall see, and this is significant. While our common sense of law appears simply to observe reality, it is also *constitutive* of reality. Thus, law in our society is maintained in the form in which it is *because* of our perception of law, *because* of our common sense. Paradoxically, as we shall later see, this may be so even if our common sense of law can be shown not necessarily to correspond with what in fact happens.

But to return to the common sense of law. The aspects we have considered can all to some extent be subsumed within the concept of 'the Rule of Law'. The idea of the Rule of Law as it exists in many capitalist democracies has been regarded by most British writers since the 19th century as one of the most significant distinguishing features of British Government and the British Constitution in its protection of freedom. Such regard is well brought out by Charles Dickens in *Our Mutual Friend* (1976, pp 178–79), when one of his characters explains the benefit of the British Constitution although he might well have been speaking of the Rule of Law:

'"I merely referred", Mr Podsnap explained, with a sense of meritorious proprietorship, "to Our Constitution, Sir. We Englishmen are Very Proud of our Constitution, Sir. It Was Bestowed Upon Us By Providence. No Other Country is so Favoured as This Country".

"And ozer countries?" – the foreign gentleman was beginning, when Mr Podsnap put him right again.

"We do not say Ozer; we say Other: the letters are 'T' and 'H'; you say Tay and Aish, You Know;" (still with clemency). "The sound is 'th' – 'th!'"

"And other countries", said the foreign gentleman. "They do how?"

"They do, Sir," returned Mr Podsnap, gravely shaking his head; "they do – I am sorry to be obliged to say it – as they do."

"It was a little particular of Providence," said the foreign gentleman laughing; "for the frontier is not large."

"Undoubtedly," assented Mr Podsnap; "But So it is. It was the Charter of the Land. This island was Blest, Sir, to the Direct Exclusion of such Other Countries as – as there may happen to be. And if we were all Englishmen present, I would say," added Mr Podsnap, looking round upon his compatriots, and sounding solemnly with his theme, "that there is in the Englishman a combination of qualities, a modesty, an independence, a responsibility, a repose, combined with an absence of everything calculated to call a blush into the cheek of a young person, which one would seek in vain among the Nations of the Earth."

Having delivered this little summary, Mr Podsnap's face flushed, as he thought of the remote possibility of its being at all qualified by any prejudiced citizen of any other country; and, with his favourite right-arm flourish, he put the rest of Europe and the whole of Asia, Africa and America nowhere.'

Dickens was, of course, writing ironically but the views expressed are not inconsistent with such famous legal writers as Dicey, or with many of the views expressed by much of the judiciary in the 19th and 20th century. Since Dickens wrote, many more states have been fortunate enough (!) to partake of the Rule of Law.

Unfortunately, 'Rule of Law' is one of those phrases or words like 'democracy' and 'liberty' of which we are all in favour, at least until we try to define what we mean, and specify relevance and limitations.

In Wade and Bradley's classic *Constitutional and Administrative Law*, they bring out well the sense of the unopposable wisdom which seems to underlie the Rule of Law. As they say explicitly, 'the Rule of Law expresses a preference for law and order within a community rather than anarchy, warfare and constant strife' (Wade and Bradley, 1984, p 97). When expressed thus, who could fail to favour the Rule of Law? But is the alternative really as posed? Do societies so unenlightened as to have 'to do as they do' really all suffer anarchy, warfare and constant strife? Obviously, they do not, and later in the book we will look explicitly at some societies where the Rule of Law would seem a most peculiar and irrelevant way of organising the world. Most readers will realise that, even within Britain, the Rule of Law is a comparatively recent development attached to particular economic and political changes in society and that, prior to these changes, British society, for all its faults, could scarcely have been characterised as anarchy, warfare, or even constant strife.

And, if indeed the Rule of Law does express a preference for order as opposed to horrible alternatives, it also expresses a preference for one particular form of order – the form of order where order is produced by following a book of rules (or at least lots of books of rules). These books of rules also contain not merely the 'musts' and the 'must nots' but also allocate power to individual office holders, to state and official bodies, indeed even to the sovereign, and place limits upon those powers.

It is this idea of allocating power but limiting its exercise which is particularly distinctive of the Rule of Law (and a very good thing too, might be the most popular reaction). So that, as Wade and Bradley (1984) point out, the Rule of Law, at least theoretically, constrains the police in their methods of interrogation; it controls the use of power by local authorities; it provides for a presumption of innocence in criminal trials (though neither necessarily nor absolutely if one considers apartheid South Africa in the first case and such legislation as the British Prevention of Terrorism Act in the second).

More significant, perhaps, is the means by which freedoms are ensured under law and the way power is allocated and rights granted. All are treated as commodities, as *things;* things which may be allotted or withheld according to law. Power and freedom and rights are dispensed and guaranteed as property – things we can possess and own.

Obviously, this is one way of seeing such abstractions, but it is quite possible to think of them quite differently. Thus, freedom might not always be conceived of as a right to do something irrespective of the interests of the community. And, although the attraction of the Rule of Law lies in its ideas of liberty and equality before the law, the reality of substantive inequality does, perhaps, make it more difficult to accept notions of liberty and equality without qualification.

As everyone knows, while the figure of justice might be blindfold, this of itself certainly does not guarantee access to justice in the first place, and even when access is granted all parties are manifestly not equal. If they were, why would one party sometimes pay her legal advisers 10 times as much as another party? Clearly, if the advice and representation were always equal there would be little point in paying the higher fee. Yet, nobody would deny that, although the correlation is not absolute, better solicitors and better counsel do provide those they represent with better chances of success.

A final point to be made of the Rule of Law is that its focus is very clearly upon individuals and their individual freedoms. The rights and freedoms which are given, are given to individuals, and they will be upheld even against the wishes of an entire community. Not every society would immediately understand how this could be sensible; nor yet, indeed, even how it could be compatible with democracy which places such emphasis upon the theory of the will of the majority. To suggest that the Rule of Law exists to curb the very rights of that majority is not a wholly satisfactory answer.

The ideas inherent in the Rule of Law are then consistent with our common sense of our world, but the Rule of Law is at least as significant for what it conceals as for what it reveals. An obvious question which we shall pursue is how it is that the Rule of Law is able to proclaim itself as intimately concerned with equality while existing in societies which rejoice in their inequalities? (The rich certainly do anyway!) Not only does the Rule of Law ignore differences in wealth and poverty but it also ignores, or purports to, class, race and gender. Does it really make sense to speak of treating such unequal people equally? Is it even logically conceivable? And, yet, one of the great sustaining myths of our society is the Rule of Law, its preference for order, and its emphasis upon formal equality.

We shall turn in Chapter 2 to consider just what sort of order might be consistent with the Rule of Law.

2   Law, Order and Reality

At this point, it is appropriate to examine a little more clearly the assumption of Wade and Bradley and the common sense that law is the bastion of order in our society. Already, it has been suggested that there are other apparently reasonably stable societies whose stability does not seem to rest upon law. Before considering examples of such societies, it is necessary to try to define what we understand by 'order' in our society. Under what circumstances might we describe our society as in a state of order and under which in a state of disorder?

Everyone will have noticed that the language of politicians, policemen, and the media, is to speak of problems of law and order. The assumption is not only that law and order are linked and connected but, more particularly, that disorder is pathological and unacceptable. The common response is to call for its elimination, often by advocating stricter policing, harsher laws and stronger penalties. Many people believe that we live in a time of great disorder and lawlessness and consequently that it has been necessary to increase police person power consistently since the Second World War; that, notwithstanding this and increased expenditure upon police equipment and prisons, the crime rate continues to rise and outbreaks of disorder, whether caused by drunken urban or rural youths, disaffected urban minorities, feckless new age travellers, or even (in the past) vicious strikers, threaten the 'very fabric of our society'. The accepted, if implicit, premiss, is that disorder is disfunctional and pathological and that a central role for law lies in its control and elimination.

Many studies have in the past attempted to discover the source of this pathology and disorder; to explain why some individuals become criminals, why some individuals become insane, why some people become football hooligans, even why some people divorce, and even indeed why some people become or are homosexual. These studies have been directed to discovering why, at least as the inquirers saw it, individuals become deviant and pathological.

But, of course, two obvious points need to be made about such studies. The first is that what we understand as order is assumed to be unproblematic. Thus, order is seen as natural and desirable, and ordinary and normal. Order is what is labelled normal, disorder is what is labelled abnormal. Is this the case? A very different way of considering order is to suggest that it is the concept of order rather than that of disorder which is problematic. If, instead of asking why some individuals become criminals, why some become insane and why some become (or are born) gay, we ask instead why *everyone* is not a criminal, what defines most of us as sane, and why heterosexuality should be accepted as normal and homosexuality as deviant, and very different questions arise. The major question now becomes: 'Who drew the map which persuades us which questions to ask?' This makes it necessary that, in due course, we consider *why* it is that order is seen as unproblematic and how it is that our notions of order and normality have arisen.

A second related question has two aspects. First, who is able to define what is an ordered or normal situation and why? Secondly, is the same definition always given or does it depend upon the perspective of the observer? Thus, to take an obvious example from the past in the UK, if one considers the miners strike of 1984 and in particular the disorder caused (according to much of the media), by lawless miners, violent pickets, and their unruly supporters, the position seems clear. Yet, if one looks at the events from the miners' perspective things were very different. They perceived the police role as one intended to prevent the miners from being able to secure their jobs and communities by ensuring an effective and solid strike. From this perspective, it was the policing which threatened order.

It is clear that social order is not an absolute. Other societies experience neither order nor disorder as do we. Indeed, to many societies our society must seem basically and fundamentally *disordered,* and not least in its explicit preference for competition. Central to our economy is the idea that the most richly rewarded should be those who can successfully destroy their competitors. Even the idea that the most richly rewarded in society should be those who are most generously endowed with intelligence and privilege, which enables us to reward the 'leaders of industry' with an annual income in excess of £1,000,000 and a nurse with, perhaps, £17, 000, regardless of their actual needs, might not seem inherently ordered to an outside observer.

This relativity of what is ordered and what is disordered is nowhere more effectively brought out than in a quotation used by RD Laing in *The Politics of Experience* (1967, p 59) concerning a classroom experience:

> 'Boris had trouble reducing 12/16 to the lowest terms, and could only get as far as 6/8. The teacher asked him quietly if that was as far as he could reduce it. She suggested he "think". Much heaving up and down and waving of hands by the other children, all frantic to correct him. Boris pretty unhappy, probably mentally paralysed. The teacher quiet, patient, ignores the others and concentrates with look and voice on Boris. After a minute or two she turns to the class and says, "Well, who can tell Boris what the number is?" A forest of hands appears and the teacher calls Peggy. Peggy says that four may be divided into the numerator and the denominator.'

The observer comments:

> 'Boris's failure made it possible for Peggy to succeed; his misery is the occasion for her rejoicing. This is a standard condition of the contemporary American elementary school. To a Zuni, Hopi or Dakota Indian, Peggy's performance would seem cruel beyond belief, for competition, the wringing of success from somebody's failure, is a form of torture foreign to those non-competitive cultures.'

Order then is not an absolute. Its definition will vary both from society to society, and from group to group, and even perhaps, from individual to individual. Even the desirability of order is sometimes questioned.

In the film *The Third Man*, Harry Lime says in his parting speech:

'In Italy for thirty years under the Borgias they had warfare, terror, murder, bloodshed – they produced Michelangelo, Leonardo da Vinci and the Renaissance. In Switzerland they had brotherly love, five hundred years of democracy and peace and what did they produce? ... The cuckoo clock!'

Anyone who knows anything of the history of the period will know just how inaccurate that quotation is (apart from anything else, the cuckoo clock was apparently invented in South Germany), but the point of the quotation is not unimportant. It suggests that a dynamic and creative society might thrive on what can be seen as disorder, although whether a 'dynamic and creative' society is to be valued is quite a separate question.

More importantly, perhaps, we are suggesting that what might be described as disorder might depend upon the viewpoint of the observer, and, secondly, that what is described as disorder might be so described, or labelled, because it is in the interest of the person, or groups, so describing it, that it be accepted as disorder. These arguments do call into question not only Wade and Bradley's statement about the Rule of Law but also the commonly held belief that without law there would be little order.

While it is reasonably clear that no two societies will have the same perception of what constitutes order, what is more remarkable is that in every society there is a concept of order against which disorder appears destabilising, and threatening, and represents conflict which requires resolution. It is also significant that there seems to be a constant relationship between the social idea of order and the existing social (and political) order. It is unfortunate that 'order' has so many meanings but the suggestion is that there is a clear relationship between the *social idea of order* as peace, and calm, and lawfulness (if the society has law), together with a lack of conflict, and people doing what is expected of them; and the *social order* which is the way we are ordered in society – as in our society for instance as rich and poor, Lords and commoners, ladies and gentlemen, men and women, white collar and blue collar workers. Disorder is very often defined as challenges, whether direct or indirect, to the social order. (There is one qualification which it is necessary to make to all of the above. The word 'society' has been used in an unacceptably broad and imprecise way. Its use will be refined later but, for the moment, it is sufficient simply to be aware of the problem and to realise that very often when we speak of the needs of society, or the interests of society we are actually speaking not of society but of those with power in society.)

Thus, for example, in the UK, with its emphasis upon democracy and its acceptance of a liberal capitalist economic order, it is clear that *disorder* is

13

defined in relation to this order. Disorder is officially perceived (at its most trivial, that means perceived by the officials) as conflicts which threaten that order, whether directly by, for example, strikes or demonstrators refusing to obey the law, or indirectly perhaps by thieves who, in refusing to recognise and accept rights over things, threaten the property order.

That is probably obvious as long as one accepts the social and political order as unproblematic but a very important question immediately arises clearly related to our earlier qualification about the use of the word 'society'. That is: 'whose order is being maintained?' or rather the question might be more usefully put as: 'in whose interest is it that a particular order is maintained?' That question will always receive an answer which is specific to the time and place about which it is asked. Probably, all social orders serve the interests of persons or groups within society differently. Only very rarely do we observe societies where the order itself does *not* dictate that some members are likely to have a much easier existence than others. In spite of Harry Lime's understanding of the world, even the Swiss have never had such a society.

Thus, notions of disorder are always related to ideas of social order. Ideas of social order are extraordinarily diverse but it is not truly tautologous to suggest that each society depends, for its continued existence in that order, upon an acceptance by those with power, that that order is sensible. This makes it necessary later to consider how it is that people in such diverse societies see their own social world as common sense and other social orders as peculiar.

The relevance of this is that it suggests the major and central method of maintaining order in any society is by making order common sense. While many might argue that it is really law and force which maintain order, and while it is true that many disputes and challenges to order, such as crime, are resolved by the application of force, a moment's reflection should persuade us that, although force is an element in the maintenance of order, it could not be the *central* element. This is not least because there is an inherent contradiction in the use of force to maintain order. (One may think of the US commander in Vietnam who made the memorable statement that, 'In order to save the town, we had to destroy it'.) This is because the more it is necessary to use force to maintain order the less the order so provided becomes part of common sense. The use of force to maintain order is itself disorderly and destroys the acceptance of the social order as unproblematic. There are many obvious examples illustrating this in the break up of Yugoslavia and events in Kosovo in particular, to Northern Ireland.

In Northern Ireland, where the lack of a shared perception of an acceptable order required (hopefully, the past tense is appropriate) the constant use or threat of force to suppress disorder, the effect was to further polarise communities and confirm significant numbers in their antipathy to the order they saw as imposed and unacceptable. Within the UK, the same phenomenon was observed in 1981 during the inner city riots and subsequently where the police, whose authority was not accepted, chose to resort to force to regain it.

In Western states enjoying the Rule of Law, law clearly has a part to play in the maintenance of order but it is not simply in the allocation of power, creation of rules and in its ability to resolve disputes. Rather, it is perhaps most centrally because the institution of law itself has become a part of our 'taken for granted' world. Most people approve of a lawful society and perceive lawfulness as a virtue and most of us most of the time identify with the lawful. The typical response to the question 'Should we obey the law?' is 'Of course!'. It is this identification which means that the application of force is comparatively seldom necessary.

Perhaps, also, what obviates the need for more force is that for whatever reason (the reason will be discussed later) many people do have some feeling of 'freedom under the law'. Although we have emphasised that common sense is coercive, there is nevertheless apparent room for individual difference in perception. Everyone does not have to agree about everything all of the time. That notwithstanding, we will, hopefully, come to see that although there is room for debate, that room is circumscribed by a consensus. Participation in debate demands acceptance of the fact that there *is* a consensus. Not all things are debatable and many arguments in our society would make no sense. Thus, if having been accused of the theft of a motor car the accused attempted to argue that her need for the car was greater than that of the owner who owned two other cars anyway, this is not a permissible argument because it conflicts with common sense about property.

To insist upon such arguments may indeed lead to a label of not merely bad but mad. The criminal accepts the legal definition of her offence, the mad person denies it.

And importantly, beyond the social control of law, we have the social control of psychiatric definitions. The parallels and relationship between law and psychiatry are sufficiently significant to require further discussion. Both have the ability to officially define situations which come before them. At the crudest level, there are similarities in the way in which we treat those we label as mad (insane) through psychiatry and those we label as bad (criminal) through law. Both are interpretations of behaviour which are *official* interpretations made by specialists. Parallel consequences may follow. While the criminal may be incarcerated as punishment designed, at least in theory, to reform, the insane may be incarcerated in not very different conditions to receive treatment in order to conform. It is not, incidentally, insignificant that most people, given the choice of label – 'bad' or 'mad', criminal or insane, prefer to be bad. While in law insanity provides a complete defence to a criminal charge giving the court the discretion to make a hospital order for treatment, almost no defendants elect to use the defence voluntarily. It may be that the stigma of insanity remains greater than that of criminality. To be sent to a 'hospital' for the criminally insane provides a double stigma with little prospect of early release.

15

In each situation of criminal behaviour and insanity, the person involved is a deviant in the sense of having deviated from what society defines as lawful or normal. (Again, of course, it is not really society which defines this; it is those who have been allocated the power within society to define this.) Equally, what makes a person criminal or insane differs widely from society to society. Criminals are, by definition, those who have broken the criminal law and it is clear that their deviance is a product of the rules. If there were no law against the conduct there would be no breach of the criminal law. This is a point of significance when one considers criminal statistics and is well made by reference to the effect of prohibition in the US. Upon the passing of prohibition laws after the First World War, it became an offence to buy, sell, possess or consume alcohol and consequently a very large percentage of the population became vulnerable to being declared officially deviant (criminal). So, transforming individuals into criminals is firstly a function of rules. If we had no criminal law, we would have no criminals. The easiest way to decrease the rate of crime is to legalise what was previously defined as criminal, whether it be homosexuality, or possession and supply of drugs.

Similarly, with insanity, what is perceived as insanity varies not only in time but also from society to society. We have evidence in the UK of a tendency in the early part of this century to define unmarried women who became pregnant as insane and evidence also to suggest that women who did not conform to the sexual stereotype were given treatment. For men, it is not very long since masturbation was thought either to lead to, or to be symptomatic of, psychiatric illness, and homosexuality, either male or female, often led to incarceration for psychiatric treatment.

The definition of insanity in other societies is by no means coincidental with our own. Although in our world faith in God is usually approved of, anyone who claims to have direct knowledge of the Deity is a prime candidate for mental care. It is sane to believe; it may be mad to know. People who claim to hear voices from God or the gods are greatly over-represented in our mental hospitals, whereas in other societies and at other times some at least would have been regarded as prophets or wise women or men. Poor King Lear who found wisdom through madness would, had he been living in the 20th century, have been likely to have had his thoughts and emotions suppressed with Valium or electro-convulsive therapy.

When many years ago one of the authors, while living in New Zealand, discovered that that country had almost the highest incidence of mental illness in the Western world, it was a matter of great surprise. New Zealand seemed then a particularly 'well-ordered' society. It was only when the author came to Europe and found many people 'manifesting behaviour' in the street, which would almost certainly have led to incarceration, diagnosis, and treatment had they resided in New Zealand (such behaviour as talking aloud to oneself, sleeping rough, even being dirty and unkempt) that the reason became clear.

New Zealand was a very well ordered society! (The only suspicion is that the wrong people were hospitalised.)

Again, we saw in the old USSR that insanity was often defined by dangerous political beliefs which probably seems preposterous until we see such films as *Family Life*, directed by Ken Loach, or *One flew Over the Cuckoo's Nest*, by Ken Kesey.

The argument is that the ways by which we define disorder are by no means objective. Not only is 'normal' culturally defined but many have observed the 'abnormality of normality' which allows us to accept that normal *men* have killed in excess of one hundred million of their fellow normal beings in this century alone. The figure does not include the millions who have starved while normal people sought to destroy their food mountains.

What is crucial in the definition of abnormality is power, the power to have one's definition accepted, again a point well made by RD Laing in an extract from *The Politics of Experience* (1967, pp 88–89):

'The old way of sampling the behaviour of schizophrenics was by the method of clinical examination. The following is an example of the type of examination conducted at the turn of the century. The account is given by the German psychiatrist Emil Kraepelin in his own words.

"Gentlemen, the cases that I have to place before you today are peculiar. First of all, you see a servant-girl, aged twenty-four, upon whose features and frame traces of great emaciation can be plainly seen. In spite of this, the patient is in continual movement, going a few steps forward, then back again; she plaits her hair, only to unloose it the next minute. *On attempting to stop her movement*, we meet with unexpectedly strong resistance; *if I place myself in front of her with my arms spread out in order to stop her*, if she cannot push me on one side, she suddenly turns and slips through under my arms, so as to continue her way. *If one takes firm hold of her*, she distorts her usually rigid, expressionless features with deplorable weeping, that only ceases so soon as one lets her have her own way. We notice besides that she holds a crushed piece of bread spasmodically clasped in the fingers of the left hand, which *she absolutely will not allow to be forced from her*. The patient does not trouble in the least about her surroundings so long as you leave her alone. *If you prick her in the forehead with a needle*, she scarcely winces or turns away, and leaves the needle quietly sticking there without letting it disturb her restless, beast-of-prey-like wandering backwards and forwards. To questions she answers almost nothing, at the most shaking her head. But, from time to time, she wails: 'O dear God! O dear God! O dear mother!', always repeating uniformly the same phrases."'

Laing comments:

'Here are a man and a young girl. If we see the situation purely in terms of Kraepelin's point of view, it all immediately falls into place. He is sane, she is insane: he is rational, she is irrational. This entails looking at the patient's actions out of the context of the situation as she experienced it. But, if we take Kraepelin's actions (in italics) – he tries to stop her movements, stands in front of her with arms outspread, tries to force a piece of bread out of her hand, sticks a needle in her forehead, and so on – out of the context of the situation as experienced and defined by him, how extraordinary they are!'

Another feature common to law and much psychiatry (here, we exclude psychotherapy and refer particularly to medical psychiatry with its use of drugs and medical treatment) is that very often the problems are decontextualised and individualised. (This is also no less true of non-criminal law cases than of criminal ones.) In the case of psychiatry, just as in law, if the problem is to be amenable to a translation into the legal or psychiatric world, the problem must be put into an appropriate form. What this means in law is that we must extract the relevant facts which allow a legal label. This means that in selecting the legally relevant facts we inevitably leave out much of the social context of the event. Lawyers usually have much more interest in *what* was done rather than *why* it was done (although of course certain legally selected kinds of intentionality are considered relevant) – often to the amazement of clients. This selection of facts however is necessary if the law is to be able to resolve disputes. Theft, for instance, is an appropriate legal category if five points can be proved – namely an appropriation, which is dishonest, of property, belonging to another, with the intention to permanently deprive. If these five elements of the offence are proved any other social circumstances surrounding the incident such as the wealth or poverty of the perpetrator, become irrelevant.

Similarly, many doctors and psychiatrists when confronted with patients with mental problems will want to isolate symptoms which allow the application of a suitable medical label, whether clinical depression, schizophrenia or whatever. Yet, the isolation of these symptoms from their causes – symptoms which in themselves are often regarded as sufficient to justify treatment with strong drugs – will provide a solution to the problem of the disordered individual. If a drug is believed to beneficially affect depression it will often be prescribed even though little or no investigation has been made into the cause of the problem.

These many parallels are not coincidental. Both institutions are concerned with the maintenance of order and the problem of the disordered individual and the perceived threat of disorder to society. That they *translate* behaviour by selecting facts or symptoms into official categories is highly significant as we will see when we consider the role of specialists in any society. What will become clear will be that, as members of any particular society, we are not all equally powerful when it comes to having our definitions acknowledged. Legal, psychiatric, medical and religious experts (specialists all) have dominated cartography in most societies and have thus been able to define and reinforce particular realities.

We have argued then that order is not an absolute and that it has a meaning which is always relative. We have argued too that the very idea of order is seldom without political content and that what is to be regarded as order depends both upon the perspective of the individual and upon the interests of those with the power in society. The perception of what *is* order, is likely to vary dramatically from those with wealth who seek order, which secures their property, as patently desirable; to those with no wealth and often no paid employment who see order in terms of being provided with access to sufficient wealth to survive. While dominant notions of order are intimately connected to notions of social order, few social orders bring equal benefit to all in society.

We have also considered the institution of psychiatry looking at its parallels with the legal institution. In particular, we observed the psychiatric method of coping with disorder, or disordered individuals by diagnosing or labelling the 'disorder'. The diagnosis led to certain and significant consequences particularly the right and ability to 'treat' the pathological condition of the individual defined as disordered. Being able to do so however is dependent, first, upon some decontextualising of social facts (that is, selecting symptoms), and, secondly, upon psychiatry being able to interpret those facts not simply in an arbitrary way but rather an authoritative way. We turn now to consider how it is that psychiatry has this power and also to explain the significance of this for law and legal method.

Although the institutions of law and psychiatry have been mentioned, it is necessary to say rather more about institutions and to consider the process of institutionalisation. The obvious features of the legal institution as opposed to the law are, first, concerned with personnel; secondly, with physical places; and, thirdly, perhaps with a distinctive way in which things are done. Thus, we have judges, juries, barristers, solicitors, court officials, police, prison officers and prison inmates; we have courts, chambers, solicitors' offices, police stations and prisons; we have procedures, appropriate clothes, and appropriate language. Within the legal institution, there is a plethora of institutions. A prison is an institution in itself as is a court. What then distinguishes an institution from any arbitrary number of people with no particular connection and why is it significant? What do those within any institution have in common?

The first characteristic of an institution is that its members have roles – roles which are assigned by the institution and which in themselves are coercive. At their most extreme, roles can persuade individuals to do things which they would never contemplate in their ordinary social life. From the judge who pronounces a sentence of death and returns home to play with his grandchildren, to the soldier who kills the enemy without feelings of personal responsibility, it is the role which makes their actions possible.

To understand the importance of institutions and roles in a study of law, it is necessary to consider a little further the idea of reality. In this discussion, we will draw extensively upon Berger and Luckmann, *The Social Construction of Reality* (1967), a book which many students find difficult but ultimately rewarding. Because of its language about which we will say more shortly, it can appear intimidating. When it defines an institution as a 'reciprocal typification of habitualised actions by types of actors', many readers may want to stop reading immediately but in this case the sociological 'jargon' used by Berger and Luckmann is used in order to economise with words rather than to expand a text unnecessarily.

The overall purpose of the book is also rather daunting. The authors are attempting to understand how it is that people, and peoples, make their worlds real, and how it is that members of any society are able to take for granted as natural so much of what appears quite peculiar to members of other societies. Thus, they are concerned to analyse reality and to ask where our sense of reality comes from and how it is maintained.

Many people might consider that question quite unnecessary and perhaps even absurd. So obvious is what is real that even to question what *is* real can seem ridiculous, and perhaps even dangerous since we know that psychiatric wards are filled with people who are unable to recognise what is real. Reality itself is of course coercive for that very reason. If something is real, then to suggest that it is not is at worst insane and at best 'unrealistic'. Constant injunctions permeate our lives to 'be realistic', or 'face up to reality', or even in direct slang 'get real!'.

But, the argument here is that it is necessary in any study of law to try to analyse reality, for the law it is after all, which can be used to resolve and define what is real, both in fact and law. Each day, the courts define the facts of the case and, once the facts have been defined, there is little possibility of disputing them further. The courts not only define what is the case but also what happened. Once the courts have defined what happened, that *is* what happened and facts which are found can seldom be challenged. Appeals against findings of fact are both rare and almost always unsuccessful and the 'mere fact' that evidence was available which proves that the court's finding of fact did not correspond with what happened is usually irrelevant.

Nevertheless, even to say that reality is a social construct, and that reality is created and maintained by people, might at first sight seem strange. Most people, except the philosophers, typified as unworldly, accept that our physical surroundings exist as a fact and are real, and most people feel much the same way about the reality of the world of human beings. Reality is after all the taken for granted world which we understand and share with others in our society. A moment's reflection however reveals how apparently arbitrary and contingent our real world is. There are a myriad of ways of organising a society. Not only is Pascal's observation to the effect that what is truth on one side of the Pyrenees is error on the other, manifestly true but even today entirely different and incompatible ways of seeing the world co-exist. What is common place to a Sufi Muslim in Turkey is bizarre beyond belief to a bank clerk in the Bronx and vice versa.

Thus, for almost every member of every society, the way in which things are done where *they* exist is ordinary, and the way in which things are done in other societies is quite peculiar. We are sensible and they are absurd; though to them of course the position is reversed.

As Berger and Luckmann state, this stupendous diversity of cultures and social worlds, decreasing though it may be, is something which clearly distinguishes the human species from other animals. All other animals inhabit their own 'species worlds' with only comparatively minor differences. The world of the dog, or the cat, or the elephant, does not leave open vast possibilities for diversity.

One observed and obvious reason for this is that human babies are born at a much earlier stage of development than many other animals in the sense that the world they are to occupy is not circumscribed. Whereas a kitten will become a cat, any human baby has the potential to be a Cheyenne Indian, a Maori, a Kurd or an American, each of whom inhabits radically different worlds. So, every baby has the potential to become a fully paid up, card-carrying member of any society, anywhere. It is only after birth that one is socialised into a particular human society.

Hence, as Berger and Luckmann note, it is the plasticity and the malleability of the human organism which is distinctive and impressive. The baby only becomes human as it not only inter-relates with a particular natural environment, but with a specific cultural and social order. It is through the relationship with this particular cultural and social order that the baby becomes Chinese, French or whatever. In one slightly depressing sense then, every child's socialisation can be seen as a destruction of potential or, more emotively, as a brainwashing exercise though of course no child could survive as human without it.

Recognising then that each child's everyday life seems ordinary to it because of the reality of the world with which it interacts, how is it that this reality is created and maintained?

The suggestion is that central to the creation and maintenance of reality are institutions. In a rather easier book than *The Social Construction of Reality*, namely, *Invitation to Sociology*, Peter Berger defined an institution as 'a distinctive complex of social actions' (Berger 1966, p 104). Thus, we can speak, for instance, of class, marriage, or organised religion as constituting institutions.

In their consideration of institutions and the process of institutionalisation, Berger and Luckmann use the time-honoured model of two people meeting on a desert island. The use of desert islands to explain phenomena is not one calculated to inspire confidence, and economists in particular seem to use whole archipelagoes of desert islands to arrive at very dubious conclusions. (There is a well known joke about economists on desert islands in which a chemist, a physicist and an economist were marooned on a desert island with one can of baked beans to eat and no can opener. The chemist suggested that, if they built a fire and heated the beans, he would be able to predict the exact moment when the can would explode. The physicist said that, if this could be done, he would be able to predict the trajectory of each bean so that none would be lost. They then turned to the economist and asked what his contribution might be. His reply began: 'Let us assume we have a can opener ...!')

In Berger and Luckmann's example, a man and a woman of quite different cultures, background and language meet on the desert island and begin to 'interact'. The authors have already pointed out that all human activity is subject to habitualisation, by which they simply mean that individuals tend to develop ways of doing things and tend to do the same things in the same way, and, finally, they are often coerced by the habits they have developed. So, by way of example, if one is in the habit of having cereal for breakfast, breakfast is something which can be done almost thoughtlessly. One does not spend time each morning wondering *whether* to have breakfast and one does not consider the overwhelming number of possibilities for food. Thus, the possibility of eating roast duck, or sponge cake, or wichita grubs simply does not present itself. The habit is coercive to the extent of making such possibilities unthinkable.

The obvious reason for habitualising so many of our actions such as when and how we eat, when and where we sleep, what sort of clothes we wear, is that it leads to an economy of decision making. Most of our daily activity can be performed almost unconsciously and certainly thoughtlessly, leaving capacity for more significant decision making.

In the desert island example, each individual not only observes the habitualised actions of the other, but as well begins to typify those actions of the other. That is, when something is regularly done by one party, it is not merely observed by the other, but motive is inferred, and as actions are repeated so regularly, the meaning and the significance are inferred. Ideally, the observer in fact infers what the actor implies, and thus we arrive at the reciprocal typification of habitualised actions in the sense that each party typifies the regular actions of the other and as well as observing the act, understands its meaning.

Because of this interaction and attribution of meaning, the desert islanders begin to adopt roles towards each other. For whatever reason (and it might be natural skill, it might be preference, or it might reflect what each did before arrival), it is likely that some tasks will be divided, and even when co-operation is required to complete a task, each party will habitualise his or her contribution to the task. Most jobs on the desert island could be performed by either, even though, if the routine is sufficiently habitualised, this might seem unlikely even to the parties. The consequent reciprocal typification of habitualised actions is not yet at this point institutionalisation. While the reciprocity allows the interaction to become predictable and itself becomes habit and begins to be ordinary, it is also the means by which the individuals construct not an individual world but a social one with shared meanings and with roles. At this stage, it is open to the individual to alter the division of tasks, should circumstances change.

But, if a child is born into this situation, the roles and interaction that have developed between the parents appear to the child not as 'a way of organising' but 'the way in which things are organised'. The roles which each parent has adopted historically appear to the child as 'the way things are' and the child is faced with the reality of his or her world.

A direct quotation from Berger and Luckmann is relevant (1967, p 76):

> 'With the acquisition of historicity, these formations also acquire another crucial quality, or, more accurately, perfect a quality that was incipient as soon as A and B began the reciprocal typification of their conduct: this quality is objectivity. This means that the institutions that have now been crystallised (for instance, the institution of paternity as it is encountered by the children) are experienced as existing over and beyond the individuals who "happen to" embody them at the moment. In other words, the Institutions are now experienced as possessing a reality of their own, a reality that confronts the individual as an external and coercive fact.'

The crucial point is then that the world of institutions (the world where things are done in particular ways) becomes, and is experienced as, objectively real; as indeed it is. The climax of the desert island model should be the recognition that, although society is created and maintained by people, people experience society as something outside of themselves as an objective reality which in turn creates and produces people. Or, as Berger and Luckmann express it, more sexistly if not more succinctly: 'Society is a human product. Society is an objective reality. Man is a social product.' There is a dialectical relationship between individuals and society. People create institutions but are in turn moulded by institutions.

What we said earlier of institutions now becomes relevant. Institutions are coercive because of their very reality. They require us to play appropriate roles and roles which fit the reciprocal typification. As university teachers, we have expectations of how students will conduct themselves, and they in turn have expectations of our roles, and, within wider or narrower boundaries, we are each constrained in our conduct. If we are utterly incompetent in our roles, observers might even deny that we are a part of the institution. Typical expressions which convey this point are 'he's no father to that child' or 'she is no wife to that man'.

All of us have many different roles to play depending upon which institution we are being a part of at any given time. Sometimes, the roles we are expected to play conflict, which leads to difficulties. The strain of fulfilling different role expectations simultaneously can be exhausting as any student is likely to know if he or she has returned home with members of the student peer group only to have to play the student role, and the child of the family role, at once. The greater the differences in the role expectations, the greater the strain. Furthermore, roles are always at their most difficult when they are being played before they have been internalised. For the young barrister who cannot escape an appreciation of the absurdity of court ritual and dress, the role can be almost impossible, particularly if he or she is also anxious about the required level of legal knowledge.

One further point concerning roles will become directly relevant later. Very often in life, individuals undergo major role changes. They may change either their role in an institution or even join a new institution. Such major role changes are very often accompanied by ritual. This is a point clearly expressed by Michael Banton in *Roles* (1965, pp 93–94):

> 'For an individual to move from one role to another is not always an easy matter. It requires that he know the rights and obligations of the role to which he is moving and that he change his behaviour accordingly. It also requires that other people recognise his change of role and modify their behaviour towards him in corresponding fashion. Role-changing therefore creates problems for social relations: (a) the greater the change for the individual (b) the more people there are who meet him in both his old and his new roles and therefore have to modify their behaviour. These two difficulties are both met by the same device, that of ceremonialising the changeover. Ceremony helps the individual who is changing roles to appreciate that this is a critical moment; for a little while it lifts him out of himself and helps him to feel as if he himself has changed in some way; this facilitates his psychological reorientation. Ceremonial also brings together a man's associates and impresses on them that he has changed roles so that they are able to make a parallel reorientation.'

So, in our society one often sees considerable ritual attached to marriage, to death and, at least traditionally, to birth. The object of the ritual is to get the meaning of the transition across not only to the person making the change but also to others who are affected by the change. Sociologically, a 'successful' marriage ceremony is one where the couple have actually been reorientated both towards each other and towards family and friends with new obligations and new privileges and responsibilities. Through ritual, the initiate ideally *becomes* the role which is demanded. This is obviously another use of magic which is relevant to the law. If it is at its clearest in a coronation ceremony where a great deal of magic (ritual) seems necessary to change a person into a sovereign (not least the crowning and anointing), it is only slightly less obvious in legal cases both civil and criminal. In civil disputes, the pomp and majesty of the robed judge lends authority to the decision handed down. In a criminal trial, the ritual is used to successfully change a defendant into a criminal. If all goes well, not only is the label successfully applied so that the observing world recognises the defendant as a criminal, but if it is *really* successful the defendant him or herself will accept the label as real, and play the new role of convict.

24

These ceremonies are magic in the sense that, if they are successful, a man really may be turned into a king, or a woman into a queen. The reality is a social fact and to disbelieve might even be a sign of mental instability. We will develop this point when in later chapters we turn to consider some ethnographic materials concerning dispute resolution in other societies.

Why is it however that we have no alternative but to accept the reality of social facts? This has much to do with the process of socialisation, the process by which after birth one is integrated into becoming a member of any particular society. Berger and Luckmann distinguish two different sorts of socialisation. Primary socialisation is the process of integrating a baby and child into a particular social world, while secondary socialisation is the process whereby a supposedly socialised child is integrated into a new institution or institutions, whether it be the army, the legal profession, the university, or a bank. In any case, the task of socialisation is much the same, namely to integrate an individual so that in its society or institution the world it inhabits is subjectively meaningful. That is, it is a part of the real, and taken for granted, world.

For Berger and Luckmann this process involves externalisation, objectification and internalisation. Fortunately, all these words may be translated. Internalisation of meaning is only the final stage or phase in making the ordinary unproblematic. Something obviously has to be available to be internalised and it is here that we see the relationship between externalisation and objectification.

We have already observed in discussing institutions and institutionalisation, that in any institution the members play roles; that is, they behave in predictable ways, or in ways which are observable, often to outsiders, but always to new entrants to the institution. Thus, whether the new recruit joins the army, the university, or the legal profession, it is immediately clear that different people in the institution have different roles and, in joining any such institution, it is necessary to appreciate the roles of others in order that the new recruit understands his or her own ascribed roles in the institution. The roles played by the members are observable because they are *externalised* or played out and the playing out is the externalisation.

Once familiar, these patterns of conduct appear as more than mere patterns. Rather, they become objectively real social facts which are as objectively real as the natural world. In turn, their reality and their objectification are reinforced by what Berger and Luckmann call 'linguistic signification' or as we might say 'language'. It is through language that things and social facts come within the common sense reality of everyday life:

> 'As a sign system, language has the quality of objectivity. I encounter language as a facticity external to myself and it is coercive in its effect on me. Language forces me into its patterns. I cannot use the rules of German syntax when I speak English; I cannot use words invented by my three-year-old son if I want to communicate outside the family; I must take into account

prevailing standards of proper speech for various occasions, even it I would prefer my private 'improper' ones. Language provides me with a ready-made possibility for the ongoing objectification of my unfolding experience' [Berger and Luckmann, 1967, p 53].

This objectification – the objective existence of the externalised roles – is in turn internalised by almost all who join the institution. The new barrister, the new sergeant, the new university student all come to *live* the role rather than merely play it. It is internalised as real. If it is not, the playing of the role remains difficult. This is a point which is central to much of Woody Allen's humour, and not least in the film *Play it Again Sam*.

And, of course, as each integrated new member of the institution lives the role which has been internalised, so too does the externalised role appear as objective to the new members.

It is important to remember that socialisation within society obviously does not lead to uniformity. Not only is the child's world created by significant adults but, while every child in each society has a similar socialisation, each also has a unique socialisation. The social reality that comes to be shared is similar, particularly in language, but there are significant differences. There are marked differences between the socialisation of children of different classes, different religions, and different ethnic groups. Even within a society children of different classes in many senses inhabit different worlds. As it is with different societies, here too what is ordinary for a child of one class will be extraordinary for another.

But, the effect of primary socialisation is to give the child an identity and a location with a name, an address (usually) and a network of people as relatives and friends. It is through the obtaining of approval from significant others that the child learns who he or she is. This statement remains true regardless of the view one takes of the 'nature versus nurture' debate. While each child is unique, to be brought up in a different society would make him or her fundamentally different. The child's genes cannot dictate the world with which it must inter-relate.

What then is the significance of such a phenomenological understanding of society for those interested in law? The crucial point which might well seem obvious (but which is certainly not so to most law students) is that social order comes not primarily from rules, from law, and from sanctions, but that social control is primarily located in shared reality. The social order and, indeed, social control depend primarily upon the objectification of social reality which in turn depends upon a world of institutions, each with a history, each the product of human society, and each of which in turn appears objectively real to the members of that society, and by that fact coerces them. Thus, we see that law might be a system of social control very much less important than the shared reality.

A second point is that an understanding of the role of law might be more easily obtained if it is accepted that the legal institution is created and maintained by people but then in turn acts upon people as though it had an existence independent of those who created it.

There is one further question which needs to be addressed in any consideration of the creation and maintenance of order and this concerns the concept of legitimation. 'Legitimation' is in itself a word with legal connotations. It is poorly and excessively narrowly defined in the *Oxford Dictionary* as 'the action of making lawful'. This is not the meaning of the word as used by sociologists, anthropologists or philosophers. Rather, to legitimate something, is to justify it by reference to some authority. Much of jurisprudence has concerned itself with questions concerning the legitimation of law. All law students are quickly taught that propositions of law themselves require legitimation, which is a reference to the authority which justifies the proposition, whether this authority be statute, common law, or a civil code. Law itself provides legitimation for much of what happens in our society. When we discussed psychiatry, we could have observed that it is the law which legitimates the psychiatric world. The authority necessary to justify most coercion, and the compulsion which enables enforced treatment, is to be found within law.

Law, too, however, like any other institution itself requires legitimation. There has to be a way of justifying and explaining and an answer to the question: 'why do we do things in this way?' One major legitimation for law derives from democracy. Hence, such statements as: 'law exists and should be obeyed because it has been created and passed by democratically elected representatives'. Although this legitimation could be criticised in its own terms (because of the theory of democracy as the will of the majority, and the very different reality in that very few governments in the West are ever actually elected by the majority of the electorate), such criticism is less significant to us than the realisation that there is nothing inevitable about democracy as the legitimation for law. It is, of course, a comparatively recent phenomenon and before democracy, law was legitimated by a democracy of limited suffrage and long before that became law, legitimation had been derived from a sovereign with 'divine right'.

The legitimation of laws through secular justification (including scientific knowledge) is comparatively recent. In most societies, the particular way in which things are done is legitimated through myth and through the supernatural, whether gods or ancestors. What is relevant to us is to see the necessary connection between the legitimation and the way things are done, and to consider the role of law in justifying and reinforcing the official way of doing things.

3   Reality, Anthropology and Dispute Resolution

The reasons for our decision to introduce the Berger and Luckmann thesis from *The Social Construction of Reality* in the last chapter may still not be entirely clear. We hope to remedy this in the following chapters. Those who do read that book itself will unfortunately be disappointed if they expect the authors' 'phenomenological' approach to be readily accessible in its own terms. We have oversimplified, in order to introduce the key ideas for our purpose (the issue of how reality is created and maintained) and have attempted to translate some of the sociological ideas, which can appear daunting. But, the fact that they do use so much language which is difficult is itself significant. The explanation is not simply that sociologists have sought to 'legitimate' (that is, give authority to) their work by using difficult language even though that criticism can be made of much sociology, and certainly is by those who are cynical of sociology as a discipline (one natural scientist once unfairly observed that sociology is at the stage that chemistry was when it was called alchemy). Rather, to try to describe our reality is difficult and more difficult than describing, at least from an external point of view, the reality of other societies, simply because we are constrained in our analysis of what reality is by our 'knowledge' of what is real.

And, as we have suggested, what is *real* is, to some extent at least, objectified and rendered uncontroversial by language, shared words with shared meanings. Very often, those who try to step outside those shared meanings lack the language to do so. Philosophers, sociologists, mathematicians, political theorists and of course poets have long had to develop some sort of 'meta-language' (that is, a language outside of day-to-day language) in an attempt to talk *about* what is taken for granted and our common sense. A little later, in an attempt to get an external perspective on our reality, we will be referring to anthropological articles and books in order to try to observe indirectly what is almost impossible to see directly. Before doing so, however, we want to explore a little further the uses of the concept of legitimation. As we said, while law is an important legitimating device, even legitimating devices require legitimation. There must be some answer to the person who says: 'with what justification?' when told that it is the law which requires him or her to act in a particular way.

Although a typical legitimation in our society would involve a justification with reference to ideas of democracy, in most societies, the institutions ('the particular way things are done') are legitimated through myth and through the supernatural. An old adage which makes the connection between human institution and sustaining myths, states simply that: 'God created man and man

29

returned the compliment!' Gods are used to legitimate particular socially created worlds. Thus, if the gods are to be relevant, they must reflect the ideals and mores of any particular set of believers. The gods must make sense of the situation in which the believers find themselves.

Hence, the Greek gods legitimated (explained and justified) Greek morality and social organisation and also provided explanations for when things went wrong, which could then be attributed to divine intervention in the affairs of humans. More contemporaneously, we can see Hindu gods legitimating a caste way of organising society; we can see the Protestant God legitimating the centrality of the individual, Catholic theology legitimating patriarchy and, until recently, and perhaps most remarkably of all, the Dutch Reform Church actually managing to legitimate apartheid.

This adage, objectionable though it may be to those blessed with faith, is only a part of the story. Even within religions there are sects who use Deities to legitimate a particular kind of morality. To illustrate this, Berger, in *Invitation to Sociology*, focused upon the so-called Bible Belt of the US, with its particular kind of fundamentalist protestantism which is preoccupied in its preaching with the sins of the flesh (promiscuity, adultery and particularly and often homosexuality) while, at the same time, the accumulation of money and possessions beyond all need is regarded as laudable, and entirely compatible with Christian virtue. From the outside, at least to many observers, it seemed curious that in the 1980s Jimmy Swaggart, the great gospel preacher, could live in fantastic luxury surrounded by poverty, without demur, hesitation, or condemnation, and yet lose all status, prestige and respect because he had committed adultery! More recently, President Clinton's 'dalliance' with Monika Lewinsky appalled America in a way that reductions in welfare spending did not. In due course, we will explain further the relationship between religion and property distribution but, for the moment, it is sufficient to note that religion as practised, and protestantism as interpreted in the Bible Belt, can be said to legitimate a particular property régime viz capitalism, which if not exactly laissez faire is certainly capitalism with minimal social obligations. (Incidentally, by 'property régime' we simply mean the way in which property is organised in any particular society. Later, we will specifically consider common sense about property which is itself of course a social construct, rather than a natural phenomenon, in that things exist naturally but humans are necessary to turn things into property.)

It is because gods are used in this way to explain and justify and to make comprehensible those things which are incomprehensible (especially death) that gods themselves have a paradoxical tendency to die or transform along with the societies they legitimate. And, at the risk of a minor diversion, it is important to explain this a little more because it says something not only of gods but also of other legitimating institutions, especially the law. One theory which seems irrefutably true is that it is not possible to change gods while preserving in a continuing form an existing, on-going society. The inevitable result of missionary success, no matter which faith is being proselytised, is that the society in which the success is achieved is irrevocably changed for better or for worse, and often in ways which are quite destructive, and almost always in ways which are quite unforeseen. Although, for example, Christian missionaries might have felt that their only role was to achieve conversion and to save souls, the objectively observable result was to make social life and organisation as it had previously been, impossible. From such simple propositions as to the sort of clothing which was appropriate, and which parts of the human body Christian decency demands be covered, to the idea of the nuclear family with one man and one woman married for life being the only hallowed status; such things as these altered the very institutions which created real worlds. To change legitimations necessarily changes the institutions which are legitimated, and thus reality itself is changed. In turn, changes in reality demand new legitimations. The effect upon peoples of losing their gods in the face of demonstrably stronger gods, has always been traumatic but many peoples have been unable to resist. The question of which were able to resist and why, and which were unable to resist and why, is interesting but not entirely relevant. The relevance of this to law is that any legitimating institution must, if it is to be consensually accepted, legitimate the social reality. Law which does not do this will have to be explicitly imposed upon an unwilling society.

An understanding of one further concept developed by Berger and Luckmann is necessary before we attempt to consider our own reality. Ideas of primary and secondary reality (merely concepts designed to help provide an understanding) distinguish between the world of common sense (primary reality) or the 'taken for granted world' which most of us share, and the world of secondary reality. The idea of secondary reality implies that, in order to explain things which are not readily explicable by common sense, societies develop specialist institutions which have the attribute of being able to explain that which common sense can not. In particular, we have institutions of specialists who tend to have a monopoly over areas of specialised knowledge. Clearly, both law and psychiatry are such institutions, as is medicine, anthropology, sociology and religion.

The central thesis of the secondary reality is that it is an interpretive reality – able to interpret problems from the everyday world into a secondary reality in which the problem will ideally be resolved, but at the least will be made meaningful. Phenomena can thus exist in both the primary and secondary reality. So, for example, a headache exists in the taken for granted world. We all know what it is to experience a headache and in our society most of us also know that a first and obvious remedy is aspirin. But, if the headache persists, or is really dreadful, or constantly recurs, we seek an interpretation of the problem, and in our society probably from a doctor but in other societies possibly from a witch doctor, a priest or an acupuncturist. In our world, the problem is likely to be interpreted as something such as a migraine, a brain tumour or neuralgia. The medical diagnosis is the specialist interpretation of the common phenomenon.

Similarly, in law, what appears in the day to day world as senseless violence, becomes a meaningful legal category. Through the specialist interpretation of the police and lawyers a 'senseless' killing becomes perhaps murder or manslaughter; hitting someone is given meaning as assault and battery, or assault occasioning actual bodily harm. Indeed, a significant part of becoming a member of such a specialist institution is learning to put appropriate interpretations upon otherwise meaningless events – meaningless only in the sense that as observed, in the everyday primary reality, the events are incomprehensible and have no solution. The interpretation of the events makes them explicable, and sometimes even resolvable.

The function of secondary reality then is to place meaning upon things which, in the taken for granted world, cannot be explained. Naturally, through being able to interpret, the specialists gain power and if their interpretations are accepted as authentic they are authoritative (and are in fact 'real'). Often, specialists are very jealous of their monopoly over a secondary reality. Not only do witch doctors hate impostors or those who suggest that their access to remedies is greater, but priests in churches consistently over the years, particularly when their power was greatest, have vehemently opposed those who pretended to their role (as exemplified by John Bunyan's experiences!); and barristers are utterly indignant at the prospect of having to lose their monopoly of wisdom in the courts. Traditionally, the British Medical Association has been firmly against homeopathic medicine and, until recently, acupuncture and acupuncturists. One of the great disappointments of university life is how possessive even academics are about their own area of specialism whether they be sociologists, anthropologists, historians or even lawyers, each of whom often seems to feel threatened in some way if someone else speaks intimately about *their* area of expertise.

We make this point partly to exemplify the distinction between 'taken for granted reality' and the 'interpreted by specialists reality' and partly to pre-empt criticism, particularly from anthropologists, of our use of their material. While we will be discussing ethnographic material, we will be using it in a fairly distinctive way. On occasions, it will be oversimplified and on many occasions it will be out of context. The point about our discussions using anthropological materials, however, is not really to make points about the societies as represented by anthropologists at which we will look. We will consider how some things are claimed to be done, or to have been done, among such peoples as the Azande, the Ibo, the Nuer, the Asante or the Inuit (Eskimo) peoples by anthropologists not with any intention of commenting upon or evaluating other societies but in order to make points about our world by looking at theirs as described by Western anthropologists of varying quality, sensitivity and knowledge. Thus, even if there were no correspondence between worlds as described and as they exist, for our purposes that would be inconsequential. Indeed, even if all anthropology had been written by science fiction writers who had never left darkest Queensland that fact would be unimportant because we are attempting to use it to stand outside our own world and talking about other people is one way of doing this. Those who have read Jonathan Swift's *Gulliver's Travels* will readily understand this point.

Obvious though this point may be, it is nevertheless necessary to be aware of the controversy that has engulfed anthropology. This is not merely to achieve 'PC' status (political correctness), but because the controversy does have lessons for all would-be drafters of maps and it is particularly clear that in reading anthropology the answer to: 'who drew that map?', or in this context: 'who says things are the way they are described and why and with what authority?' is of the utmost importance. What we are implicitly suggesting is that much ethnography tells us more about the anthropologist, and his or her world, and his or her ideology, than about the thing which is being described.

It is not an exaggeration to suggest that anthropology has recently been undergoing a crisis which is not yet resolved and may in fact be irresolvable. A first problem concerns how any individual can make sense of other 'societies' without imposing quite unjustified generalisations and yet these generalisations are usually what the anthropologist would consider as the significant results of the study. Thus, in much of older anthropology we read statements that a moment's consideration will necessarily question. When, in a famous book, *Witchcraft, Oracles and Magic Among the Azande*, the anthropologist Evans Pritchard talks of the Nuer people of what is now the Sudan and tells us how *they* are, and how *they* behave and what *their* characteristics are – namely, proud, aggressive and leaderless – two questions immediately arise. First, is every individual Nuer possessed of these characteristics? The answer is obviously negative. Secondly, in many anthropological generalisations the analysis and often indeed even the research is completely, if unself-consciously, male orientated. Very often, women are almost invisible and the generalisations refer to society as though it were composed only of men. This fact is well illustrated in a quotation from Clifford and Marcus, *Writing Culture* which is a book concerning itself with the hidden politics of ethnography. Speaking of a famous ethnographic text – Lienhardt's *Divinity and Experience: The Religion of the Dinka* (1961) James Clifford observes (Clifford and Marcus, 1986, p 17):

> '... it comes as a shock to recognise that Lienhardt's portrayal concerns, almost exclusively, the experience of Dinka men. When speaking of "the Dinka" he may or may not be extending the point to women. We often cannot know from the published text. The examples he chooses are, in any case, overwhelmingly centred on males. A rapid perusal of the book's introductory chapter on Dinka and their cattle confirms the point. Only once is a woman's view mentioned, and it is in affirmation of men's relation to cows, saying nothing of how women experience cattle. This passage introduces an

equivocation in passages such as "Dinka often interpret accidents or coincidences as acts of Divinity distinguishing truth from falsehood by signs which appear to men" (p 47). The intended sense of the word "men" is certainly generic, yet surrounded exclusively by examples from male experience it slides towards a gendered meaning ... Terms such as "the Dinka" or "Dinka" used throughout the book, become similarly equivocal.'

A further point is of relevance. Recently, those concerned with the methodology of anthropology have been asking critical questions about the relationship between the anthropologist and his or her object of study. Earlier, we used a quotation from RD Laing where he quotes the German psychologist describing and demonstrating the condition of a woman in deep mental despair, and observes that pathological though her condition may be, the conduct of the psychiatrist is even more so. Yet, we start and proceed with the assumption that he is sane and she insane. While it is not quite the same with the anthropologist, what is apparent upon reflection is, first, the power of the anthropologist to define what is. It is his or her role to mediate and translate other *peoples'* reality, but in doing so the anthropologist is in a position of complete power made even greater by the use of the 'objective' and 'scientific' description. As written, the possibility of inaccuracy does not arise as accurate descriptions must be 'truthful'(!) – yet, this cannot be achieved because every significant anthropological description involves a translation not only from one culture to another, but through one pair of eyes trained in a peculiarly Western tradition of anthropology, which looks for what it expects to find in the sense that it is impossible to look with innocent eyes which deny experience. Until recently, there was usually the assumption that the 'people' studied have themselves no interest in the politics of the relationship between anthropologist and informant and that those studied do not play games with their resident anthropologist. Of course, they do. Many of the peoples studied could not but have been well aware that their inquisitor was a part of a colonial regime attempting to obtain power over them – a point well brought out in one analysis of Evans Pritchard's work with the Nuer by Renato Rosaldo:

'Evans Pritchard's simultaneous account of, and lack of accountability to, the political context of his fieldwork appears particularly disconcerting in the one instance where he and a Nuer man enter a textualised dialogue. The fieldworker attempts a British introduction by asking Cuol his name and the name of his lineage. Cuol in response uses a number of manoeuvres to resist giving both names and in the process asks: "Why do you want to know the name of my lineage?" and "What will you do with it if I tell you? Will you take it to your country?". The narrator interprets the conversation in the following terms: "I defy the most patient ethnologist to make headway against this kind of opposition. One is just driven crazy by it. Indeed after a few weeks of associating solely with Nuer one displays, if the pun be allowed, the most evident symptoms of 'Nuerosis'... The narrator depicts Cuol's "opposition" complexly. It is at once bull-headed, admirable, and perverse. His opposition is enjoyed as an assertion of Nuer values of freedom and autonomy, and it appears perverse because it subverts "innocent" ethnographic enquiry. Furthermore, it is measured against a norm (which probably is alien to the Nuer) of courteous conduct that requires strangers, on first meeting, to introduce themselves by giving their names. The narrator finds that the fault in this unhappy encounter lies with Nuer character, rather than with historically specific circumstances. Yet the reader should consider that, just two pages before, Evans Pritchard has described how a government force raided a Nuer camp, "took hostages and threatened to take many more"... Cuol had, not a character disorder, but good reasons for resisting inquiry and asking who wanted to know his name and the name of his lineage' [Clifford and Marcus, 1986, p 91].

Yet another problem for anthropology concerns the visibility of the anthropologist. To read many ethnographic materials one has the impression of a people being observed by a god who is invisible, omnipotent and even omniscient. But, the very methods of anthropology deny the possibility of the anthropologist being an unnoticed observer. Not only need they observe (and this means that they must strive to be at the centre of significant events), but they must also question. Here, the Heisenberg principle cannot but be relevant; viz to observe is to affect. The very fact of observation will almost invariably alter the behaviour of the observed, and the alteration will be increased in the presence of recording equipment and cameras.

Lastly, it is necessary to consider the conundrum which faces anthropologists and sociologists who attempt to obtain external perspectives upon their observed society. This relates back to what we suggested much earlier in that it is difficult to see *through* rules if one sees through rules. Here, we are referring to the possibility of cultural translation and we are suggesting that it is supremely difficult, and perhaps even impossible to understand another reality without becoming a part of that reality. Thus, for example, for a secular Westerner to study an Islamic society is possible at one level, but obviously not at another, since what is real and crucial in making sense of the world for a Muslim (the existence of God, the role of the Prophet and the sanctity of the Quran) will not be real to the observer. One cannot see through Islamic eyes without being a Muslim. At the same time, if one is a Muslim, one cannot comprehend the perspective of the non-believer. This was well demonstrated in the fierce debate over the publication of Salman Rushdie's *Satanic Verses*. We can then observe others' reality but until it is internalised it cannot be real for us, but while it is not real for us we lack a vital aspect of comprehension.

With these caveats, we now turn to a portrayal of a way of understanding the world which is dramatically different from ours, to briefly consider the Azande, a Central African people and their belief in witchcraft. A belief in witchcraft is central to Azande society and even Evans Pritchard, when living with them in the 1930s observed that to live in that society left one with no alternative but to accept the reality of witchcraft, so central was it to the Azande comprehension of the world. The Azande notions of witchcraft are used to explain things for which in our own world we have little explanation beyond 'bad luck', or mere or sheer coincidence. While we tend to be satisfied by the explanation that there *is* a physical cause for every physical act whether we can identify it or not, the Azande would be far from satisfied. If a particular shelter which falls down through termite action should fall at a particular time on particular heads we would probably be satisfied with the explanation of coincidence. The Azande however would not question the significance of the actions of the termites but would argue that witchcraft caused it to fall as and when it did. This, in turn, gave meaning to the event, because if the sorcerer could be identified, the witchcraft could be countered. Thus, the Azande made sense of their world through the legitimating secondary reality of witchcraft which made sense of the otherwise inexplicable. For participants in the society, disbelief was not an option because the evidence of the witchcraft was everywhere apparent.

To identify an event as one caused by witchcraft was however only a beginning. Its identification was important because it could lead to its elimination. This was achieved through the process of divination by which the diviner could identify from whence came the witchcraft. It was recognised that witches were often unconscious both of the fact that they *were* witches and also of the harm they were doing, and that they could be purged of the badness within them. Furthermore, if accusations were made by one person against another, for instance of adultery, again the diviner was called in to determine the truth of the accusation. There is on film a recording of such an accusation of adultery and its determination. The accusation having been denied the parties were referred to a divination with the aid of chickens. The diviner asked questions before the chicken (as the medium through which the ancestors reveal truths) and then proceeded to feed the chicken poison, in the knowledge that if the chicken died the answer would be an affirmative one and if it did not die the answer would be negative. (With one chicken per question, the process can be prolonged and expensive!) Once the chickens have 'spoken', it is usually simply not possible for the parties to demur because *the truth has been established* (whether or not it corresponds with what 'actually' happened).

At first sight, nothing could be further removed than chicken divination from our method of dispute resolution. Our system is, after all, rational, and theirs merely superstition. Further, an acute or cynical anthropologist might well want to observe that the reality for the Azande of the objectivity of the chicken divination, is actually more apparent than real. Conversely, however, an Azande anthropologist making a study of our courts might want to make the same point notwithstanding courtroom ritual and the beliefs of both litigants and observers. What do courts and chickens have in common?

To be a successful chicken diviner, the diviner must (as must a judge) come to conclusions which are not, regularly, completely inconsistent with public opinion.

If the diviner is to be regularly consulted (for which he is paid), the diviner will have to be respected for his accuracy in his divination. To the extent that he (the diviners are invariably male) can influence the outcome of the divination by, for instance, using larger chickens or less poison, it could be said (from an external perspective at least) that the diviner can in fact use the chicken divination and ritual to *legitimate* the decision he considers appropriate. The major point is that this ritual does give an explanation of illness, it does determine whether adultery has taken place and by whom, and does attribute blame. In addition, the diviner's decision was fail safe. If it was demonstrably wrong then it was clear to all that someone had interfered with the divination; it was the process which had been interfered with rather than defects in the process itself.

Perhaps, what might surprise external observers of Azande divinations most, is that the Azande consider that the divination provides an objective answer to the questions that have been posed and an answer which is usually then beyond question. But, of course, within 'Rule of Law societies' members generally believe that in the civil as opposed to the criminal courts at least, the *law* (rather than a divination) is applied, which leads to objective answers. A vital point to remember is that with *very* few exceptions no lawyer would either bring a case to court, or alternatively defend such a case, unless he or she considered the case to be legally winnable. What that means is that, in almost every case heard in the High Court and certainly in every civil case heard on appeal, the case would not be being heard but for the fact that barristers involved on both sides thought it possible that the court could decide the case, consistently with the law, as they had argued it. Nobody goes to court to bring a case or to defend a case which there is no prospect of winning. What is involved in chicken divination and the law courts is less the determination of an issue than the legitimation of the decision. For the Azande, the decision is legitimated by the chicken, for us the decisions are legitimated by the law with the accompanying courtroom ritual. Law students in a common law jurisdiction cannot but be impressed by the fact that almost every reported civil appeal decision could have been decided otherwise in a manner which was yet consistent with precedent (past cases); otherwise the case would simply have been unarguable. This is not to suggest that rules do not usually dictate outcomes. It is rather to acknowledge that the 'trouble' cases which come before the court upon appeal provide a need for an authoritative resolution and this is particularly difficult because there are (manifestly) arguments on either side.

We observed earlier that the Azande consider the chickens not simply as chickens but rather as a medium through which their ancestors may speak. The decision is not made by a mere mortal but by the ancestors who speak through chicken and diviner. It is not too fanciful to suggest that something of the same process occurs in common law courts. The judge or judges translate the message from the law reports, which are often themselves the words of the ancestors, in that what is applied, often comes from judges long dead. In England, the legitimation comes from the rules and from past cases, with the Azande it comes from chickens. Neither rules nor chickens dictate the result; they legitimate it.

When we suggested that the divination was fail safe because if it was wrong, the explanation was that someone had interfered with the divination, this too has parallels and reverberations. Time after time, when miscarriages of justice are exposed in our criminal courts the explanation is not that the method is wrong but that something interfered with the method whether it be perjury, improper use of evidence, or any other breach of the rules leading to a 'not good divination'.

When Christianity came to the Azande, most of the Azande converted at least nominally, but nevertheless in times of crisis, illness, or strife, the oracle is still consulted. Christianity did not provide the practical advice the Azande required. If religion is to be internalised, it has to provide the legitimation which people require to make sense of the inexplicable. The point in passing to be reiterated is that when new gods are accepted by existing societies, if they are to be successful not only must the society adapt, but so too must the gods.

A final point arising from Azande society warrants mention. The divinations are used not only to resolve problems which we would usually categorise as 'legal' but also sickness which we would categorise as 'medical'. If it seems bizarre to us to use the same method to diagnose the cause of severe illness as to determine whether adultery had taken place it is worth remembering that because law and medicine are secondary realities (and thus human creations) there is no *natural* categorisation. What is defined as illness, and indeed what is identified as crime or its equivalent, varies from society to society, as do all social problems which require translation.

It is appropriate to end these comments on Azande witchcraft with a quotation taken out of context, not about the Azande, but by an anthropologist writing in 1926 (Malinowski, 1926, pp 92–94) which nevertheless offers an insight into the use of oracles, divination and sorcery. It also suggests a central feature of both official secondary realities in general and chicken divination and law in particular:

> 'In many, in fact most cases, black magic is regarded as the chief's principal instrument
> in the enforcement of his exclusive privileges and prerogatives. Such cases pass, of
> course, imperceptibly into actual oppression and crass injustice, of which I could
> mention also a number of concrete instances. Even then, since it invariably ranges itself
> on the side of the powerful, wealthy, and influential, sorcery remains a support of
> vested interest; hence, in the long run, of law and order. It is always a conservative
> force, and it furnishes really the main source of the wholesome fear of punishment and
> retribution indispensable in any orderly society. There is hardly anything more
> pernicious, therefore, in the many European ways of interference with savage peoples,
> than the bitter animosity with which Missionary, Planter and Official alike pursue the
> sorcerer. The rash, haphazard, unscientific application of our morals, laws, and customs

to native societies, and the destruction of native law, quasi-legal machinery and instruments of power leads only to anarchy and moral atrophy and in the long run to the extinction of culture and race.

> Sorcery, in fine, is neither exclusively a method of administering justice, nor a form of criminal practice. It can be used both ways, though it is never employed in direct opposition to law, however often it might be used to commit wrongs against a weaker man on behalf of a more powerful. In whatever way it works, it is a way of emphasising the status quo, a method of expressing the traditional inequalities and of counteracting the formation of any new ones. Since conservatism is the most important trend in a primitive society, sorcery on the whole is a beneficent agency, of enormous value for early culture.'

Clearly, Malinowski's perspective is that of one who sees order as unproblematic and desirable, no matter how oppressive the powerful, wealthy and influential. It is significant that he says that because sorcery supports the vested interests, it is also supportive of law and order! But, the crux of what he says is that the legitimating secondary reality of sorcery reinforces a particular social order. Divination, and the fear of divination, in itself provides an important element of social control; and that social control is inherently conservative in reinforcing an existing social order. Because all the diviners are male and because they have the power to resolve the conflicts, the order which exalts the role of men is sustained. Malinowski attacks those who attempt to destroy the power of sorcery because they have not understood its role in social control. While we would not want readers to think that the description of such societies as 'primitive' or examples of 'early culture', for the reasons we discussed earlier, is acceptable, or even sensible, the explanation of the conservative features of sorcery, stands. So too does the point that legitimating realities legitimate an existing social order.

To make quite different points, we remain with the peoples of the Sudan but move to the Nuer people who live in the South. Evans Pritchard also spent time with the Nuer and his observations did in fact significantly alter British policy with regard to dispute settlement, by his observation of what had hitherto been invisible. By all accounts (though remembering necessary anthropological cynicism), when the British took over the administration of territory which included the Nuer lands, Nuer society seemed, at least to British eyes, to be a society in which disputes seemed endemic. To the British, there appeared to be considerable personal violence and widespread cattle theft. Evans Pritchard himself observed while living with the Nuer that:

> 'As Nuer, they are very prone to fighting, people are frequently killed. Indeed, it is rare that one sees a senior man who does not show marks of club or spear. A Nuer will at once fight if he considers that he has been insulted, and they are very sensitive and easily take offence. From their earliest years, children are encouraged by their elders to settle all disputes by fighting, and they grow up to regard skill in fighting the most

necessary accomplishment and courage the highest virtue' [Quoted in Moore, 1978, pp 95–96].

Having quoted Evans Pritchard, it is necessary to add that more recent observation of Nuer society has suggested that, beneath such manifest disorder, the Nuer did have ways of resolving disputes which were rather more subtle than simple violence. They were not, however, methods calculated to appeal to British administrators using as they did, prolonged arbitration, often with no clear-cut and enforceable decision and often leading to direct restitutive action together with a curse which would be effective for an aggrieved party.

The fundamental attributes of the British legal system were singularly lacking. There were no secular courts, there were no independent judges, no clear procedure for dispute resolution, and not even very visible leaders or people with power in disputes. For whatever reasons, and some reflect less favourably upon the British administrators than others, the British found such apparent chaos unacceptable and decided to regularise Nuer justice. They did not however attempt anything so crass as an imposition of British laws, rather they sought to identify the customs which they saw as being insufficiently upheld by the Nuer themselves. The underlying thesis was that if such customs could be given the force of law, this would allow for dispute settlement which would at once, both authoritatively and finally, resolve the trouble (and coincidentally make clear the beneficial quality of British administration!).

Needless to say, things did not work out exactly as planned. Nor yet was it the first occasion in which the British had rather mixed results in trying to translate native custom into law. Indeed, as early as Warren Hastings' period of administration as the first Governor General of British India (1774–85) in order to regulate and regularise custom, an attempt had been made to legislate for the Hindu population the provisions of the Dhamashastra – the Hindu code containing the rules of behaviour supposedly for all castes. (Although this might appear to have been an act of benevolence, the alternative explanation is that the real intention was the significant one of gaining control of dispute resolution because authoritative dispute resolvers always and necessarily have considerable power.) If the British expected Hindu gratitude for their legislation and that Hindus would consequently obey the law rather than the Dhamashastra, they were unjustifiably optimistic. The change from religious custom to law was objected to by all castes – even by the Brahmins who had traditionally obeyed the Dhamashastra anyway. Their objections were twofold. First, when they had voluntarily obeyed the rules in the past, there was clearly religious merit in doing so. If they were now to be compelled to do that which they had been doing voluntarily, their conduct might not change but the religious merit was lost. Their other objection was that one significant distinguishing feature of the Brahmin caste was that it did comply with the code in the Dhamashastra. If all were now to live by it, the distinction would disappear.

For other castes, the change was, if anything, even worse. The Dhamashastra had always been applied by them with discretion according to their particular needs. It was regarded as a code for guidance to be applied when practical. For it now to be enforced was to force them to obey a not wholly relevant code, without obtaining merit, and with sanctions for non-compliance!

That experience should have been relevant to the administration of the Nuer. To change custom into law inevitably has implications which are not readily foreseeable. While the British perceived obvious advantages in making law certain, its application regular, and the system of dispute resolution efficient, the Nuer, unfortunately (for the British), neither saw their disputes in terms which would allow of such clear-cut and rapid resolution, nor did they see these objectives as being what dispute resolution was about. Because Nuer society was based upon highly complex kin relationships and an intricate system of obligations (obligations which were often allowed to lie dormant but which could be made active), the Nuer failed to perceive their disputes as did the British. The Nuer method of controlling disputes was not intended to pronounce guilt or to enforce deterrent punishments. It was based on the notion of arbitration and their idea of justice was indistinguishable from their idea of social obligation and a religiously sanctioned moral order and hence the notion of the effective curse over the land of wrongdoers. The problem with an imposed settlement under the British system was that it did not effectively finally resolve anything, and this was particularly true if the solution was inconsistent with either kinship obligations, or with the religious implications of the dispute. For the Nuer, satisfactory dispute resolution was that provided by arbitration, conducted by persons of religious prestige, and determined with respect to other existing obligations.

Thus, what we see very clearly is that the legal method of translating a problem and decontextualising it simply did not work because the context remained and had to be lived with. While it is of the essence of legal method that it operates by ignoring what it defines as irrelevant or extraneous matters, to the Nuer, these aspects were an integral feature of the dispute, and, if ignored, the problem could not be considered resolved. The result of the court 'resolution' was that a case would often and quickly return to the courts in a new guise.

What happened then was that, although the British considered (perhaps) that they were beneficially legislating Nuer custom, this was not the way the 'consumers' perceived it at all. The Nuer simply did not see questions of order and justice in legal terms. Their obligations were not seen in terms of external rules, and ideas of guilt and innocence were altogether too simplistic. It was hardly surprising that the British reported, with some indignation, that they were still having trouble in 1918 persuading the Nuer to obey what the British administrators considered the Nuer's own rules!

With hindsight, it seems obvious that what the British were imposing was in no sense compatible with the Nuer tradition. In attempting to impose a legal

41

conception of custom, the British were in fact imposing a quite different way of understanding the world. Whereas law depends upon disputes being between individuals, Nuer disputes always involved the community. What affected any person had implications for those to whom the individual had ties of kinship. Whereas the separation of individuals from their social world is something that law requires for efficacy, it makes little sense to the Nuer.

Illustrative of this is the fact that one of the central problems faced by British administrators was the problem of enforcing full payment of debt when Nuer custom seemed to suggest that it should be payable. In fact, although custom suggested this, full payment was not, traditionally, insisted upon and for two subtle but non-legal reasons. First, to insist on full payment could activate the dormant obligations which we mentioned earlier which could lead to further disputes. But, in addition, to insist upon full payment would be to estrange irrevocably creditor from debtor and all ties of obligation would be broken. As one astute author (Johnson, 1966, p 74) observes:

> 'The courts in both Nuer and Dinka societies may have reaffirmed some obligations, but they were not necessarily ending disputes. Rather, they were proliferating disputes by insisting on the premature activation of social obligations. To a certain extent it can be said that in Nuer society, as in other Nilotic societies, the potential obligation, the uncollected "debt" helps to link individuals and different segments of the community together. The community is held together by "a willingness to share, give, loan and accept compensation for wrongs" and to this extent the moral community takes precedence over "the theoretical rights of individuals". The courts' insistence on precise and punctual repayment of obligations seems to have emphasised, in practice, what was owed the individual rather than the community. To fulfil one's obligations completely is to sever a link; to repay one's full debt ends a form of relationship. To *insist* on full payment is a sign that the relationship is broken.'

To conclude this chapter, we want briefly to consider a little more the distinction between law and custom. In an article by Stanley Diamond entitled 'The Rule of Law versus the order of custom' (1942), a number of relevant points are made – points which are also of relevance to the following chapter. Diamond suggests that, to us (dwellers in Rule of Law societies), custom is unimportant and something which is challengeable because it belongs to the past, but, for what he calls 'primitive' society (we would say societies which do not have the same concepts of law and state!), custom plays something of the same role as does magic for the Azande, in that there is no compulsive submission to custom. Customs are not followed in such societies 'because the weight of tradition overwhelms a man ... a custom is obeyed there because it is intimately intertwined with a vast living network of interrelations, arranged in a meticulous and ordered manner'. Thus, custom is very much part of the social reality, the shared commonsensical, taken for granted, everyday world which it is even difficult to talk *about* because it is so ordinary that the thought of disagreement does not arise.

Diamond also points out that it is a grave error to think of the law as known, certain and definite, while custom is vague and uncertain. Custom may certainly be somewhat flexible (as may law) but customary rules if they are part of the common sense world do have to be known and internalised. Because they are not sanctioned by organised political force, serious disputes about the nature and content of custom would destroy the integrity of society. The contention is that laws may be invented and stand a good chance of being enforced, while custom obviously cannot be created in this manner.

To summarise, then, what we have tried to explain in this chapter has been the relevance of legitimation to law, the idea of law as a secondary interpretive reality, and the problems of understanding the means by which other cultures resolve disputes. At the same time, it is important to understand the relevance of the dispute resolution mechanisms of other cultures in understanding our own law and appreciating its singularity not least by considering law compared with custom. All of this is relevant to the following chapter in its consideration of notions of property.

4   Making Rules, Making Property and Translating Disputes

We saw in the last chapter a crucial distinction between custom and law, in that custom is consensual while law is imposed; and, while custom is a part of social reality, law is a part of the secondary interpretive reality. In order to consider this relationship further and to begin a discussion of the relationship between law and property, we will quote a short story from Llewellyn and Hoebel *The Cheyenne Way* (1941, p 127). This is a 'case' which apparently took place among the Cheyenne, who were American Plains Indians.

In the first history, there is Wolf Lies Down, owner of horses:

'While Wolf Lies Down was away, a friend took one of his horses to ride to war. This man had brought his bow and arrow and left them in the lodge of the horse's owner. When Wolf Lies Down returned, he knew by this token security who had his horse, so he said nothing.

A year passed without the horse's return, and then Wolf Lies Down invited Elk Soldier Chiefs to his lodge because he was in their society. "There is this thing", he told them. "My friend borrowed my horse, leaving his bow and arrow; there they are yet. Now I want to know what to do. I want you to tell me the right thing. Will you go over and ask him his intentions?"

The borrower was in another camp well distant, yet the chiefs agreed. "We'll send a man to bring him in, get his word or receive his presents", they promised.

The camp moved while the messenger was gone, but he knew of course where it would be on his return. The soldier returned with the borrower, who was leading two horses, "one spotted one ear tipped". He called for the four Elk chiefs on his arrival. The chiefs laid before him the story told by Wolf Lies Down.

"That is true", the man assented. "My friend is right. I left my bow and arrow here. I intended to return his horse, but I was gone longer than I expected. I have had good luck with that horse, though. I have treated it better than my own. However, when I got back to camp I found my folks there. Our camps were far apart and I just could not get away. I was waiting for his camp and mine to come together. Now, I always intended to do the right thing. I have brought two good horses with me. My friend can have his choice. In addition I give his own horse back, and further, I am leaving my bow and arrow."

Then up spoke Wolf Lies Down, "I am glad to hear my friend say these things. Now I feel better. I shall take one of the horses, but I am giving him that one he borrowed to keep. From now on we shall be bosom friends".

The chiefs declared, "Now we have settled this thing. Our man is a bosom friend of this man. Let it be that way among all of us. Our society and his shall be comrades. Whenever one of us has a present to give, we shall give it to a member of his soldier society".

"Now we shall make a new rule. There shall be no more borrowing of horses without asking. If any man takes another's goods without asking, we will go over and get them back for him. More than that, if the taker tries to keep them, we will give him a whipping."'

In this story, we see the Elk Soldier Chiefs using the dispute to make a new rule against horse borrowing which was to apply for the future, together with a sanction, the whipping, in the event of non-compliance. The custom by which property could be borrowed by token acknowledgment was ended, or would have been if this rule was upheld. Property, which had been in some sense commonly held, at least to the extent that it could be borrowed by acknowledgment, would have become private property with the owner's rights exclusive.

Pertinently, in Hoebel's *The Law of Primitive Man* (1967, p 169) when discussing the Cheyenne, he observes:

> 'A fair amount of *petty pilfering* took place in the camp but *theft* was never made a legal issue. A known *thief* was publicly shamed with the remark, "If I had known you wanted that thing I would have given it to you". Gift giving was a high virtue and good Cheyenne were not supposed to value their material possessions too highly. Hence, they did not strive to discover the less proper person who lifted that which was not theirs.'

Interesting though that description is, however, it is equally significant that the only words with which Hoebel can describe this relationship with property is in the italicised terms of 'theft', 'thief' and 'petty pilfering' – all involving actions which contradict and threaten private property ownership, but which might not be incompatible with other ways of controlling and distributing things. That is, the moment we observe in *legal* terms the understanding of another society, we impose upon it a meaning which, while to us it might seem obvious, has connotations which may simply be meaningless to the people described. Yet, to Llewellyn, the unauthorised appropriation of things makes sense only as theft of property. If the situation of horse borrowing was as described in Wolf Lies Down before the ruling, it is possible to argue that property carried no such exclusive right of possession, which, if interfered with, should be designated a theft or even criminal, anti-social though it *may* have been.

It can be argued indeed that it is *our* notion of private property which most nearly equates with Azande witchcraft. So central is the idea to our comprehension of the world and to our reality that often even to suggest that private property is not natural is to invite incredulity. Just as the Azande found it difficult to talk *about* witchcraft without cynical hilarity and contempt for those who question it, so do we often react to suggestions that notions of property are socially constructed rather than natural. Because property and law are so inextricably linked, it is necessary to consider further, ideas of property , real and personal, private and common. The words of Jeremy Bentham (quoted in Gray, 1987) are worth bearing in mind: 'Property and the law are born together and die together.'

There is a legal distinction between real property or realty, and private property. Realty, roughly speaking, is essentially land and those things attached to it. Here, at least, it is reasonably easy to understand that not all societies see the land as something which is capable of ownership. Obviously, if there is land in abundance for all, as in the Sahara or in the Arctic, there is, traditionally at least, little concept of ownership of land.

But, not only is there no need to define ownership, the very idea of individuals owning land is utterly bizarre to some peoples. At its most extreme and emotional, this view has never been better put than in a reply purportedly from an American Indian Chief, Chief Seattle, when in 1854 he received an offer from Washington for the purchase of a large area of land peopled by the Indians. It is a statement which exemplifies a very different relationship of people to land from that which is orthodox to us with our legal knowledge of title and rights. Its authenticity need not concern us as the attitude remains significant. Yet, the questions that are posed are questions which really do require answers.

Chief Seattle's reply begins:

'How can you buy or sell the sky, the warmth of the land? The idea is strange to us.

If we do not own the freshness of the air and the sparkle of the water, how can you buy them?

Every part of this earth is sacred to my people ...

We know that the white man does not understand our ways. One portion of the land is the same to him as the next, for he is a stranger who comes in the night and takes from the land whatever he needs.

The earth is not his brother, but his enemy, and when he has conquered it he moves on.

He leaves his father's grain and his children's birthright are forgotten. He treats his mother, the earth, and his brother, the sky as things to be bought, plundered, sold like sheep or bright beads.

His appetite will devour the earth and leave behind only a desert.'

And, adds Chief Seattle:

'Whatever befalls the earth befalls the sons of the earth ... This we know. The earth does not belong to man; man belongs to the earth. This we know.'

Even so, it might be argued, this attitude to land tells us little about our own relationship to land, where we have a long tradition of individual land ownership although it is worth remembering JJ Rousseau's observation about land in the 18th century (quoted in Gray, 1987):

'The first man who having enclosed a piece of ground bethought himself of saying 'This is mine!' and found people simple enough to believe him was the real founder of civil society. From how many crimes, wars, murders; from how many horrors and misfortunes might not anyone have saved mankind by pulling up the stakes, or filling up the ditch and crying to his fellows "Beware of listening to this impostor! You are undone if you once forget that the fruits of the earth belong to us all, and the earth itself to nobody!"'

And, as a final quotation of pertinence, we go to Robert Tressell's *The Ragged Trousered Philanthropist* which not only calls into question the naturalness of the ownership of the land but makes some suggestions (which might or might not be acceptable) about the political nature of ownership. In the excerpt (Tressell, 1965, pp 163–64), one of Tressell's characters is speaking:

'Poverty is not caused by men and women getting married; it's not caused by machinery; it's not caused by 'over-production'; it's not caused by drink or laziness; and it's not caused by 'over-population'. It's caused by Private Monopoly. That is the present system. They have monopolised every thing that it is possible to monopolise; they have got the whole earth , the minerals in the earth and the streams that water the earth. The only reason they have not monopolised the daylight and the air is that it is not possible to do it. If it were possible to construct huge gasometers and to draw together and compress within them the whole atmosphere, it would have been done long ago, and we should have been compelled to work for them in order to get money to buy air to breathe. And, if that seemingly impossible thing were accomplished tomorrow, you would see thousands of people dying for want of air – or of the money to buy it – even as now thousands are dying for want of the other necessaries of life. You would see people going about gasping for breath, and telling each other that the likes of them could not expect to have air to breathe unless they had the money to pay for it. Most of you here, for instance, would think so. Even as you think at present that it's right for a few people to own the Earth, the Minerals and the Water, which are all just as necessary as is the air. In exactly the same spirit you now say: "It's Their Land", "It's Their Water", "It's Their Coal", "It's Their Iron", so you would say "It's Their Air", "These are Their gasometers, and what right have the likes of us to expect them to allow us to breathe for nothing?" And, even while he is doing this the air monopolist will be preaching sermons on the Brotherhood of Man; he will be dispensing advice on "Christian Duty" in the Sunday magazines; he will give utterance to numerous more or less moral maxims for the guidance of the young. And, meantime, all around, people will be dying for want of some of the air that he will have bottled up in his gasometers ...'

The object of these quotations is simply to reinforce the obvious but well hidden fact that while land exists naturally, property in land, or land ownership, is a socially constructed fact which requires legitimation. And, although the quotation from Tressell may seem extreme, it might well have been even more so had it alluded to the remarkable phenomenon in our society of land being 'owned' by individuals who have never seen and might never see the object of their ownership and yet whose rights, derived from ownership, might be far greater than the rights of families who have dwelt on the land for generations.

All this, hopefully, is reasonably obvious and clear but it does have implications which we will consider later. A crucial point is that the translation of land to property does not alter the realty but it *does* alter the reality. What property is about is only indirectly about the object of ownership. Rather, it is about *rights against other people* over the land. What then becomes crucial is what we mean by 'rights' and we should begin to see that our definitions of property require law for the enforcement of property rights when challenged, and their guarantee where not. Thus, what is central to property, indeed that which creates property from things, is rights, but the idea of rights might itself be intimately connected with law.

Leaving the discussion of realty and its ownership we should now consider personal property. It will be obvious that things, possessions and, property are three separate concepts. We may possess without owning and particularly when others have ready access (often without permission being necessary) to possessions, it is clear that to talk of exclusive property rights is misleading as also is the language of 'petty pilfering' and 'theft'.

Of course, just as land exists naturally and property over land or ownership of land is a social construct which does not alter the land itself, so too of personal property. Things exist in any social world, but what is not fixed is the relationship between person and thing. As CB Macpherson put it in *Possessive Individualism* (1962), property is not objects themselves but, as with land, rights in, or to, things. Although we often equate property with *private property* (an exclusive individual right), there is no inherent reason why this should be so. But again what is also significant is the distinction between possession and ownership. The implication of ownership is that the owner has a claim that will be enforced by society or by the state; by custom, or convention, or law.

Macpherson observes that the concept of ownership is often justified or legitimated in very circular terms (not unlike Azande explanations of witchcraft!). As he says, 'the perennial justification of any institution of property is that property ought to be an enforceable claim because property is necessary for the realisation of man's fundamental nature or because it is a *natural* right'. And so far have we internalised the naturalness of private property that as he says 'property is not thought to be a right because it is an enforceable claim' [as in fact it is], but rather 'it is an enforceable claim because the prevailing ethical theory holds that it is a necessary human right' (Macpherson, 1962).

When expressed in these terms, the effect ought to be to force us to question why it is that property is understood as it is in our society and, perhaps even more, to consider in whose interest it is that property is perceived in this way. It is not least because of the 'naturalness' of property (which in turn implies necessary inequality) that concepts of distributive justice, or equality, have seldom held sway in property-owning regimes.

Furthermore, because property is about enforceable claims, it is (in Macpherson's terms) a *political relation* between persons because *every system of property is a system of rights of each person in relation to other persons*. Because property requires enforceable rights this implies that there must be some body to enforce these rights and in modern times, in 'Rule of Law' societies this has been the state. Significantly, if the idea of property is to be one with effect, it will always require the potential for enforcement, but not by the owner of the rights (even if at his or her behest or request), but rather by somebody other than the owner. Because for us it is usually through law that these rights are legitimated and may be enforced it can be suggested that there might be a dialectical relationship between property and law in that our understanding of property is dependent upon law but so too is much of our law dictated by the demands and needs of private property. Although we will return to this relationship, it may at this point be worth considering that it may be law which allows us not only to objectivate property – to see things *as* property (thus, *my* house, *your* dog, *her* elephant) but it may be too, that we need law to *alienate* property, that is, to change the property in the thing from one person or body to another.

We return now to the story at the beginning of this chapter concerning Wolf Lies Down. Were the Elk Soldier Chiefs acting in a 'legal' way? A first point to be made is that there is no need to lay down a rule if there is complete agreement about how people should conduct themselves over horse borrowing. Transparently to be a horseless Cheyenne for whatever reason, particularly to be one who also knows that current Cheyenne conduct dictates that when necessary one goes to war, as did Wolf Lies Down's friend, is tedious beyond measure, and possibly also ridiculous and humiliating. And, it might seem even worse if the person from whom one might borrow a horse, were he present, actually has spare and unused horses! Yet, if the rule were to be applied, this would be the outcome, or rather it would have been but for the fact that the sanction of the whipping seems to have been envisaged not for the borrowing but for the refusal to return.

The crucial point remains however, namely, that to lay down the rule, 'There shall be no more borrowing without asking' reflects conflict which necessitates a ruling and a ruling is given which clearly favours horse owners over the horseless.

We do not know the subsequent history, if any, of the ruling. It would only amount to a legal a way of dealing with disputes if it were subsequently applied to cases of unauthorised horse borrowing. This, in turn, would imply that, for whatever reason, the Elk Soldier Chiefs had the power to lay down such a rule. Rules as such (without the constant application of force) are obviously only effective if those who are to be affected accept the authority of the rule giver. Because this is a general point, it is worth considering under what circumstances rule givers have authority.

The Elk Soldier Chiefs might have had that power for perhaps one of five reasons. The least likely but most obvious would be that the Elk Soldier Chiefs had sufficient force at their command to ensure that it was well known that any infraction of the rules would indeed lead to a whipping. This is however improbable because there were only four Soldier Chiefs for each Soldier society and they would have had to rely upon assistance to enforce the rule if so required.

Secondly, the Elk Soldier Chiefs might have obtained the power to lay down rules if they had access to a legitimating religious world as did the Azande diviners. In many societies, selected medicine men, priests or shaman have the ability to effectively curse those who disobey injunctions and break rules, particularly about places or things, which are declared taboo or tapu. Or, indeed, the rule might be effective if people believed that the rule was transmitted through the priest figure from the Deity as in the case of the Ten Commandments, or Joseph Smith's golden tablets which revealed God's will to the Mormons. (It may be excessively cynical (but not irrelevant) to observe that Moses's laws in Palestine were upon stone, Joseph Smith's tablets in the US were of gold!) (Those who understood the point about God being created in man's image will appreciate this!)

Thirdly, the authority of the Elk Soldier Chiefs could have been derived from tradition with a significant history of accepting rulings from this particular body, or conforming with the custom of how things are done. When we considered institutionalisation, we saw how tradition might be a very strong source of legitimacy.

The Elk Soldier Chiefs might also have been able to make such a ruling because of the particular esteem in which those particular chiefs were held. The Elk Soldier Chiefs were chosen for their prowess, strength and courage and it might be that their charisma alone sufficed to create the rule.

Finally, it is possible that the created rule reflected popular sentiment and seemed right and proper as a modification to an old custom based on reason. It is relevant to consider the source of the authority of all rule givers because rules invariably, if they are to be effective, require legitimation. There must be some answer which satisfies the question: 'why should I be bound to obey that pronounced rule?'

It is manifest then that, if rules are to be effective, they must be accepted and legitimated. Although theoretically it might be possible for the rule to be accepted because the Elk Soldier Chiefs did a great deal of whipping, as we observed earlier, the more force which is required to support a rule, and the more often the sanctions are applied, the less like a law the rule seems and the more like a simple exercise of superior force. Rules are at their most effective, and so is law, when it is accepted that it is wrong to break them; that is, when conformity with law or rules becomes a value in itself. If members of a society can be persuaded to the belief that it is wrong not to obey the law, then the importance of sanctions fades and the transparency of the exercise of power fades also. When a society becomes accustomed to obedience to rules laid down in particular ways, that very custom of obedience comes itself to be coercive and rule obedience to be a value in itself. So much is this the case that, as we have observed, in our own societies to continue with the same arguments against policy when that policy has been translated into official rules (that is, law) is regarded as almost unthinkable and tantamount to rebellion. This is well exemplified by opposition parties constantly pledging to resist laws which they regard as bad 'by all lawful means'; which in fact usually means accepting the law no matter what its outcome.

What we hope this illustrates is that the fact that there is an official rule, itself provides an answer as to what is correct conduct. The rule laid down in the case of Wolf Lies Down becomes the resolver of issues of horse borrowing. The magic of this process is that an official rule comes to govern future cases not because it is necessarily the best solution to a new situation but because it is the official rule. One of the implications of this is that such rules will then affect the outcome of cases to which they are applicable even though the social reality or the need for the rule might have changed.

What the case of Wolf Lies Down illustrates then is one potentially legal method of dealing with conflict whereby those in society with authority determine the outcome and use the opportunity to pre-empt future conflict by promulgating a rule for subsequent events. In fact, we do not know how the Cheyenne responded to the rule. It is probable that they continued to regard horse borrowing as negotiable in spite of the rule, because for most Cheyenne-like societies custom was always more important than official rules.

While continuing to pose questions related to private property, we want to consider a singularly different form of dispute resolution from that suggested in the Cheyenne example. To do so, we turn to the Inuit (Eskimo) people whose practices make further comment upon our own. Obviously, and significantly, the Inuit lived, and to some extent still do, in conditions very different from those of the Plains Indians. Until recently, Inuit life was always close to the edge of survival. In many ways, and certainly through European eyes, it was a grim life and the most popularly known facts – that the Inuit sometimes practised infanticide and sometimes put the aged out on to ice-floes to die – are misleading. It nevertheless does give some idea of the problems commonly faced. Such deaths were only caused when the entire life of the community was threatened by starvation.

More importantly for our purposes, however, the Inuit existed without most of the political and governmental structures that often exist in such communities. 'Leaders' or the 'Headman' possessed no fixed authority, had no formal position and were neither elected nor formally chosen. 'When other men accept his judgment and opinions he is a headman; when they ignore him he is not.' The only Inuit word meaning 'Headman' is not a flattering one ('ugiman') and is actually pejorative.

The Inuit property regime was not one that we would recognise. In respect of game which was killed, all who took part in the hunt had rights. The accumulation of property beyond that required to satisfy need, was regarded as unacceptable. The entrepreneur who accumulated too much property (that is, kept it for himself) was looked upon as not working for the common good: 'so that he became hated and envied among the people' (Hoebel, 1967, p 81). Ultimately, such an accumulator would be forced to give a feast and to distribute all his goods upon pain of death in the event of a refusal. 'Nor might he ever again undertake to accumulate goods. Should he postpone the distribution too long he was lynched and his goods distributed among the people by his executioners ... Prolonged possession of more capital goods, than a man could himself utilise was a capital offence in Western Alaska and the goods subject to communal confiscation – elsewhere, the ethics of generosity and hospitality were enough to see to it that he who had, gave' (Hoebel, 1967, p 81).

Parenthetically, it is not insignificant that Victorian 'Christian' anthropologists found this ethos of generosity and hospitality and the rules against the accumulation of property, as evidence of a lack of moral development! When the Encyclopaedia Britannica observed of the Eskimo, in the 1870s, that: 'long habit and the necessities of their life have also compelled those having food to share with those having none – a custom which, with others, has conduced to the stagnant condition of Eskimo society and to their utter improvidence', it seems, at least in retrospect, incredible that the inconsistency between the legitimating Christian world and the practice of accumulation and speculation was invisible to such authors. Of this we will say more when we consider the cargo cults of Papua New Guinea. This Encyclopaedia Britannica entry is an excellent example of imperial anthropology which sees property regimes only through its own cultural spectacles.

An extended extract reads as follows:

'The Eskimo cannot strictly be called a wandering race. They are nomadic only in so far that they have to move about from place to place during the fishing and shooting season, following the game in its migrations. They have, however, no regular property. They possess only the most necessary utensils and furniture, with a stock of provisions for less than one year; and these possessions never exceed certain limits fixed upon by tradition or custom ... Long habit and the necessities of their life have also compelled those having food to share with those having none – a custom which, with others, has conduced to the stagnant condition of Eskimo society and to their utter improvidence.

Moral and Mental Character –

So far as a nation can be characterised in a few words, it may be said that the Eskimo are, if not in the first rank of barbarous races, not in the last, and that, though they want some of the mental endowments of races like the Polynesians, they are equally free from many of their vicious traits. Their intelligence is considerable, as their implements and folk-tales abundantly prove. They display a taste for music, cartography, and drawing, display no small amount of humour, are quick at picking up peculiar traits in strangers, and are painfully acute in detecting the weak points or ludicrous sides of their character. They are excellent mimics and easily learn the dances and songs of the Europeans, as well as their games, such as chess and draughts. They gamble a little – but in moderation, for the Eskimo, though keen traders, have a deep-rooted antipathy to speculation. When they offer anything for sale – say at a Danish settlement in Greenland – they always leave it to the buyer to settle the price. They have a dislike to bind themselves by contract. Hence, it was long before the Eskimo in Greenland could be induced to enter into European service, though when they do so now-a-days they pass to almost the opposite extreme – they have no will of their own. It is affirmed by those who ought to know that any sort of licentiousness or indecency which might give rise to public offence is rare among them. In their private life their morality is, however, not high. The women are especially erring; and in Greenland, at places where strangers visit, their extreme laxity of morals, and their utter want of shame, are not more remarkable than the entire absence of jealousy or self-respect on the part of their country-men and relatives. Theft in Greenland is almost unknown; but the wild Eskimo make very free with strangers' goods – though it must be allowed that the value that they attach to the articles stolen is some excuse for the thieves. Among themselves, on the other hand, they are very honest – a result of their being so much under the control of public opinion. Lying is said to be as common a trait of the Eskimo as of other savages in their dealings with Europeans' [1875, vol 8, p 545].

Upon this, there is little need to comment! Two other central features of Inuit life were, first, the necessity of cooperation and collaboration if survival was to be ensured, and, secondly, what seems to have been a remarkably high level of violence; almost invariably between men and usually, regrettably, about men's claimed rights of possession over women. (The 'erring' women were not always tolerated in their 'erring' as the Encyclopaedia Britannica might suggest!) Killing itself was not translated as a crime. When violence occurred if the perpetrator was thought to be unjustified, he might simply be killed or the people might simply withdraw from the violent man, and as we have observed, a life alone is not possible in such an environment.

In other disputes, the Inuit used what at first sight seems a ludicrous method of dispute resolution; dispute resolution by so-called 'song-duel'. The song-duel is an important form of dispute resolution but it is not the only form. It stands alongside boxing and head-butting contests as a means of resolving disputes not involving homicide. Clearly, in both boxing and head-butting competitions the facts which have led to the dispute are completely irrelevant. Like trial by battle, there is no concern with issues of justice but only with a resolution, whatever that might be. He who wins acquires vindication and esteem; he who loses, loses standing in the eyes of the community. Song-duels are altogether more subtle in their operation (they could hardly be less!) because of the participation of the community which they allow. While there is a plethora of forms a song-duel may take, depending upon local custom, a typical song-duel will take place in a public gathering with each of the disputants (or his representative) singing in turn a song of contempt and abuse directed at the opponent. Like the boxing or buffeting contest, the song need have no relevance to the dispute in hand or its facts. Rather, it is concerned to score points through ridicule and it is said that singing skill may equal or outrank gross physical prowess. It also seems that the choice of the song-duel as a means of resolution is chosen, not surprisingly, by those who are clearly physically weaker than the adversary.

The singing is highly stylised with traditional patterns of composition and it has been suggested that the Inuit's best songs of abuse do have quite highly developed property rights attached to them! Indeed, the better known and more predictable the song, the greater will be the ability of the audience to participate, appreciate and empathise. Such empathy is generally expressed by violent but friendly digs in the ribs of the good singer. The winner is he who can win the audience or simply silence his opponent.

There are a number of features of the song-duels which are relevant to our consideration of law. Unlike the Elk Soldier Chiefs who lay down a ruling, in the song-duel, it is the community that decides victor and vanquished. Even more significantly, the winner of the song-duel wins the dispute even though neither the case itself nor the facts of the case are ever alluded to. The rights and wrongs of the social dispute are determined not by a discussion of the merits of the case but by talking about something else which *can* be decided!

The great advantage of this process is that a social dispute to which there is simply no ready or obvious solution which would be accepted as correct by both parties is *translated* into a form which is amenable to decision. It is because of the very insolubility of the social problem that the problem is not faced but rather sidestepped. Just as a contest of physical violence, such as trial by battle, or boxing, *does* provide a solution of sorts, so does the song-duel but in a more subtle way.

Admittedly, at first sight this bizarre process for resolving disputes seems to be of little relevance to our perception of our way of dealing with disputes but several points need to be made. The most obvious is that in our experience most law students on first visiting the courts, and particularly the courts hearing appeals are immediately impressed (as often are the litigants themselves) by the fact that the court does not seem to be hearing argument 'about the real issue'. Rather, what they experience is a debate over what seems to be a technical point of law. It is, of course, just such legal points that determine cases.

A second obvious point is that just as the Inuit has, or often may have, a nominee to sing his song, so of course does the litigant in a Rule of Law jurisdiction have his or her barrister or legal representative to sing his or her song for him or her. Significantly, although one of the principles of justice in such societies is that all are equal before the law, it is well known and understood that all legal representation is not of the same quality or competence. A true generalisation is that the more one can afford to pay one's advocate the greater will be the prospect of success in the court. The better the payment, an Inuit may say, the better the song. Anyone whose instinct is to question this proposition need only consider why some barristers or advocates are able to command fees greatly in excess of others. And, to read autobiographies or biographies of great legal figures is to read of figures (certainly in the common law jurisdictions) who gained fame, wealth and prestige through winning cases against prediction.

Although one might consider that any analogy between Inuit song-duels and Western courts is fundamentally flawed and misplaced, because the result of the song-duel seems much more arbitrary than court decisions, this almost certainly underestimates the Inuit. There is little doubt that an Inuit with a very strong social case is in a strong position to sing a powerful song to which the community will be sympathetic. If the merits of the case were overwhelming the wrongdoer would hardly welcome a song-duel.

We have suggested that the sidestepping of the issue renders the dispute resolvable, but the sidestepping, or the translation itself may also, to an extent, defuse the issues. It is easier to be detached from the social issue while fully participating in the song-duel. In writing about the duels, one author (Hoebel, 1967, p 96) noted that:

> 'In spite of the nastiness of the insults hurled it is good form for neither party to show anger or passion. And it is expected that the participants will remain the best of friends thereafter.'

And, as long as the issue which resolves the dispute is not the social issue itself, a losing litigant is always able to blame his loss on a badly sung song (or an incompetent advocate) rather than being forced to accept the very real humiliation that his own case lacked justification.

Finally, the participation of the community is also significant. Not only does the participation have the effect of controlling the formalised conflict (in the pressure upon the participants to retain self-control) but it also exerts group pressure on the participants not to irrevocably disrupt the community. They are under pressure to abide by the community rules and in many song-duels winner and loser, in spite of the decision, are expected to be reconciled and as a token of the reconciliation they will exchange presents. Thus, the community strength is reasserted by reintegrating the parties in conflict back in to the community. The song-duel then serves a function beyond the interests of the parties in that it reasserts the unity of the community.

In summary, then, it is impossible not to see the advantages of side-stepping the issues in a dispute. Although there is an obvious 'downside' to the method in that underlying social issues *may* remain as we saw in the Nuer world, this process (if accepted by the litigants) does turn an irresolvable dispute into one which may be resolved. It may defuse the issue, and through the participation of the community it may allow the reintegration of the parties.

The Western world, of course, as we have observed, also translate issues into a form with which the legal order can cope and as we have said, a large part of the lawyer's craft is in being able to define the issues. Having translated the dispute, we are in turn constrained, if not governed, by rules which may not always appear appropriate. Because the Inuit example seems so exotic, it makes points about our own system of dispute resolution more easily than domestic examples. Nevertheless, it is important to realise that examples of such sidestepping can be found universally. It would of course be possible to quote examples of trial by battle or trial by ordeal, although in the latter at least, it was believed that divine intervention would ensure an accurate result.

To exemplify the significance of the Inuit song-duels to Rule of Law societies, we shall briefly consider two English cases one of which is concerned with criminal law and one with civil. The first, *Ashford v Thornton*, is very much a case which marks the transition, albeit a late one, from the explicit avoidance of issues to the new format which decides hard cases by reference not to social facts but to structured legal categories and technicalities. *Ashford v Thornton* is a case decided in 1818 in which it was held that under some circumstances trial by battle was still available to an accused. The Chief Justice Lord Ellenborough held, in words which take us back very explicitly to rule magic, as follows:

'The general law of the land is in favour of the wager of battle, and it is our duty to pronounce the law as it is , and not as we may wish it to be. Whatever prejudices therefore may justly exist against this mode of trial, still as it is the law of the land, the Court must pronounce judgment for it.'

Incidentally, but as a matter of interest, the authorities considered, in reaching that decision, the law of Normandy all the way back before the Norman Conquest of 1066.

Ashford v Thornton also provides us with an (admittedly) extreme example of the translation process used by law to put questions into a resolvable form. The application against Abraham Thornton at the behest of William Ashford, the deceased woman's brother was put in the following terms:

'For that he the said Abraham Thornton not having the fear of God before his eyes, but being moved and seduced by the instigation of the devil, on the 27th day of May, in the 57th year of the reign of our Sovereign Lord George the Third by the grace of God, &c with force of arms at the parish of Sutton-Coldfield in the county of Warwick, in and upon the said Mary Ashford spinster, in the peace of God and our said lord the King, then and there being feloniously, wilfully, and of his malice aforethought, did make an assault, and that the said Abraham Thornton then and there feloniously and wilfully, and of his malice aforethought, did take the said Mary Ashford into both his hands, and did then and there feloniously, wilfully, violently, and of his malice aforethought, cast, throw, and push the said Mary Ashford into a certain pit of water, wherein there was a great quantity of water, situate in the parish of Sutton-Coldfield aforesaid in the county aforesaid, by means of which said casting, throwing, and pushing of the said Mary Ashford into the pit of water aforesaid by the said A Thornton in form aforesaid, she, the said M Ashford in the pit of water aforesaid with the water aforesaid, was then and there choaked, suffocated, and drowned, of which said choaking, suffocating, and drowning she, the said M Ashford, then and there instantly died. And so the said A Thornton, her the said Mary Ashford in manner and form aforesaid feloniously and wilfully, and of his malice aforethought, did kill and murder against the peace of our said lord the King his Crown and dignity' [*Ashford v Thornton* (1818) 106 ER 149].

While we would not now expect to see charges framed in such a way, this *reductio ad absurdum* does make manifest the legal method of translating social events into legal format.

The second English case which we can use to illustrate both the sidestepping of the issues and the way law justifies decisions by referring to pre-existing rules is the case of *Thompson v London and Midland Railway* [1930] 1 KB 41 which, although over 60 years old, seems almost contemporaneous to lawyers.

The facts of that case as heard by the court were that the tragic Mrs Thompson had wished to travel for a day's outing from Manchester to Darwin on the London and Midland Railway. Mrs Thompson could neither read nor write and she requested her niece to purchase her rail ticket for her. When the niece bought the ticket, she might have seen on the front of the ticket the words: 'excursion. For conditions see back.' Had Mrs Thompson's niece then turned the ticket over she would have seen a notice to the effect that the ticket was issued subject to the conditions in the rail company's timetables. The timetables were on sale at the ticket office and one of the conditions attaching to the issue of excursion tickets, according to the timetable was that all liability for injury to excursion passengers, however caused, was excluded.

Without being aware of these conditions, Mrs Thompson set off for Darwin. Unfortunately, when the train arrived at Darwin and its arrival was announced to passengers, Mrs Thompson stepped out only to discover that there was no platform outside her door as the train in which she was a passenger was longer in length than the Darwin station platform. Mrs Thompson was injured in the fall and sought compensation from the railway company. The *legal* issue of the case did not concern itself with Mrs Thompson's injuries except extraordinarily indirectly. Mrs Thompson must have been amazed to discover what the question of her compensation turned upon. The legal question to be answered by the court was: 'was the clause excluding liability for injury, to be found in the timetable which was available at the ticket office, a part of the contract of carriage entered into by Mrs Thompson via her niece as agent and the railway company?'

The court held that Mrs Thompson was unable to recover. They did so by referring to previous cases and the rules that they had laid down. The questions they asked were not concerned with what seemed the most socially relevant facts – the injury to Mrs Thompson and her need for compensation – but rather to the rules and circumstances under which it would be held that a party to a contract had had 'constructive' notice of the existence of a clause which purported to limit liability. Having said that it must be conceded, that, to many law students, the legal question will seem the obvious one. So commonsensical has contract become that many on hearing the facts of Mrs Thompson's case will want to know immediately the terms which governed the transaction. It is not frivolous to suggest that such Rule of Law common sense is objectively no more sensible (nor yet less so) than the Inuit's acceptance that a song-duel which talks about something almost utterly unrelated to social facts is an appropriate way of resolving social disputes.

For a more modern and equally striking example of the 'translation' process at work, readers may wish to turn to the decision of the European Court of Justice in *SPUC v Grogan* [1991] 3 CMLR 689. The case arose out of a decision of the Irish Supreme Court to grant an injunction to restrain a student organisation from publishing and distributing guides to abortion clinics in the UK. It appeared to raise fundamental questions relating to the protection of human rights and to necessitate a balancing of the 'right to life' contained in the Irish Constitution on the one hand, and freedom of expression protected by Community law on the other. Translated into a form susceptible to adjudication by a reluctant European Court, however, the case was deemed to hinge rather upon the meaning of 'services' within the European Community Treaty and the capacity of the Irish restriction upon the provision of information to interfere with the cross-border supply of services in the Community's internal market. Ultimately, the decision of the Court was predicated upon the fact that the students responsible for the distribution of the information were not financially rewarded for their activities and hence not economically tied to the clinics in the UK whose services they were advertising. For the European Court, 'buying' an abortion was seen in the same light as the purchase of an insurance policy.

To summarise this chapter then, it has been our argument that many of the features which make our legal system seem obvious and sensible are in fact contingent – contingent in the sense that they are no more nor less logical than other ways of understanding the world which to us at first sight seem absurd. We have suggested that the taken-for-granted property regime is not natural, not only socially constructed, but constructed in a way which is of benefit to some (the property owners) and of detriment to others. Yet, this benefit is legitimated by creating and maintaining the appearance of the naturalness of property. When Proudhon observed that 'Property is Theft', he was making a point which at one level at least was doubly subtle. Proudhon's phrase implicitly recognises both the law's legitimation of property and the law's ability to legitimate some ownership and to deny other possession the title of ownership because of the means of acquisition. When Angela Davis, in a stirring but finally futile statement in the US in the 1960s, claimed that the real criminals were not the people in prisons across the US but were rather those who had stolen the wealth of the world from the people, she was echoing Tressell, Proudhon, and even Lenin, but, it has to be said, with rather less lasting effect.

We then attempted to understand how it might be that rules can be made by one body for another and what is it which provides rule makers with authority. Why do rules made by others feel coercive and under what circumstances? And why do such rules seem to carry with them the value of obeying – why do we obey rules because they are rules, rather than because they are merely appropriate to a particular problem?

Finally, by way of stark comparison both to the Cheyenne property regime and to their dispute resolution system we looked briefly at Inuit social organisation and their song-duels. Such cursory consideration was intended to provide us with ways of seeing more clearly some of our own techniques for resolving problems exemplified in English law. Those who would maintain that while contract is rational, customs are irrational, would do well to read again the extract from the Encyclopaedia Britannica.

5   Defining Disputes and Comprehending the World

What the examples of dispute resolution in the last chapter had in common was that they all led to resolution through a translation of social facts into a form which could be resolved. At its most extreme, this meant dealing with the conflict by talking about something completely unrelated to the social dispute. Although all societies have ways of dealing with disputes which are intractable, and threaten or disrupt the life of the community, there are communities which attempt this task without translation. The means by which they do this, the limitations inherent in such an approach, the objectives such attempts seek to achieve, and the reasons for attempting to resolve the social problem in the social world, are all of significance in a consideration of law in our own Rule of Law world. The initial points we wish to make will be derived primarily from three sources. The first will be concerned with the use made by the Kpelle people of the 'moot' as discussed by Gibbs in 'The Kpelle moot: a therapeutic model for the informal settlement of disputes' (1976); the second will consider the preservation of order among the Ba Mbuti Pygmies as discussed by Colin Turnbull in *The Forest People* (1984), and the third will consider Bohannan's analysis of Tiv justice in *Justice and Judgment among the Tiv* (1957).

The Kpelle are a people who inhabit central Liberia in West Africa. The Kpelle moot, as described by Gibbs, is a complete contrast both to courtroom method and to song-duels. It is not however the only way of dealing with 'trouble cases' amongst the Kpelle; they also have courts which are explicitly coercive and authoritarian and which are used when a case is unlikely to be resolved by moot. Significantly, the moot procedure tends to be used when it is considered important for the community that the parties to the dispute be reconciled. The task for the moot then is in many ways a more challenging one than the task for a court, for not only must the problem be resolved but the parties themselves must accept the outcome as genuinely correct. Because of this, it would be a mistake to see the moot as less coercive than the court though it is certainly less explicitly so, and its coercion is of a different kind and quality.

The moot is a method of dispute resolution which does not depend in any sense on a duel between the parties. Rather, the aim of the moot is a reconciliation of views to provide, or attain, a uniform perception of a dispute – a perception shared both by the participants and even the parties to the dispute. A successful moot is one in which perception is reorientated so that it is shared by all. The dispute is resolved within society, without translation. The issues considered are the social issues themselves. This is because, as reconciliation of the parties is an important goal for the community, the dispute must 'really' be eliminated rather than simply ended. To do this, it is necessary to actually change the perception of the problem by at least one of the parties but probably both.

In itself, of course, this goal constrains the conduct of the moot, as the decision reached must be one which will not irrevocably alienate any member of the community. Thus, there is a constant emphasis upon reconciliation and compromise. How does a moot set out to achieve such apparently desirable goals? According to Gibbs, it is because of the moot's therapeutic nature; therapeutic in the sense that it acts as therapy 'gently' persuading the parties to merge their perception of what has occurred. This reorientation is then sealed by a delicate exchange of goods and gifts; delicate in that the level of gift giving is intended not to embarrass the giver who in turn is the recipient of a gift from the other party. A successful moot ends with the party who has had to make the greater change in perception (that is, whose perception was found more 'incorrect') receiving group approval for capitulation and the other party approval for magnanimity in victory.

As described, the moot is a remarkably informal institution. It is, in Gibbs' words: 'an informal airing of a dispute which takes place before an assembled group which includes kinsmen of the litigants and neighbours from the quarter where the case is being heard. It is a completely ad hoc group...' (Gibbs, 1967, p 279).

There is a person of prestige (significantly male!) who acts as mediator and commences the proceedings with a blessing upon both parties (who are there 'voluntarily') and the community. Each party is given the opportunity to speak, though he or she may be interrupted by either the mediator or any participant. Supposedly, although unrestrained, the proceedings remain orderly although those who speak out of turn may be fined (the fine being alcohol for the moot participants). After all who wish have been heard and had questions asked of them, the mediator 'expresses the consensus of the group' at which point the exchange of gifts takes place and the 'losing' party provides rum or beer, which is consumed by all present.

The procedure of the moot is designed to achieve this necessary reorientation. Everything may be said, and indeed there is encouragement for the parties to say whatever they will whether, in our terms, strictly relevant or not. The advantage of this is twofold: first, all causes for dissent can be faced and eliminated; and, secondly, as Gibbs says, the more neurotic the things which are alleged the more important it is that the allegations are dealt with by the community. Obviously, the pressure upon the parties to the dispute to accept the decision of the community is immense. As we have said, the procedure is begun with an appeal to the Deity for blessing upon parties and community, but it also perhaps has the effect of suggesting that to refuse to accept community views is an infringement of, or a challenge to, that blessing.

At one level, this means of resolving disputes is surely attractive. What, after all, can be better than a genuine reconciliation of the disputants, particularly if the whole community's solidarity is also reemphasised? And, to some extent, this sort of reconciliation and reintegration is reminiscent of the way in which many family disputes are resolved. There is often a basic recognition that that which a family has in common is more important than individual conflicts.

Nevertheless, further consideration might give rise to some hesitation about the Kpelle moot being unequivocally wonderful. Just as in the case of the Azande divinations, here again the mediator is invariably male, and the ideology which is being reinforced is that in which men are obviously dominant. This is a society in which men may have more than one wife and can inherit a wife from a brother regardless of the wife's wishes. And, although it might seem that the moot is singularly free from rules, the norms upon which the moot operates may be no less coercive – indeed, they might be so coercive that anyone who questioned them would obviously be a suitable case for referral to the court which can impose decisions when a moot is unsuccessful (and again the court is dominated by the chief, again invariably male).

And as a final comment, it is worth referring back to the comparison between law and psychiatry in Chapter 2 which ought to make us hesitate about the inherent value of therapy, and therapeutic goals. The result of a moot is obviously exceptionally coercive. To lose in court is to lose a case; to lose in a moot leaves one with little alternative but to accept the view of the community. Further, it is possible to walk away from the court having lost a case and still feel sure that one was right notwithstanding. In the examples provided by Gibbs, even a woman who has been adjudged in dereliction of her wifely duties to a husband whom she finds repellent, is left with no choice but to accept that her correct role is as a servile piece of male property. To reject that judgment, that role, and that therapy, would be to reject Kpelle reality; the reality of Kpelle society as reinforced by court, moot and man. Furthermore, every time the parties to a moot are reconciled in conformity with this ideology, the ideology is itself strengthened because the correct way of seeing the world, and consequently of acting, has been demonstrated both to disputants and to the community. There is a scene in a Ken Loach film *Family Life* (based on the work of RD Laing) in which one of the 'deviant' young women observes presciently of her position in a mental asylum: 'You've got to see it their way if you want them to help you.' The consequence in a moot, of refusing to see it 'their' way, is actually to put oneself outside of the society within which one exists and from which one obtains identity; an horrific prospect to all except the truly disordered! (joke).

Leaving this aside, however, the significance of the moot is that it does very clearly describe a situation in which problems are resolved in the community. The resolution does not involve translation and it is here appropriate where reconciliation is important.

Colin Turnbull's book about the Ba Mbuti Pygmies is well worth reading in its entirety and it is singularly free of the anthropological jargon which so often gets in the way of understanding. Perhaps, the most significant criticism of Turnbull's methodology as an anthropologist (a criticism with which we do not identify) is that he has rather too much empathy for the people he is observing and cannot resist becoming a player in the social drama which he is supposed (academically speaking) to be watching. Consequently, this is an entertaining and romantic book in which one fears cynically but hopefully wrongly that the Pygmy world may have been idealised. For those of us who prefer to believe it in its romanticism, there is always the sobering thought that such has been the destruction of the Pygmies' beloved rain forest to satisfy the needs of export and industry that this question will anyway be forever unresolvable. Turnbull's book was published in 1961 and since then destruction in the name of development has been devastating.

The Pygmy Forest people live in the North East corner of what was the Belgian Congo, to the West of Uganda. The Pygmies live within the rain forest but they also emerge to take temporary employment for the local non-Pygmy population with whom they have an almost symbiotic relationship. Indeed, one of the themes of the book is the manner in which the Pygmies maintain self-pride and confidence (not to say arrogance) in the face of an apparently subservient role to the local population, whom they have, at various times, to serve. (Irrelevantly but interestingly, this is perhaps one of literature's (and life's) eternal themes – the fact that servants know so much more about masters and their private lives with all their indignities and absurdities, than the masters know of the servants! Servants paradoxically encompass masters, in a way in which the converse is unimaginable.)

In the chapter concerned with disputes in Pygmy society, Turnbull indicates directly many of the features of the relationship between societies where disputes are resolved without translation and those which rely upon a separation between law and society. Here, when disputes arose, there were no conflict specialists as one might find in our courts. Rather, as Turnbull (1984, p 102) says:

> 'There were no chiefs, no formal councils. In each aspect of pygmy life there might be one or two men or women who were more prominent than others, but usually for good, practical reasons. This showed up most clearly of all in the settling of disputes. There was no judge, no jury, no court. The negro tribes all around had their tribunals, but not so the pygmies. Each dispute was settled as it arose, according to its nature ... In a small and co-operative group no individual would want the job either of passing judgment or of administering punishment, so like everything else in pygmy life the maintenance of law was a co-operative affair.'

While we might query the use of the phrase 'the maintenance of law' since what is described seems scarcely legal in character, we would also want to observe that the real reason disputes had to be resolved quickly and effectively was twofold. First, as in our Inuit example, the groups of Pygmies were heavily interdependent and co-operation was necessary for survival. The second related reason was that as the Pygmy depended upon the successful hunting of game for their survival, any significant disruption within the community would also disrupt the hunt by frightening away game.

One story in particular illustrates very well the pressures upon a tightly knit hunting community to remain together. The story concerns a young Pygmy man Kelemoke who is discovered in what to the Ba Mbuti Pygmies was an incestuous relationship with his cousin. Turnbull being caught up in the noise and concern asked his informant to explain the furore:

> 'He looked very grave now, and said that it was the greatest shame that could befall a pygmy; Kelemoke had committed incest. In some African tribes it is actually preferred that cousins should marry each other, but amongst the Ba Mbuti this was considered almost as incestuous as sleeping with a brother or sister. I asked Kenge if they would kill Kelemoke if they found him, but Kenge said they would not find him. "He has been driven to the forest" he said "and he will have to live there alone. Nobody will accept him into their group after what he has done. And he will die, because one cannot live alone in the forest. The forest will kill him. And if it does not kill him he will die of leprosy." Then, in typical pygmy fashion, he burst into smothered laughter, clapped his hands and said, "He has been doing it for months; he must have been very stupid to let himself be caught. No wonder they chased him into the forest." To Kenge, evidently, the greater crime was Kelemoke's stupidity in being found out' [Turnbull, 1984, p 104].

Theoretically, then, Kelemoke will die because one cannot live alone in the forest. But, of course, as Turnbull is told, once Kelemoke has been driven into the forest food is secretly taken to him by his friends and after three days he comes cautiously back to the camp where he is accepted as though the deed (or deeds!) had never taken place and, according to the book, Kelemoke supposedly never 'flirted' with his cousin again. The *threat* of punishment is ever present but the demonstration of its possibilities is sufficient. And, as is observed, it is difficult for the group to maintain an ostracising punishment for long because the size of the communities emphasises the interdependence in a hunting community.

It is not surprising that the worst offence that can be committed in Pygmy society is an act which threatens the group. We see this in another of Turnbull's stories about one Masolito who, in return for some distinctly unbrotherly conduct, tries to enlist from the group support for his position. Because of the noise for which he is responsible, it is Masolito who incurs the wrath of the *Molimo* (the semi-supernatural method of punishment) because as Turnbull says: 'he is guilty of the much more serious crime of splitting the hunting bands into opposing factions' (Turnbull, 1984, p 110).

So great is this emphasis upon the wellbeing of the camp that:

'Disputes are generally settled with little reference to the rights and wrongs of the case, but more with the sole intention of restoring peace to the community' [Turnbull, 1984, p 110].

And the person most guilty in this society is the person who disrupts the camp, particularly to the extent of causing noise which will disrupt the hunt. This emphasis on preserving the wellbeing of the group is well illustrated too in Paul Bohannan's book on the Tiv to which we will shortly turn.

But, the forest people of the book are distinguishable from most other peoples in one important way of significance for our discussion of women and law in later chapters. Regularly, in anthropological material not only is the role of women distinct from that of men but also when women do appear in their own right rather than as 'male appendages', it is usually with an explicitly inferior status (though that inferiority is male defined). Quite often, women appear simply as the property of men who seem able to exercise almost absolute control. Later, we will consider the significance of this division between male and female roles, and the almost constant subordination of women. Although it is again possible to romanticise the role of women in Pygmy society, one feature which is noticeable and significant is the extent to which roles are shared and interchangeable. Because of the size of the groups and because of the lack of an accumulative property regime, specialisation had not arisen and men had not appropriated roles of power in relation to women.

As a final example of attempts to resolve disputes within the community, we turn to the example of the Tiv Jir. At the time, when Bohannan was studying the Tiv, they were a tribe of subsistence farmers living in Northern Nigeria. There were some 800,000 Tiv and they were usually to be found living in local groups (though spread over the farmland) of between 150 and 1500 people. The area which each group or subgroup inhabited was called the Tar and the word 'Tar' is a name which designates both an area and a group or subtribe belonging to that area. This, for each member, is the primary Tar. As well as that, there will be adjacent groups who together form a larger Tar, and the largest Tar of all contains all the subgroups and is known as Tar Tiv or Tiv land.

From the opposite dimension, the Tar is the country, the land of the Tiv and it contains many 'utar' defined by lineages into which the Tar divide themselves 'and in terms of which they see some of the most significant of their relationships with one another'. Until the intervention of the European, there were no Tiv courts but only the moots or the Tiv Jir, beyond which there were elaborate non-jural means of self-right enforcement, particularly armed raids and self-help.

As Bohannan (1952) says:

'Moots both traditionally and at present [1952] are concerned primarily with disputes *within* a social group, courts (imposed by the colonial power) are concerned with disputes between social groups or between individuals in different social groups.'

The first aim of the courts was to settle those disputes that were no longer permitted to be settled by self-help which might include violence. We might conclude from this that, as with the Kpelle, it might be the case that a moot, since it involves the reorientation of perception, might only be acceptable in a situation of great social cohesion where imposed solutions would be likely to lead to continuing resentment.

The Tiv Jir, or moot, is a mechanism which not only resolves disputes but reinforces society through a ritual handling of the problem *within* society. The problem does not become the preserve of specialists and it is not isolated in its facts but is rather simply a part of the ongoing social world. There are a number of points illustrated by the Tiv Jir. As with the Kpelle, when contrasted with a British legal system the Tiv Jir does seem remarkably informal. It lacks most of the attributes of our legal system, with no officials, no procedures and no clearly defined rules. The Tiv moot as with the Kpelle is intended to achieve not the clear cut decision of the court, but rather, essentially a compromise. As with the Kpelle (and with the Inuit), a large number of the local community takes part in the Jir with everyone having a right to contribute. Whereas our courts are expected to be isolated and removed from the community, the Jir is essentially a community operation.

What, then, is significantly different in the Tiv Jir from the Kpelle moot which necessitates such repetition? The answer lies in three major points to be made. The first is in the significance of the way in which the Tiv talk about a case which goes to the Jir. They do not speak in terms of solving a case, or resolving the dispute, or deciding the case, or judging the case or even determining blame. Rather, they speak in terms of 'repairing the Tar' – the goal is to repair damage to, or trouble caused by the social group designated by the Tar concerned. When there is social trouble within a Tar, it is spoken of by the Tiv as something 'spoiling the Tar' and the object of the Jir is to 'repair the Tar' by resolving the trouble. There is the recognition that disputes which require moot 'handling' are those which damage the community.

There is a danger of oversimplifying this idea of repairing the tar because it also has other meanings in terms of the use of magic and various rituals (unfortunately involving more sacrificial chickens) and it is also used to give meaning to things which, like disputes, are not readily understandable, such as death and disease. But, to repair the Tar is to adopt a means of ensuring the harmonious continuance of the community.

The second point of significance intimately concerns this idea of repairing the Tar. It concerns Tiv notions of truth and falsehood. In Tiv language, the two antonyms to the word 'yie' (meaning lies or falsehoods) are 'mimi' and 'vough'. 'Vough' corresponds closely with our notion of judicial truth, namely something which is verifiable and/or which corresponds with 'what happened'. The notion of vough is also of importance in the court resolution of conflict in Tivland. But of 'mimi' which is much more prominent in the Tiv Jir we have no exact equivalent. It has some of the ambiguity Bohannan observes of our word 'right' in that it means both the morally good thing and also the socially correct thing. It does *not* necessarily imply the factual truth of 'vough'. To quote Bohannan:

> 'In considering the evidence presented to the *jir*, one must always keep in mind the similarities and distinctions between the two words *mimi* and *vough*. We must also realise that each speaker also weights these words from his own point of view. Therefore, an accuser in a Tiv court action may "speak *mimi*", but this does not mean that we can, translating, say that he is telling the truth. He is, rather, telling that version of the story which does least damage to social relationships from his own point of view. He might, at a later date,even admit that he did not "speak *vough*". The accused in his turn will "speak *mimi*" but *mimi* is not the same thing from his point of view as it is from that of the accuser ... Tiv judges do not expect principal litigants to speak vough but only to speak *mimi*' [1957, pp 49–50].

And Bohannan goes on to say that no Tiv would blame a witness for telling what we should consider untruths if by doing so the criterion for 'mimi' was maintained; and that is so even though witnesses are usually expected to use 'vough'. Truth in Tivland, says Bohannan, is an elusive matter because smooth social relationships are deemed of higher cultural value than mere precision of fact. We cannot judge Tiv litigants or witnesses in our terms. They are not liars, as to us they might seem, but their truth differs from ours. 'Mimi' is best translated as 'the best truth' as opposed to 'the truest truth'. Truth, for the Tiv, is not an objective and value free notion, as is our judicial truth supposed to be.

The third point of significance concerns, not the way the Tiv see facts, but the way in which the Tiv see and understand their rules and prohibitions. For us, as we have argued, 'The Law' confronts us as a massively real institution which takes on the appearance of separateness from, and independence of, the very people who created it. Our laws take their validity from the fact that they are a part of this legal institution and world – a part of 'The Law'.

The Tiv however do not have anything which equates with our legal institution. Their rules do not derive legitimation from being a part of the legal reality. One consequence of this is that such rules as they do have, appear as individual rules (Bohannan would say 'laws') which they call 'tindi'. While as Bohannan says: 'European Courts determine the facts and then determine what laws, customs and precedents are involved' (1957) because the Tiv 'tindi' does not have that authority tindi may be seen as a law but the institution of law is unknown. Thus, tindi are isolated prohibitions or injunctions and although they may be individually important they do not have the same form as our law, because they are not part of a system. Because of this fundamental difference, the appropriateness of designating such prohibitions as laws, as Bohannan does, is in doubt, but the point is well made that isolated rules do not command the same authority as rules which are part of an institution of law.

The objective of the Jir is, as we have said, to settle a Jir with the agreement of the litigants and the community. To settle it otherwise is unacceptable. The idea of settling a Jir 'by force' is the worst fate that can befall a Jir. So strong is the pressure to accept the conclusion of a Jir that even the imposition of a fine or even imprisonment must be agreed to, and approved of as appropriate, by the person affected, if the decision is not to be considered arbitrary. If the person to be imprisoned objects, then the case will be reconsidered. If however that person is the only one who considers the penalty unjust, there are, so to speak, ways of persuading the recalcitrant to 'accept' the justice of the sentence. It is possible for the elders to threaten to withdraw their protection from witchcraft.

A final point concerning the Tiv is best put by Bohannan when he speaks about the difficulty for us with our ethnocentricity (starting from the premiss that our world is normal and one against which to judge others) to make sense of what is going on without imposing our own sense of order upon other people. He says (1957, p 69):

'It would be possible, once one had elicited all the rules which one could find in all the cases, to arrange them into some sort of order and set them forth as the procedural law of the Tiv courts ... The error would be that the arrangement is not part of the Tiv way of looking at it, and hence would be false.'

In each of these three examples of dispute resolution within the society itself, untranslated, and without the use of specialists, we see the decisions reached being validated not by a secondary legitimating world, but by consensus and consent directed to ensuring the continued order within the particular society. For this to be possible, it is obviously necessary that there should exist in such a society a high level of orthodoxy with limited possibilities for the acceptance of deviance. Societies which are able to resolve disputes in this way will almost certainly be closely knit groups, without a high differentiation of interests. Nevertheless, one must observe that even among most such groups there is, or there appears to be from an external perspective, a distinction in the interests and power of men and women.

The requirements of legitimation are very different when disputes are resolved by translation. As we saw in the case of the Azande, for these decisions to be sustained, there must be an acceptance of the authority of the decision for some reason. An example which illustrates even more clearly both this need and at the same time suggests insights into our own judicial process is to be found in the use by the Ibo people of Nigeria of oracle usually in the form of a magical voice emanating from a bush, by which to resolve intractable disputes. What we see here is that if disputes that are not consensually resolvable, are not authoritatively resolved by access to a secondary reality of religion, magic, law or whatever then the most probable outcome will be violence, in which the problem will be resolved in favour of the more powerful. Without such mechanisms the bigger stick determines the victor. Resolution of disputes through violence is always problematic however in that high levels of violence in a society threaten its very existence and also in that violence is not only self-defeating but is itself the ultimate method of resolving a dispute by sidestepping. Such a resolution has no direct relationship to the dispute itself, and will often bear no relationship to what is seen as the correct decision by the members of the society.

If, however, the dispute may be translated then, as in the case of the Azande, a decision may be reached which is consistent with the morés of those with the power in any society. Our discussion of Ibo oracles is largely derived from Simon Ottenberg's article 'Ibo oracles and intergroup relationships' (1958) not because it is the best description of the phenomenon in most senses, but because it very much suits our purpose in that, accurately or not , his description, if over simplified, is also immediately, if misleadingly, comprehensible and accessible. Ottenberg writes of the Ibo oracles from an explicitly external perspective in which the social fact of the oracle is quite invisible. For Ottenberg, the oracle is simply a person concealed and revealed only as a voice in a bush, who pontificates upon disputes in a way which is accepted by those who have consulted the oracle and are gullible enough to believe in its powers. Though, perhaps, that description could be paralleled by an acute Ibo anthropologist observing our own court room drama, and suggesting that the person in the strange garb, with or without a wig, and possibly even wearing a maroon dressing gown, is merely a human being rather than a judge. Of course, to the Ibo people, the oracle is not a human voice in a bush; to them, the oracle is the magical provider of justice.

The oracle was very much a place of last resort for disputants who stood to pay dearly if they were unsuccessful. Historically, the fail safe device which effectively made the oracle incapable of incorrect decision lay in the sanctions applicable to an unsuccessful litigant. Although a fine might have been thought appropriate in very minor cases, in more major cases (and in order to make the journey to the oracle cases would generally have been serious), the loser could forfeit his life or be sold into slavery. Thus, the sanction against consulting the oracle was very substantial. In Ottenberg's words: 'If the consultation concerned a dispute and the decision went against a person he might have to pay a fine to those controlling the oracle; he might be sacrificed to the oracle, or more likely be sold into slavery. If the decision was one in which a person was indicated to be a witch, or sorcerer, or a thief he would generally either be sacrificed or sold into slavery' (Ottenberg, 1958). Obviously, then, only the most intransigent disputes were actually brought to the oracle and there was an obvious incentive to resolve disputes informally within the community.

To us, of course, the idea that litigants should lay their case before a bush with a human voice seems bizarre, and to Ottenberg it appeared only a sham, yet what might he (and we) say of our own courts. Transferring his understanding of the oracle, he could not fail to observe the authority granted by the surroundings and trappings to the judicial figure. A judge is *not* simply a person dressed up in a peculiar way. The surroundings and trappings allow him (or her) to *become* a judge. What the bush does for the voice to make it into an oracle, the surroundings, the clothes, and the style, together with the court procedures, all operate to turn a human being in to a judge – at least for the people socialised to see the reality.

Secondly, an Ibo anthropologist would quickly have realised why it is that more people do not consult our judicial oracle and why it is that it is often said that the best lawyers are those who manage to keep clients out of court. In Britain, where losing litigants are usually required to pay not only their own costs, but those of the victor as well, the effect will often be simply ruinous. There is, in all Western jurisdictions, almost invariably (except sometimes in the case of those legally aided), this very significant sanction against consulting not only the judicial figure, but even the initial, but still expensive legal specialist.

Thus, it is clear that the decision of a specialist is often legitimated, by actually making the specialist something more than a merely wise mortal.The creation of a judge is no less magical than the creation of an oracle, but what is significant is that we are able to identify magic when practised by others, but not by ourselves.

A little more needs now to be said about legitimation and its role in making the world around us sensible. To do so, we will move from Africa to New Guinea to consider cargo cults and one particular story of a leading figure in those cults. To have any appreciation of the significance of cargo cults, it is necessary to understand a little of what the coming of the Europeans meant to the peoples of New Guinea. The appearance of Europeans in New Guinea effectively challenged almost every aspect of the New Guineans' ways of comprehending their world. Whereas they had had gods which reflected their comprehension, suddenly they were faced with European missionaries who brought word of a quite different god – and one who was apparently believed in by people who had access to the most miraculous and fantastic things; things indeed which, until seen, were quite unimaginable. It seems that it was (not unreasonably) not at first realised by the indigenous New Guineans that the European goods to which they were introduced were really human products because for them it was simply inconceivable that such things could be made by mere people. How could *people* produce ships, and machines, and guns, and books, and cloth? The answer was so far outside experience as to be utterly beyond imagination. The only 'reasonable' explanation, then, was that the goods were created and provided by the European God. (This, of course, is a clear example of the point we made earlier that things which cannot be explained in the common sense world, may require interpretive explanations placed upon them from secondary specialist realities.)

It also seems that the access that the missionaries had to such goods in turn was likely to have reinforced the perception that there was a relationship between religion and material products. It also seems that the missionaries themselves did not go out of their way to dispel this view. (Perhaps, their problem was similar to the dilemma Endo, in his novel *Silence*, suggests faced the Jesuit missionaries in Japan in that they realised that the bible in its Latin, if translated literally into Japanese, would have little appeal because it did not address the issues which the Japanese wanted a religion to address. At the same time, if the bible were freely translated to deal with that difficulty could it still be said to be the word of God?) Anyway, it seems that after initial difficulties in persuading natives to convert to Christianity the suggestion that if Christianity were followed wealth would also follow was effective. Moreover, Marvin Harris fairly points out that the missionaries' role must have seemed rather confusing to people who were used to the belief that wealth brought with it both obligation and the possibility to be a 'bigman', namely the opportunity to obtain status, prestige and approval by providing feasts and giving away wealth. Indeed, for many, the sole reason for accumulating wealth beyond personal need, was so that prestige could be acquired through the redistribution of the excess wealth. Harris also observes that in their world the worst thing that anyone could be was a 'stingy bigman', and it must have seemed to them that the missionaries kept for themselves that which ought to have been redistributed (Harris, 1977, p 100). He does not point out, but it is undoubtedly relevant, that the native view of the obligation of 'bigmen' to redistribute wealth is obviously completely consistent with Christian doctrine, and of course the New Testament constantly enjoins Christians to give away their wealth if they are to become true followers of Christ. Here were the missionaries living with wealth unimaginable to the natives, preaching the message of Christian charity and love for one's neighbour, and yet giving away almost nothing. The confusion in the minds of the natives is fully comprehensible.

Attempts to make sense of the situation may be perceived in one story told by Harris of the New Guinean, Yali, a study of whom provides a central part of Peter Lawrence's book about cargo cults *Road Belong Cargo*. Yali was a native who had won the respect of the Australians who were administering Eastern New Guinea, for his valour in the Second World War and for the fact that, unlike many of his compatriots, he had remained faithful to the Australian administration rather than transferring allegiance to the conquering Japanese. By all accounts, Yali was an impressive figure. Peter Lawrence (1964, pp 126–27), in an extract which also says a lot about Lawrence's self-perception, says of him:

'One of the most significant of Yali's experiences – especially his wartime experiences – was that they gave the unprejudiced Europeans who liked and supported him a one-sided appreciation of his character and outlook. When he first came to their serious attention during and after 1945, he impressed them at once as an exceptional native. He was of fine physique and much taller than the average native of the Southern Madang District, well spoken and dignified without ever being impertinent. He was always scrupulously clean and well turned out, bathing regularly, and wearing a spotlessly white singlet or shirt and immaculately ironed shorts.

These externals set aside, Yali had even greater qualities. [!] In the first place, he had a deep sense of responsibility. At the beginning of the Japanese invasion, when many policemen on the mainland were openly deserting, Yali remained loyal.

In the second place, Yali gave the impression of almost complete Western rationality. He genuinely liked Europeans, took pleasure in their company, and wanted nothing more than to count them among his friends. His close personal associations with them as *Tultul* of Sor, policeman, and soldier, and his reputation as a war hero, gave him ease of manner in their presence. He could talk about service and administrative affairs, and his experiences in Australia with a degree of seeming sophistication. Thus, generous Europeans regarded him as a native who had really seen into their world: who had grasped some of the essential concepts at the basis of their own culture – hygiene, organisation, and hard work.

Yet, this was only a surface image ... Yali's was the tragedy of all men who want to assimilate an alien culture, but can see only its externals and hence never leave their own behind.'

(Note: this extract needs to be read several times if its extraordinary ideology is to be truly appreciated!)

Yali's early beliefs are difficult to summarise not least because they proved to be infinitely malleable, constantly readjusting to encompass more perceived phenomena. In essence, however, they were an interpretation of the bible, which at once explained the 'cargo-less' predicament (poverty) of almost all natives, the 'cargo' of the Europeans and prescribed a means of obtaining a share of the cargo. The belief was that God created the world, placed Adam and Eve in Paradise completing their happiness by providing them with cargo (such as tinned meat, steel tools, and tobacco in tins, and matches); that they forfeited their place through having sexual intercourse and lost access to cargo, that after the flood Noah and his family survived and would all have once more had cargo, as indeed did Shem and Japheth (Noah's sons) and all their descendants (the white races), but Ham, Noah's third son, the ancestor of the New Guineans, offended God and was sent cargo-less to New Guinea, where he and his descendants had to do without. It was also believed that in due course his descendants would return to the ways of God and cargo would then be provided.

Beliefs of this kind are not, it has to be said, unusual in many millenarian movements among peoples newly converted to Christianity who are yet unwilling to abandon their traditional cultures, but they are significantly less absurd than they may at first appear. The natives who came into contact with the missionaries were faced with startling differences between what they observed, and what they were told they were seeing. Even leaving aside Lawrence's questionable statement that some of the essential concepts at the basis of European society are 'hygiene, organisation and hard work' there are several significant contradictions in Yali's perceived reality which required resolution.

In particular, Harris suggests there were three central contradictions which were made explicit when Yali was rewarded for his loyalty by a visit to Australia. The cargo cult explanation for the goods which they were unable to acquire was that the Europeans had kept from the natives the secret of cargo, by which they initially meant that the Europeans prevented the gods delivering the god-made articles to New Guineans, and then later in Yali's time, that although the goods were the products of humans the secret of their production was that given by the gods to Europeans who then refused to give the natives a share of the products. The missionary promise, which was quite unfulfilled, was that once the natives became Christian then if they worked hard, material reward would follow. They did. It didn't. Even so, this was how wealth/cargo ownership was legitimated.

When Yali visited Brisbane in Australia, he might well have seen just how unclear the link between work and cargo, or work and wealth was. The people who went to work in the factories each day might have seemed to get very little of the cargo and might well have appeared to live in more poverty than those who did things which could only, with difficulty, be identified with work. Even if he did not, however, two events are known to have impressed Yali significantly. The first was his visit to Brisbane zoo and later to an agricultural station. In the zoo, he was impressed less by the range of animals than by the fact that they were so well treated and that furthermore there was information about evolution. Evolution did not seem compatible with the missionaries' Christianity, yet it was consistent with the pre-Christian pagan beliefs of his people, which had been treated with scorn by the Europeans! And why, if they were not of totemic significance, would the animals be treated so well? Unable to accept the explanation that some Europeans believed in the Bible as incontrovertible truth, while others held other views even within a fixed social group (so far was such divergence of belief alien to his own society), Yali came to a new conclusion. The care shown the zoo animals, the animal husbandry in the agricultural station, and the care lavished upon pets in Brisbane, could only be explained by the recognition that for Europeans, Christianity was only one part of the world which hid the secret of cargo. The missionaries had not been open with them. Europeans too, just as his own people, had multiple totemic origins. As well as Adam and Eve and the *Moñki*, there were others claiming descent from the animals.

The second event of significance was Yali's visit to the Queensland museum. According to Lawrence, Yali's party were impressed not at all by the mechanical exhibits from Western society. What did impress were the exhibits from their own society – not only face masks, and bows and arrows, but statues of old gods. A member of the party from Madang asked a crucial question: 'Why', he asked the European officer conducting them, 'do the missionaries urge us to root out the "satans" and then other white men come and collect all these things invented by the "satans" and put them in this Museum?' (Lawrence, 1964, p 132).

Indeed, the very 'false gods' they had been urged to destroy by the missionaries, which had previously been revered, were here to be found in positions of status and dignity, in glass cases and with attendants in white coats to look after them! How was Yali to reconcile the apparent contradiction?

In fact, these events led to Yali emphasising the role that the pagan gods had in the cargo beliefs, and it provided further evidence that the Europeans had duped the natives in order to continue withholding the cargo that was rightfully theirs. It did provide an explanation of why Europeans had cargo, and made sense of the clear deceptions practised by the Europeans against the natives. Most satisfyingly of all, perhaps, it provided what has been described as a 'tremendous feeling of self-respect under European domination'. 'As an intellectual system it [cargo] explains European economic superiority with much greater logic in native eyes than any description of Western financial transactions, industrial research and factory organisation with all their complexities and seeming [sic] contradictions can ever hope to offer. To reject the cargo belief completely for untried schemes the logic of which is not at first apparent, would involve renewed dependence on the white man and hence a sacrifice of pride' (Lawrence, 1964, p 269).

What is the significance of this rather strange episode for a study of law? First, although we do not have Azande, Ashante or Nuer anthropologists in some ways Yali, in trying to make sense of another culture, is in the role of a New Guinean anthropologist. And, what Yali sees is significant for us as well as for him. Just as any anthropologist, Yali can see only what can be understood in his own ideological framework and what is consistent with his experience of the world. In translating the European world, he sees he inevitably gets some things wrong, but not unreasonably so (in particular, the role of gods in the creation and distribution of cargo). Yet, though this is an error, it makes more sense of cargo distribution than did a belief in work bringing cargo. Indeed, this is something Yali *does* get right in that he sees that some of our sustaining legitimations do not appear to correspond with reality.

Secondly, when Yali is faced with contradictions in what he perceives, and contradictions between what he thinks he sees and what he is told he sees, and contradictions in the reality he is expected to internalise he resolves the problem by moving to a different frame of reference, namely that of religion. Phenomena which cannot be explained or made sense of in the ordinary world have to be given meaning in an interpretive reality – here the world of the gods and ancestors.

Thirdly, Yali along with most New Guineans found the European concept of property difficult to comprehend, but as we have already argued a society's property regime and ideology, is crucial for the interpretation of the world. As we observed, to a Madang native the only purpose of property accumulation was in order to obtain status by redistribution. The idea of accumulation of wealth as an end in itself is a difficult one for many people, as indeed it should perhaps be for us.

A final related point which Harris makes cogently is that there really is a mystery about cargo. Whereas the rather problematic conclusion of Lawrence's book concerns itself with how to eliminate cargo cults: 'We must so coordinate and introduce our programmes of development that the mass of the people have no alternative but to accept them as the only logical solution to the problems of modern living' (1964, p 273). Harris says that to write of the cargo cult leaders as rogues or idiots might be cogent 'if there was not in fact anything mysterious about how industrial wealth gets manufactured and distributed. But, in point of fact', he goes on, 'it is not easy to explain why some countries are poor and others rich, nor is it easy to say why there are such sharp differences in the distribution of wealth within modern nations' (Harris, 1975, pp 99–100).

It is also true that, in *Road Belong Cargo,* Lawrence sees the problem of Yali's understanding in his belief that cargo is the result of ritual rather than industrial production with all that that implies. Yet, it has to be added that confusion between ritual and reality is not confined to New Guinea. We too place emphasis upon ritual in the hope that it will provide. The attempts of Western industrialists to imitate Japanese corporate methods (from early morning company songs to corporate loyalty) seem oblivious to the fact that only the Japanese are Japanese. Perhaps, we also see the problem of confusing ritual with reality when we observe the UK's answer to the paucity of university graduates. Rename polytechnics 'universities' and the problem is solved (apparently!).

6   Women and Subordination

In this chapter, we want to explore the relationship between the status of women in any society and the prevailing form of order. We have been looking, in this book, at several different types of society and at theories about what is a 'natural order', as opposed to an imposed order, an opposition between consensus and conflict, and the role of law in reproducing or maintaining, constructing or destroying the existing order. By looking at the way in which women are treated in actual societies or in social theory, some of the issues may become clearer, even if solutions remain as tenuous as ever.

We have already referred to the dangers of what might be called cultural imperialism or the imposition of inappropriate interpretations on the behaviour of people in other societies. For example, Llewellyn and Hoebel's use of the terms 'theft' and 'petty pilfering' in their account of the Cheyenne, terms which presuppose a private property regime and which would have been foreign to the Cheyenne themselves, may distort comprehension. For those who are concerned with the role of women in other societies, there is the added danger of androcentrism to be guarded against (a danger to which we referred in Chapter 3). By this, we mean that, until quite recently, male anthropologists have tended to rely on male informants among the people they have been studying and have not asked the questions which women might want asked. Thus, if male anthropologists ask husbands in a polygamous society what they think about the marriage system, they are likely to get very different answers from the answers given by women to women in the same society. Polygamy is considerably more popular with husbands than it is with wives. Again, it is clear from Gibb's account of the Kpelle moot that women were certainly present and were often at the centre of the dispute, but it is not at all clear whether equal weight was given to the views of young women as was given to the views of old men in the discussion, and the fact that the disputes so often involved the re-education of women into their appropriate roles is not seen as significant by Gibbs.

Androcentrism is not confined to anthropologists however. It is as much a feature of theorising in political philosophy and about law as it is about anything else. Even Berger and Luckmann are not exempt from criticism on this score. They repeatedly use the term 'Man' in such formulations as 'Man occupies a peculiar position in the animal kingdom', 'Man has drives', 'Man is a social product'. This use of the term 'Man' with a capital letter is often merely shorthand for 'human being' but it is a dangerously confusing shorthand because it posits Man as the norm of human being and Woman as either subsumed by the term Man or as 'the other', the abnormal. It is a usage which was very common among political philosophers such as Hobbes or Locke or Rousseau who, on closer examination, actually meant men rather than human beings when they wrote 'Man', but who considered the fact that they had excluded women from their discussion as so self-evident that it did not need justification or explanation. In this way, in societies in which males are dominant, much knowledge which lays claim to being objective and neutral, turns out to be 'male knowledge'. That is to say, male experience is accepted as the norm and from it a generalised, apparently universal knowledge is abstracted. It is important to be aware of this kind of slippage in meaning between 'Man' and 'human being'. Sometimes, it is inadvertent and sometimes it is deliberate but it is usually significant.

For many feminists, two features of societies are important in the explanation of social order. These are the sexual division of labour and the subordination of women. We want now to look at these two recurring characteristics of societies.

In his book, *The Origin of the Family, Private Property and the State*, Engels (1972) suggested that the sexual division of labour is natural and complementary. Writing of pre-state societies he says:

'The division of labour is purely primitive, between the sexes only. The man fights in the wars, goes hunting and fishing, procures the raw materials for food and the tools necessary for doing so. The woman looks after the house and the preparation of the food and clothing, cooks, weaves, sews. They are each master in their own sphere: the man in the forest, the woman in the house. Each is owner of the instruments which he or she makes and uses: the man of the weapons, the hunting and fishing instruments, the woman of the household gear' [Engels, 1972, p 218].

There are problems with Engels' picture which stem from the inadequacies of the anthropological materials available to him and probably also from his own Victorian assumptions about women's place in the home. Evidence from contemporary hunting gathering societies (Lee and Devore, 1968), which is all the evidence we are able to secure which will throw some light on acephalous societies, shows that the women in such societies, far from waiting by the fire for the men to return with something for them to cook, actually provide between 60% and 80% of the food consumed by the group. Not only that, but it is the women's contribution which is the more reliable, based as it is on the gathering of roots and fruits and berries and the snaring and trapping of small animals and fish, whereas the men's contribution from hunting may be very erratic. In addition, any suggestion that the division of tasks between the sexes is in some way natural cannot be supported by the evidence. In some societies, women will build the huts and fix and repair roofs, in others this is defined as men's work. Apart from the limited biologically determined tasks of child-bearing and lactation, the variation in the ways in which tasks are allotted between the sexes is very great. Nor can it be explained in terms of the supposed physical characteristics of the sexes such as strength or dexterity, in that women do all the heavy carrying and lifting in some societies but not in others, weaving and handicraft are likewise allocated to different sexes in different societies. In many societies, one of the most arduous daily tasks is the collection and carrying of water which may involve a long walk and the manipulation of heavy containers. This task is nearly always allocated to women. The inescapable conclusion from the evidence is that the sexual division of labour is socially constructed, it is not a natural biologically determined given, of all human societies, but is specific to any particular society, and the question arises of how it is to be explained.

It is not possible to point to a single conclusive explanation, but the sexual division of labour appears to be a mechanism by which gender differences are symbolically reinforced. By that, we mean that they serve to differentiate between the sexes in a positive way, making men and women much more 'different' than biology requires. Claude Levi-Strauss, the French anthropologist argues that:

'The sexual division of labour is nothing else than a device to institute a reciprocal state of dependency between the sexes' [Levi-Strauss, 1971, p 348].

In other words, because the tasks allotted to each sex are complementary, men and women are forced to co-operate in order to secure their subsistence. For example, among the Mbuti, the Forest People studied by Turnbull, who live in a fairly fertile environment, subsistence is derived from cooperative hunting and gathering in which both men and women participate but the sexual division of labour is organised in such a way that it is the men's job to hold the nets and kill the animals caught in them and it is the women's and children's job to act as beaters and to drive the animals into the nets. Thus, men as a group and women as a group are dependent on each other and need the performance of the tasks allotted to the other in order to survive. Men and women perform reciprocal services among the Mbuti.

But, if we look at the sexual division of labour among the Cheyenne, we will find a very different situation. Red Eagle was a Cheyenne Indian who described the sexual division of labour among his people to Bonnerjea in 1934. He said:

'Nowadays, since the white people have come to our country, a man does all the hard work but it was different before that: a woman used to do all the housework. When we moved from one place to another, as we did very frequently, she would take down the tipis, carry them and all other household things to the place we were going and when we arrived at our destination, she would not only set up the tipi but see to all other household affairs, such as cooking, gathering wood and so on. She went into the woods, cut down trees and brought the wood on her back to the tipi. A man could not do these things because others would laugh at him if he did so: these were women's work. A man did nothing but look after the horses. He would also go hunting, procure game and when needed go to war' [Bonnerjea, 1935].

In its most extreme form, as in this example, the sexual division of labour can be characterised as women doing all the work while men's work is defined as sitting round the fire, drinking home brewed beer and arguing about the possession of horses.

Another example of an exploitative division of labour is provided by the Asante market women of what is now Ghana. In a 'Disappearing World' documentary, the anthropologist, Charlotte Boaitley, discussed the Asante women's social situation with them. Although these women had carved out an area of activity for themselves in market trading, which was seen as 'women's work' by both women and men, that did not mean that there was any shift in the sexual division of labour in the home. There, women and girls were responsible for child care and, when children were a few months old, they accompanied their mothers to the market. Wives and daughters were responsible for collecting firewood and water, for cooking and cleaning and washing and baby girls were ritually presented with the tools necessary for domestic labour even if their future might include taking over the powerful and demanding role of tomato or plantain 'queen' in the market. For the Asante men, this sexual division of labour appeared 'natural' although they conceded that it was also convenient for them. A sexual division of labour often appears as 'natural' in the society in which it occurs but the extent of the variety of its manifestations leads to the inescapable conclusion that it is socially constructed. It is not a natural, biologically determined given of all human societies but is specific to any particular society at any particular time.

Does any particular sexual division of labour emerge spontaneously as is suggested by Berger and Luckmann in their account of the interaction between A and B on their desert island? Or is a particular sexual division of labour the result of power struggles, or does it operate in the interests of one group rather than another? And how is the division maintained? We are going to argue that the sexual division of labour is crucial to women's subordination in most of the societies about which we know anything: that the institution of marriage plays an important part in that subordination, and that what we will call patriarchal ideologies are used to legitimate inequality.

Throughout this book, we have been concerned with the types of order existing in different societies and with the ways in which order is created and maintained. In most pre-state societies, such as the Nuer or the Kpelle or the Tiv, the organising principle is kinship. It is through the kinship system that order is created and maintained. In theory, a social group could revolve around a woman and her children with brothers and sisters engaging in sexual intercourse with each other and thus producing a further generation. In practice, the incest taboo is an almost universal characteristic of human societies. The incest taboo means that sexual intercourse with various designated relations is forbidden, or at least that marriage between various relatives is forbidden, and also that marriage with other designated relatives is preferred. It is sometimes argued that the fact that the incest taboo is such a persistent characteristic of human societies means that it must be 'unnatural' for particular sexual relations to take place. But, what we have said about rules only being necessary where there is no consensus raises doubts about this claim, as does the enormous variation in the classes of forbidden or preferred marriage partners. Currently, there is considerable concern in this country about the sexual abuse of children within the family. The largest group of abusers is composed of fathers or stepfathers but it is the abuse of a position of power and trust in the family which gives rise to most repugnance rather than the question of whether or not there is a blood relationship between the man and the child. We are arguing that the incest taboo has more to do with rules about marriage partners than it has to do with sexual partners.

The most plausible explanation for the incest taboo is that those groups which did not practise it would have been too small and too vulnerable to disease or to demographic irregularities to survive. The groups which managed to survive were those which acquired women from other groups. This could be done by simply seizing women from another group, but seizure would invoke hostility and feuds and was only a feasible strategy if no cooperation on such questions as land or water use was desirable. A more usual strategy was the exchange of women between groups which allows for cooperation and the building of reciprocal relations and which may give access to larger areas of forest or plain on which to gather and hunt. This exchange of women was achieved through the institution of marriage which formed a knot in the network of kinship links which bound the society together. By marriage, we mean a socially recognised relationship between a man and a woman or between a man and several women or, in rarer cases, between a woman and several men; a socially constructed relationship from which various consequences in the form of social obligations flow.

One of the reasons why women were exchanged between men rather than men being exchanged between women is that if the survival of the group was thought to be at risk it would be due to a shortage of women rather than a shortage of men. That is to say, several women are required in order to produce enough children to form a viable group whereas only one man is necessary. In some societies, such as the Tiwi who live in the Melville Islands, Northern Australia (Goodale, 1971), this exchange of women in marriage was virtually monopolised by the older men who collected several wives by exchanging daughters with each other and thus derived power by accumulating the products of their wives' labour and by excluding the young men from marriage. In such a society, the imbalance is clear. Exchange of women and their reification, their transformation into objects of exchange or into a kind of property provided the conditions for women's subordination.

This reification of women as objects of exchange need not imply some sort of conspiracy on the part of men to gain power over women. Where the acquisition of more women was seen as a necessity for group survival, because of ecological or demographic factors, it would be perceived as a necessity by the whole group, by women as well as by men and in any case reification and the institution of marriage by which it was carried out do not, in themselves, bring about the subordination of women but they do make it possible.

Heterosexual pair-bonding is a feature of all societies known to us. Only when such pair-bonding is recognised by the community as conferring certain duties and obligations on the partners and on their kin does it constitute the institution of marriage. But, although the institution of marriage has existed in all known societies, the forms which it has taken have been diverse. In some societies, marriages have been formed and dissolved with the minimum of community or kin intervention. In others, the institution has been subject to strict social control accompanied by sanctions. In some societies, monogamous marriage has been the preferred form. In others, men, or more rarely women, have been allowed several spouses. Availability and ease of divorce has varied greatly as has the locality of the couples home and the ascription of their children to a particular lineage. For example, in England, marriage is monogamous, its formation and dissolution have, in the last 200 years, become the concern of the state and the obligations and duties to which it gives rise are now a matter of law. Children of a marriage were, until 1925, held to be the children of their fathers, and mothers' rights over children born within marriage were very limited. It is also customary, though not a legal requirement, for women to change their surnames to their husbands' on marriage.

For the Asante, marriage is polygamous. A man may have up to five wives. It was fairly clear from Charlotte Boaitley's documentary that this was an arrangement which was welcomed by men and disliked by women. It was an arrangement which gave the benefit of the labour of several women to the man. He lived in a house with his brothers and uncles, a fraternity of related males, whilst his wives provided food for him and his guests, took care of any children and washed the clothes and bed linen. The men argued that they needed at least two wives because of the prohibition against a menstruating woman cooking. If he did not have two wives, a man might go hungry for one week in four. The question of why men did not cook for themselves was greeted with gales of laughter. 'God never intended men to cook', the men explained, and as we have remarked before, an appeal to a deity adds a powerful ingredient to an explanation. In addition, polygamous marriage meant that the husbands could operate a sexual rota or could use their sexual access to more than one wife as a means of control. Although these women were strong and capable and could keep order in the market on the basis of royal patronage and charisma, they were nevertheless subordinate to their husbands. In part, this subordination was due to the fact that marriage is patrilocal for the Asante. That means that it is the woman who moves to her husband's village, where she is an isolated stranger whilst he is surrounded by kinsmen. As one woman said: 'what can we do to change anything? Our husbands are not of our family.' 'Another factor in women's particular situation among the Asante is the customary rules about inheritance. When a man dies, his property goes not to his widows and children, but to his sister's sons, his nephews. The institution of marriage, it is sometimes claimed, is an institution for the protection of women and children. In all societies, we would argue that this is a very dubious claim but, in the case of the Asante, the advantages that marriage brings to men are very clear in terms of control over women's labour and over their sexuality, with the added bonus that in the case of the market women, the wives are earning money for themselves and for their children.

If we look again at some of the other societies to which we have referred in this book – the Cheyenne, the Kpelle, the Tiv, the Inuit (Eskimos) and the Mbuti – we can see how rules about what constitutes a wife, what follows from the institution of marriage and so on, appear to be understood to the extent that infringements of the rules give rise to disputes.

In Llewellyn's account of *Wolf Lies Down,* we saw the Elk Soldier chiefs redefining property in horses. They were attempting to alter the traditional attitude to horse-borrowing by making a new rule. We do not know how effective this new rule was in altering behaviour. However, it is clear from another part of Llewellyn and Hoebel's book, *The Cheyenne Way,* that rules about marriage were already understood at the time of the Elk Soldier chiefs' intervention. Cheyenne men may not have seen horses as private property over which they had exclusive rights but they seem to have had a clear idea of property in wives. Llewellyn and Hoebel describe how a wife who had committed adultery or who had been disobedient or had failed somehow in her onerous duties was put 'on the prairie' by her husband. A woman put 'on the prairie' was gang-raped by her husband's soldier society and was sometimes beaten or unilaterally divorced or even killed – sanctions notably rather more coercive than the whipping promised to unauthorised horse-borrowers!

If we look again at the Eskimo song-duels, we find that all the examples collected by Hoebel are of disputes between men, and the recurring subject for dispute is the behaviour of men in relation to women. Men were accused of neglecting their wives, of luring other men's wives away and, in one case, of plotting with another man's wife to kill him in order to marry her. There is some socially recognised control over relations between the sexes because reference is made to numbers of wives and to divorce and although there are no discernible rules regarding marriage in Hoebel's account, yet clearly, through the mechanism of the song-duel, men are negotiating the norms, whilst women remain silent or receive a beating, as happened with the wife who had plotted the murder. The man involved simply had to engage in a song-duel, the woman was given a beating.

In the accounts of the Kpelle and the Tiv, a system of rules about marriage is evident, and this is what we would expect from a kinship ordered society. The disputes concern correct behaviour between men and women. In one case, in the Kpelle material, there is an instance of a rule of inheritance that a man inherits the wife of his dead brother. The dispute is about the behaviour of the various family members. The moot was called by the man, but the proceedings are very informal and relatively consensual in that everyone appears to have a chance to speak. However, the decisions are about the allocation of women, not the allocation of men. In two examples of cases from the Tiv, we see further examples of marriage rules. In the first case, the dispute is about rights to bridewealth and about the correct segments of the society from which marriage partners may be taken. Among the Tiv, women are the objects of exchange between groups. The second case concerns the distinction between a recognised mistress and a wife and the correct amounts to be paid for either and the consequences of such payments. Women are again clearly being exchanged between men, as a type of property.

Of the societies to which we have so far referred, the Mbuti are the closest to being a non-hierarchical, consensual society. Their principal method of dealing with any dispute was to appeal for quiet for fear of disturbing the forest and thus ruining the next day's trapping. One of the causes of commotion, in Turnbull's account (1984) was the violation of the incest taboo by one of the young men, who had slept with a cousin. As we have pointed out, incest taboos are a near universal feature of societies but they are clearly socially constructed rather than being based on natural or biological instincts, in that the field of forbidden or preferred sexual partners varies from society to society. The interesting point about the incest taboo among these people is that although the behaviour of the culprit was apparently a serious infringement of a societal rule, three days later, once the original fuss had died down, he casually returned to the camp when the hunters came back from hunting in the evening and no more was said about his breaking the rules. In fact, Turnbull's informant gave the strong impression that it was the discovery of the deviance rather than its existence which had upset the members of the group. *The harmony of the group was much more important to the Mbuti than the discovery or punishment of misdemeanours.* Marriage certainly existed among the Mbuti but it was not strictly controlled. Certain behaviour between husbands and wives was sanctioned by ridicule or by third party discussions, as the incident reported by Turnbull, in which a husband is criticised for sleeping with his young wife, who has just had a baby , shows. The couple were inside their hut with the door closed. The baby had been given to the grandmother to look after. Other relations of the wife were of the opinion that sexual intercourse too soon after giving birth was bad for the mother's health and would also adversely affect the mother's supply of milk for the baby. They therefore set up such a commotion that the man emerged from his hut and a fight broke out which was finally brought to an end by one of the man's other wives striding out of her hut and announcing in a loud voice that she could not sleep with all the noise going on. She added that she did not care who her husband slept with as long as she could get some rest.

In another of Turnbull's examples of disputes among the Mbuti, a young man was chased into the camp by the angry father of a girl he had tried to sleep with, but it transpired that the real offence was that he had woken up the father by crawling over him to get to the daughter, rather than that he had infringed any rule about sexual relationships (Turnbull, 1984, p 104).

Control over sexuality and over women were at a minimum among the Mbuti. Women were not reified, that is turned into things, and there was no elaborate system for their exchange. Men's and women's tasks were complementary rather than exploitative and women took part in disputes in the same way as men. The ordering element in that society is the commonly held perception that the peace of the forest and the sleep of the cooperative men and women hunters should not be disturbed.

Thus, even if we confine our attention to those societies to which we have referred, we can see a wide variation in the amount of control exercised over women, with maximum control exercised by the Cheyenne and minimum control exercised by the Mbuti. These variations can be most plausibly explained by reference to the ecological and demographic factors which made the exchange of women a necessity for the survival of some groups and by the actual organisation of the sexual division of labour which may also have been determined by environmental considerations.

We want to stress that the institution of marriage is a feature of all societies known to us but that it does not take a universal form. Can we find any explanations for why heterosexual pair-bonding should be subject to social control in so many instances? In other words, what does the institution of marriage, in its many variants, do and for whom?

A frequent answer to that question, in the past, has been that marriage provides protection for women and children. The implication is that without a man to hunt for them and fight for them women and children would not survive. Robin Fox, in a book called *Kinship and Marriage*, written in 1967 argues that:

'There is no logical reason – although there may be many practical ones – for the putative father genitor to pay any further attention to his sex partner. Why he so often does so must be explained not just taken for granted.'

For Fox, the mystery is that the father could be persuaded to stay at home in order to offer support, sustenance and protection to the mother and child. He identifies the basic unit of society as being the mother/child dyad and sees marriage as the mechanism by which the reluctant father is coerced into giving up a carefree, self-sufficient life in order to provide for them.

85

'For the greater part of human history', he writes, 'women were getting on with their highly specialised task of bearing and rearing children. It was men who hunted the game, fought the enemies and made the decisions' [Fox, 1967, p 31].

But, as we have already pointed out, this view of acephalous societies is not born out by more recent anthropological studies which demonstrate that 'woman the gatherer' was perfectly capable of providing for herself and for her children in all environments with the possible exception of the most inhospitable areas of the Arctic, without the protection or assistance of 'man the hunter'. There are no grounds for agreeing with Fox that women and children needed the product of man the hunter in order to survive. What evidence is there for his assertion that men were required to remain with women to 'fight the enemies'?

Certainly, men have tended to monopolise access to weapons in all societies and have been most prominent in warfare, but it is not clear that fighting between men can be interpreted as protection of women and children, except in the sense of the protection of possessions. And, in any case, the question arises: protection from what or whom? Unless the man stayed close to the woman and children, which would have impeded his hunting and is not generally observed behaviour, he would have been unable to provide protection from animal predators. Fighting for possession of women certainly occurred between groups but such fighting was between groups of men intent on capturing women; it cannot be defined as fighting to give women and children protection. And, as we have seen, it was usually replaced by the more advantageous strategy of the exchange of women.

It seems, therefore, that we must look elsewhere for an explanation of the origins of the institution of marriage. Fox's reliance on women's supposed need for support and protection will not suffice. The evidence from hunting and gathering societies leads to the conclusion that not only were women, at all times, capable of providing for their own needs and for those of their children but also, that for women, membership of a social group was never problematic. For any female mammal, the biological processes of giving birth and lactation mean that the young are known. In humans, the long period of infant dependency produces a relationship between mother and child which can be recognised by both. This statement should not be taken as a justification for particular child-rearing practices in our own society but it is clear that in the absence of alternative methods of feeding, the mother, or possibly, in an unusual case, an alternative lactating adult female, is a necessity for the survival of the infant. Through birth and nurturing, the woman produces a ready-made social group, capable of co-operation and mutual support, a group of the kind frequently cited as a necessity for the survival of human beings, who are social beings.

Men too could claim membership of their mothers' group but because an explicit knowledge of biological fatherhood is a late accomplishment in the history of mankind, appearing only in comparatively sophisticated civilisations, they would have had no means of claiming group membership except through the mother who would be likely to predecease them. Their sisters would by then have produced children of their own and so, we would argue, the institution of marriage, far from being necessary for the protection of women, was primarily a way of providing group membership for men.

Inevitably, there is an element of speculation in any attempt to account for the emergence of a social institution, such as marriage, which has occurred in different forms in societies all over the world, from prehistoric times to the present day. However, the suggestion that social recognition of a particular heterosexual relationship conferred much needed group membership on the man appears to make good sense in the light of the evidence of women's capacity for survival and group cohesion. Malinowski argued that through marriage and the principle of legitimacy, for which he claimed universality, the social rule was applied by which:

'... no child should be brought into the world without a man – and one man at that – assuming the role of sociological father, that is guardian and protector, the male link between the child and the rest of the community' [Malinowski, 1930, p 137].

Lucy Mair, another anthropologist, also concludes that marriage and husbands are mainly important in that they confer status on children and assign them to a particular lineage, depending on whether the society is patrilineal or matrilineal. The emphasis of these writers is on the need of the child for group membership. We would argue that that was always available to the child, through the mother. What marriage does is to extend group membership to the husband. It gives him access to the product of the women and children and a claim on the support of the next generation. As Lucy Mair herself writes:

'... a man is anxious to be the head of a numerous household, when this provides him with a large working team; to be a member of a numerous lineage when this may be necessary for defence. He looks to his sons for support when he is old and sick' [Mair, 1971, p 17].

We would argue that he also looks for support to his wife and daughters and that marriage might therefore be more accurately viewed, primarily, as an institution for the protection and support of men – man's means of gaining membership of the group and access to the labour of women and children.

We started this chapter with a warning about androcentrism in research and in theory. We need to be careful about what people mean when they talk about 'Man'. The implication often is that men's interests coincide with the interests of everyone in a society, whereas we would argue that in societies where the sexual division of labour makes control over women advantageous to men, there may be a discernible clash of interests between the sexes. We have compared the kind of communal decision making in the Kpelle moot, to the kind of decision making which goes on in the family and that seems an apt comparison. In our society, the assumption is often made that there is no clash of interests within the family but, if we open up the family, we will frequently find that it is the husband or father whose interests take priority because he is the eldest or the most economically powerful or because he is physically stronger. His views are then seen as the family's views because he is the head of the household. In the Kpelle moot, women are being resocialised into seeing things the way the majority sees them and this may well mean ignoring their own interests.

Secondly, we looked at the sexual division of labour in its various forms. In some societies, it is minimal: for example, among the Mbuti, men and women co-operate to produce their subsistence. In other societies, such as the Cheyenne, the sexual division of labour is much more extensive. Women effectively do all the work connected with the day to day survival of the group. Men's work is confined to looking after horses and engaging in hunting and warfare when they feel like it. Just as the form of sexual division varies so does the amount of control exercised over women in the form of rules about marriage. Sexual bonding seems to be most free from social control where men's and women's tasks are similar or where they are complementary. It is most stringently controlled where reification of women has been institutionalised. These variations between societies as regards control over women should not be seen in terms of an evolutionary progression. They are adaptive responses to different ecological conditions.

Marriage is the institution through which women are controlled, but marriage in itself does not imply subordination. It simply provides a potential site for subordination and for control over women's labour and over their reproductive capacity. We have suggested that it is because a clash of interest arises between men and women on the basis of an unequal division of labour between the sexes and on the basis of the reification of women through exchange that the customary rules regarding marriage and relations between the sexes are the first to be institutionalised. They come close to being capable of being described as law. However, they do not possess some of the characteristics of law in our society. They are not the preserve of specialists except in so far as they are the preserve of men rather than women. They are still seen as negotiable and changeable, part of the primary reality, rather than belonging to a separate legal reality but whether they are negotiable by the whole group or only by the men in the group is open to question. We have said that law in our society is required to secure the private rights of some against the general social interest. Macpherson's argument clarifies this aspect of law with regard to private property (Macpherson, 1978, p 53). Customary rules which govern marriage seem to us to secure the rights of men against those of women, certainly when they are at their most coercive as they were among the Cheyenne for example. In the next chapter, we will look at the ways in which these rules are legitimated in different societies, including our own.

7   Patriarchal Relations and Marriage

The word 'patriarchy' is sometimes used to describe societies in which men play a dominant part and women are subordinate. Patriarchy might be said to imply the rule of the father rather than simply the rule of men and, as we argued in the last chapter, a man cannot know that he is a father without some form of the institution of marriage. Men and women have obviously got together to produce children in all societies, otherwise we would none of us be here but, unlike women, men do not know when, or whether, they have helped to produce children. Marriage is the social institution which creates the link between a man and the children born to his wife or wives. In England, the presumption that a woman's children are her husband's has been called the strongest presumption in the law and it could only be rebutted if the husband was, for instance, out of the country at the time of the conception. By an Act passed in 1987, this presumption has now been extended to those children born to a woman after artificial insemination by a donor, provided that the woman's husband had agreed to the procedure (Family Reform Act 1987, s 27).

So, the use of the word 'patriarchy' presupposes the existence of the institution of marriage in a society and to that extent it is not totally satisfactory. It would be useful to find a word meaning the rule of the husbands, but such a word seems not, as yet, to exist. In any case, the use of the term patriarchy to define all societies in which men play a dominant part may be misleading in so far as it implies that that dominance always takes the same form and is a universal of all societies. There are those who would argue that all relationships between the sexes are inevitably oppressive to women because women's biology puts them at a disadvantage from which they will not be able to recover until technology releases them from the exigencies of childbirth. We would reject that argument on several grounds. First, the sort of evidence we cited in the last chapter about acephalous and kinship societies shows that women's biology did not prevent them from contributing, in most cases more than the men, to the subsistence of the group, in the form of gathering, house building, water-carrying and so on. Secondly, the evidence from the Mbuti shows that relations of human reproduction are not inevitably oppressive. When women are not seen as objects of exchange and when the sexual division of labour is complementary rather than exploitative, relations between the sexes may be free and voluntary. The third ground on which we would reject the concept of universal patriarchy is the same ground on which we have been rejecting the concept of a 'universal human nature' in this book. We would argue that we cannot talk about 'human nature' or relations between the sexes in a vacuum. That is to say, both are products of particular social contexts. In other words, women are subordinate and held to be of inferior status in a great many societies but their subordination takes particular forms in particular societies. In some societies, women's subordination takes the form of their total exclusion from public life: they do not take part in discussions which affect the community, they are barred from public places or prevented from, for example, voting in parliamentary elections. In other societies, women's subordination may consist in their doing most of the work which needs to be done but lacking control over what they produce. Or again, it may consist of their inability to own or control property as was the case for married women in this country until the end of the 19th century. Women's biology may be crucial in an explanation of their subordination, not because it renders women weak or ineffectual, but because it is the means by which the next generation is produced and that production has generally been considered sufficiently important to require control, either by the whole group or by individual men.

Ideologies which legitimate the subordination of women are present in many, perhaps most, societies. Bearing in mind the problems to which we have just referred, with regard to the word 'patriarchy', we are nevertheless going to call such ideologies 'patriarchal ideologies'. We want to stress that such ideologies are historically, geographically and also frequently class specific. That is to say, they vary according to the type of society in which they occur and they may also vary within any particular society, according to the interests they are designed to promote. Such ideologies range from myths about the ways in which women angered the primeval spirits and were therefore given inferior status and deprived of access to certain sacred objects, through religious concepts of woman as the cause of man's fall from grace or as a lesser kind of mortal whose main purpose is to succour or to be a helpmate to Man, to contemporary myths about women's psychological instability or penis envy or smaller brain or lack of competitive and aggressive drives.

Examples of statements which are antagonistic to women, made by those in authority, are numerous, but two examples from the mediaeval church will provide some idea of the tone of such statements. Women in the mediaeval church were told:

> 'You are the devil's gateway: you are she who first violated the forbidden tree and broke the law of God. It was you who coaxed your way around him whom the devil had not the force to attack. With what ease you shattered that image of God: Man. Because of the death you merited the Son of God had to die. And yet you think of nothing but covering your clothes with ornaments' [quoted in O'Faolain and Martines, 1973, p 145].

Or again:

> 'Women should be subject to their men. The natural order for mankind is that women should serve men and children their parents, for it is just that the lesser serve the greater.

The image of God is in man. Women were drawn from man and therefore woman is not
made in God's image' [O'Faolain and Martines, 1973, p 143].

If access to the pulpit allows such statements to be made, it is perhaps no wonder that the Churches have been so reluctant to give that access to women.

Such ideologies have been used to legitimate women's subordination in different classes at different times in different societies, but patriarchal ideologies, like any other secondary reality, do not come out of the air. They emerge in response to the actual conditions of peoples' lives. Those conditions of peoples' lives include the way they organise the production of food and clothes and shelter and also the way in which men and women organise the reproduction of children. The social relations into which men and women enter in order to bear and rear the next generation are at least as crucial as the relations they enter in order to produce food, and those relations of reproduction, in so far as they are hierarchical, are likely to produce specific legitimating ideologies, ideologies that can be described as patriarchal to the extent that they legitimate male domination and female subordination.

In the last chapter, we argued that rules about marriage are often a means by which women are deprived of power and men gain access to the labour and property of women and children. In England, marriage as defined by the Church in the 12th century and as incorporated in the common law was 'a union of one man and one woman which made of them one person, in the eyes of the law, and that person was the husband'. Under what is called the doctrine of coveture, a married woman lost her separate legal status on marriage. She gave up her right to own or to use any property. Any property which she owned on marriage became, automatically, the property of her husband. She was held to be under his protection in the same way that children are held to be under the protection of their parents. The wife was held to be under the coveture of her husband who was also sometimes referred to as her baron or lord. He was entitled to her company and to her services. At least until the end of the 19th century, the husband was entitled to restrain his wife, particularly if her departure might jeopardise his property or his honour. And throughout the 19th century, it was held that a husband had the right to chastise his wife provided that he did not beat her with a stick which was thicker than his thumb. The husband was, until the decision of the House of Lords in 1992 (*R v R* [1992] AC 599), entitled to have sexual intercourse with his wife whenever he pleased and the marriage itself constituted her consent to sexual intercourse which she was unable to withdraw without legal sanction. It was for this reason that a man could not be convicted of rape against his wife, a situation which contemporary feminists have helped to change and to which the House of Lords has finally responded.

The legal historian Blackstone, writing in the 18th century, says of the private, economical relation of husband and wife that it is founded in nature but modified by civil society. 'Nature', he says, 'directs man to continue and multiply his species and civil society prescribes the manner in which that natural impulse must be confined and regulated'. He goes on to speak of the legal consequences of marriage which he calls a civil contract. He says:

> 'By marriage, the husband and wife are one person in law, that is, the very being or legal
> existence of the woman is suspended during marriage or at least is incorporated and
> consolidated into that of the husband under whose wing, protection and cover she performs
> everything' [Blackstone, 1766, Book 1, pp 423–33].

Is it any wonder that we feel the need for a word meaning 'rule of the husbands'?

Marriage, in this country, was strictly controlled for those who had property because it might be necessary to prove the validity of a marriage in order to decide who was the legitimate heir, usually the eldest son, or to enable a widow to claim some support. But, until the middle of the 18th century, two different kinds of marriage had been recognised by the Church and by society. As well as the publicised, solemnised marriage of the propertied, there was a formless, consensual, privately negotiated marriage, consisting merely of the promises of the parties to take one another as husband and wife. This kind of marriage needed no witnesses and no priest and no formality; it was simply the exchange of promises between the couple. These promises had to be in the present tense in order to create a valid marriage on their own. The couple would promise 'I do take you as my husband/wife' and the marriage was then complete. If the couple's promises were in the future tense, as 'I will take you as my husband/wife', and they subsequently had sexual intercourse, that would also create a valid marriage in the eyes of the Church. The Church had tried to exert control over those without property by disapproving of the most formless kind of marriage for centuries, but, at the same time, it had accepted the validity of such marriages and recognised the children of such marriages as legitimate. But, in 1753, Parliament passed Lord Hardwicke's Marriage Act which rendered any marriage, other than the most formal and public kind, invalid. The Act was passed with the express purpose of preventing the secret marriages of wealthy heirs and heiresses – marriages which threatened the family property by allowing control over property to fall into the 'wrong hands'. But, the consequence of the passing of the Marriage Act was that the type of marriage which had been traditional and functional to those without property was no longer defined as a marriage.

The 1753 Marriage Act is a prime example of the discontinuity between law and custom identified by Stanley Diamond in his article 'The Rule of Law versus the order of custom' (Diamond, 1971). The legislation was passed in response to the clear interests of the wealthy aristocracy, who were alarmed at the ease with which their children could contract unsuitable marriages and at the possibility of losing control over family property. For those without property, it was at best an irrelevance and at worst a means by which they could be branded as immoral and their children could be defined as bastards. It was a 'new rule' which was designed to alter customary behaviour just as the Elk Soldier Chiefs' new rule was intended to alter Cheyenne attitudes to horse-borrowing.

The class-related development of marriage in England shows the gradual imposition of an institution, which suited the propertied class (or, at least, the men in that class) on those with little or no property, for whom it was hardly relevant. Marriage for all classes finally became regulated by the state in 1753. Can we see the same intrusion of law into personal relationships when we consider divorce? On the face of it, divorce was not a widespread response to marriage breakdown in England until the 20th century. Judicial divorce was made available for the first time in 1857 with the passing of the Matrimonial Causes Act, but its effect was limited. It allowed for divorce to be granted by the courts rather than by private Act of Parliament but the grounds – adultery by the wife or aggravated adultery by the husband – were very narrow and the expense of a suit was such that it was beyond the resources of most people. But, are we to assume that before 1857 married couples remained together, in spite of marital discord, because the only way of obtaining a divorce, which could be followed by a second marriage, was by private Act of Parliament? And how is this apparently divorceless situation to be reconciled with, for example, the marital arrangements of Henry VIII, whose six wives, as everyone knows were, in turn, 'divorced, beheaded, died, divorced, beheaded, survived'? The answer is that 'divorce' is a misleading term. In spite of the Church's insistence on the indissolubility of marriage, it had been possible, at least since the Norman Conquest, to have a marriage declared null and void by the ecclesiastical courts. Such a declaration left the parties free to remarry because the marriage was deemed never to have been valid because of some fundamental flaw which might be consanguinity, affinity, duress, non-age or non-consummation.

The method of dissolving a marriage most commonly used by the propertied was annulment on the grounds of consanguinity. This particular area of matrimonial law has been called 'a mixture of mathematics and mysticism' (Jackson, 1969, p 21). The theory of the canonists was that, although marriage as an indissoluble union had been instituted by God at the time of the Creation, no marriage was possible between persons of the same blood. By the end of the 12th century, it was possible to have a marriage declared null and void if the couple were discovered to be within seven degrees of blood relationship. When we consider that third cousins are only fourth degree blood relatives, it will be realised that such a provision could be held to cover a very wide population, on occasions when it might prove advantageous and that to be sure of the validity of a marriage at the time of its formation would have necessitated a thorough knowledge of genealogy. In 1215, the number of degrees was reduced to four, but which of us nowadays would be able to identify our third cousins?

The field of prohibited spouses was further extended, by analogy, into those relationships created by the appointment of godparents for a child and affinity was even created, according to the most extreme view, by carnal knowledge alone, so that sexual relations between an unmarried couple would create a whole new group of forbidden marriage partners. This conclusion was based on the conviction that sexual union between a man and a woman automatically made of them 'one flesh'. These rules have been called the 'idle ingenuities of men who are amusing themselves by inventing a game of skill which is played with neatly drawn tables of affinity and doggerel hexameters' (Pollock and Maitland, 1911, p 239). Certainly, the law regarding consanguinity was 'a maze of flighty fancies and misapplied logic', but the practical result was that it was possible for those with sufficient means to pay the requisite fee to escape from a marriage which might prove irksome or in some way disadvantageous (Jackson, 1969, p 21).

Apart from the grounds of consanguinity, a marriage could be declared void by the ecclesiastical courts if it could be shown that consent had been obtained only under duress, or that one of the parties was insane at the time of the marriage or that the parties were too young to be capable of consenting to the marriage. The age of consent was fixed by the later canonists at seven, but either party could avoid the marriage up to the age of puberty which was defined as 12 for girls and 14 for boys. A putative marriage could also be declared void if it could be shown to be unconsummated because of incurable impotency or invincible frigidity towards the partner. Except in the case of the impotent person, the parties to any of these annulled marriages were free to remarry as, according to the canonists, the marriage had never existed and therefore any children born would automatically be illegitimate. The couple were released from 'vinculo matrimonii' and were free to cease cohabitation because in the eyes of God there had never been such a marriage.

Divorce 'a mensa et thoro' could be granted by the ecclesiastical courts in cases of adultery, cruelty or sodomy, but this was no more than a licence to be relieved of the duty of cohabiting; it did not enable the parties to remarry. The validity and indissolubility of the marriage was not affected and the children were legitimate.

Divorce 'a vinculo matrimonii' by Act of Parliament was introduced in 1670, when the marriage of Lord Roos was dissolved and he was enabled, by statute, to remarry. There had been two previous conflicting cases of attempts to dissolve a marriage by Act of Parliament in the 16th century, but it was not until after 1670 that the law was made clear.

Throughout the next two centuries, this procedure was used about 300 times. It was a very expensive and cumbersome method of obtaining a divorce and a licence to remarry. The only admissible ground was adultery and for all practical purposes it was a method confined to extremely wealthy male petitioners.

This whole body of rules relating to the dissolution of marriage reminds us of the 'new rule' made by the Elk Soldier Chiefs. Neither that rule nor these rules could be described as the articulation of custom. They are not a response to the needs of society however defined. They are a complicated set of prohibitions, drawn up by men who would not, themselves, ever be disadvantaged by them, given that the canonists would never marry. The making of the rules would have increased the power of the Church and of the Church officials from whom permissions and dispensations had to be sought.

After 24 years of marriage, Henry VIII finally obtained the annulment of his marriage to Katherine of Aragon on the grounds of consanguinity. His main argument was that because Katherine was the widow of his elder brother, Arthur, and because that marriage, in spite of its brevity, had probably been consummated, his own marriage to her, which had produced five children and which had been preceded by a papal dispensation, was unlawful. His eventual success was, of course, due almost as much to regal bullying as it was to the niceties of canon law. He had fallen in love with Anne Boleyn and had, in fact, been living with her for several years. When he later wanted to rid himself of her and, subsequently, also wanted to be free of Anne of Cleves, he relied on the finding of a pre-contract, coupled in the case of the latter with the claim that he had not fully consented to the marriage and was therefore under duress!

An action claiming pre-contract was much the most frequent method by which those without great resources might seek to escape from an uncongenial marriage. The very insistence of the Church on the binding nature of promises in the present tense, made in private by the couple, provided a possible way out, by means of a claim that an earlier contract existed. These suits for pre-contract far outnumbered petitions for nullity in the Church courts. If one of the parties to a marriage could show that he or she had made the requisite promises in the present tense to someone else prior to the instant case, then the earlier contract would be held to prevail. It seems likely that pre-contract was used deliberately, in this way, in order to dissolve marriages.

'Some men, and even women, entered into a series of betrothals. This had advantages for the non-enthusiast. Pre-contract discouraged the formal celebration of marriages, since the announcement of banns might lead to the registering of a "just impediment" by a party to a previous betrothal, which would break up the marriage. But, the non-enthusiast could break the marriage himself at any time by declaring a pre-contract. The wise womaniser seduced a series of females after saying the magic words of contract to each and, thus, had a supply of pre-contracts to fall back on when his current adventure turned sour' [Hair, 1972, p 241].

Leaving aside the sexism implied in Hair's account, his analysis is broadly correct except that the cases show that women felt able to resort to the courts as well as men. The consequent lack of certainty about whether or not a couple were married has seemed to modern commentators to give grounds for concern and dismay. 'It needs little imagination to picture the social evils which resulted from such a state of the law', writes one. 'A person who had believed himself to be validly married for years would suddenly find that his marriage was a nullity because of a previous clandestine or irregular union, the existence of which he had never suspected' (Bromley, 1976, p 8). For those who had property or the expectation of property, certainty of the validity of marriage was, of course, always of immense importance, but what is seldom acknowledged by legal writers is that the very formlessness which so appals them was in many ways functional to those without property, especially in the event of a breakdown in the relationship, as it might offer a means of avoiding the duty to co-habit or even the possibility of a declaration that the present marriage was null and void because of a previous contract.

These multi-party suits were very numerous. They were not instances of charges of bigamy. Bigamy was made a capital felony in 1603 (1 Jac 1 C11), but this Act included provision for a defence that the couple had been apart for seven years. For this defence to succeed, it was not necessary to show that the defendant had made any efforts to discover whether or not his or her spouse was alive.

It is difficult to assess the numbers of desertions and self-divorces which occurred in pre-industrial England. Lawrence Stone argues:

'In a society without a national police force, it was all too easy simply to run away and never be heard of again. This must have been a not infrequent occurrence among the poor, to judge by the fact that deserted wives comprised over eight per cent of all the women aged between 31 and 40 listed in the 1570 census of the indigent poor of the city of Norwich' [Stone, 1977, p 38].

All the evidence from the court rolls leads to the conclusion that, for the labouring classes, before the middle of the 18th century, marriage was viewed as a private contract, between two individuals, which required no official sanction to be valid. Nor do the principles of monogamy or indissolubility seem to have been widely internalised. Couples felt able to form and dissolve their unions in their own way. Of course, matters did not always proceed smoothly and, in cases of dispute, they resorted to the ecclesiastical courts, but it is clear that at this time neither the Church nor the state had succeeded in gaining complete control over the personal relations of the people.

Before leaving this discussion of the methods by which marriages were dissolved before the divorce reforms of the 19th and 20th centuries, there is one other extra-legal type of dissolution to be considered. This is the so-called wife sale. When Thomas Hardy used the sale of Henchard's wife and baby as an important episode in his novel *The Mayor of Casterbridge*, critics complained that the incident was 'a violent instance of assault on credulity making the suspension of disbelief a resentful ordeal' (Winfield, 1970, p 224). However, Hardy had copied down several accounts of these sales from the local newspapers in Dorset and Sussex and other writers have found instances from the 16th to the 19th century.

Although for the poor, desertion was an adequate method of escaping from an unsatisfactory union and 'society was only bothered about spousal walk-outs when it was hurt financially', yet, for the lowest class of rural property owners, the class most frequently met with in the wife sale cases, some sort of public affirmation of the change of partner seems to have been required. The wife sale provided for these people a 'valuable social method of giving the husband a "no-fault" separation, which ensured economic support for the wife and created a potentially viable social relationship for the purchaser' (Menefee, 1978, p 181).

Accounts of wife sales begin to appear fairly frequently in the writings of journalists in the latter half of the 18th century. In the view of one commentator, they disclose 'a custom rooted sufficiently deeply to show that it was of no recent origin' (Kenny, 1929, p 494). They have certain features in common, in particular, the women do not seem to have been reluctant participants in the proceedings and the purchaser was often already known to the parties and was sometimes the wife's lover so that the sale was a public declaration that she was leaving her husband. In this respect, Hardy's example is atypical because the purchaser was an unknown stranger. The earlier cases were characterised by a certain amount of symbolic ritual: the wife was led to the market place (Smithfield was a favourite site for these sales) by a halter, which was placed around her neck or her waist and which was handed to the purchaser as a mark that the transaction was satisfactorily concluded. The actual price paid, which was often so many pence per pound in weight, seems to have been only a secondary consideration in these sales. The more important aspect was that the participants felt that, by this method, certain legal rights were conferred: they were publicising the end of one union and the formation of another.

The official attitude to these sales was somewhat ambivalent. Lord Mansfield treated them as the criminal offence of conspiracy to commit adultery, but very few of the cases reported in the newspapers actually came to court and of those that did come before the magistrates a dismissal with a warning was the most likely outcome. Attorneys were sometimes employed to draw up contracts of sale to lend the affair more officiality and, for purposes of practical law enforcement, we might conveniently speak of tolerated consent divorces where society suffered no immediate detriment.

It is clear from all the evidence that to infer stability of marriage from the absence of a readily available divorce procedure before the 19th century would be incorrect. The Church held that marriages were indissoluble, but in practice there were legal and extra-legal methods by which new partners could be taken. As many marriages were broken by premature death in the 17th and 18th centuries as are broken by divorce in the 20th and, for those without property, the notion that marriage was a matter for the parties alone or for their families and not a matter to be decided by the authority of the Church or state was very persistent, at least into the 19th century and arguably beyond. The law of formation and dissolution of marriage evolved in response to particular class and gender interests; not to 'the needs of society'.

In the last chapter, we stressed the importance of the sexual division of labour in explaining women's subordination and we quoted Levi-Strauss, who said that the sexual division of labour is a device to institute a reciprocal state of dependency between the sexes. For a woman in the propertied class in this country over the last few hundred years, a state of economic dependency has been imposed because marriage deprived her of any means of supporting herself. She was reduced, in the extreme case, to a producer of heirs or, if she had inherited some wealth of her own, to a means by which her husband could accumulate more wealth. The stereotypical picture of the bourgeois wife of the 18th century is epitomised in numerous restoration comedies. She is shown filling her days worrying about such earth-shattering problems as what dress to wear or which man to seduce. The picture may be exaggerated but it had its basis in reality. Such a woman was certainly subordinate to her husband but her subordination stemmed from her lack of control over property, which rendered her powerless, rather than from working for the benefit of her husband or her children as was the case among the Asante or the Cheyenne. The most that was expected from a wife in the propertied class was that she should be a status symbol for her husband and should produce an heir.

In *Little Dorritt*, Dickens (1976, p 292) draws a sharp picture of a wife whose role in life is to be a status symbol for her rich husband. He writes:

'Mr Merdle was immensely rich: a man of prodigious enterprise, who turned all he touched to gold. He was in everything good, from banking to building. He was in Parliament of course. He was in the City necessarily. He was Chairman of this. Trustee of that. President of the other. This great and fortunate man had provided Mrs Merdle and her extensive bosom with a nest of crimson and gold some 15 years before. It was not a bosom to repose upon but it was a capital bosom to hang jewels upon. Mr Merdle wanted something to hang jewels upon and he bought the bosom for the purpose.

Like all his other speculations, it was sound and successful. The jewels showed to the richest advantage. The bosom, moving in Society with the jewels displayed upon it, attracted general admiration. Society approving, Mr Merdle was satisfied.'

For the wealthiest members of that class, the bearing and rearing of children were often, in fact, separated by the employment of wet nurses and tutors and servants so that little more was expected from the mother other than actually giving birth to the babies or providing a walking display case for the husband's wealth.

By the 18th century, a clear sexual division had emerged in the propertied class the effects of which have been felt in all classes to the present day. This was a division between the public world of men and the private world of women or between the economic sphere and the domestic sphere. And, with that division, emerged new patriarchal ideologies confirming the home as woman's 'natural' place. An early promoter of such an ideology was Martin Luther, in the middle of the 16th century, who said:

'Men have broad shoulders and narrow hips and accordingly they possess intelligence. Women have narrow shoulders and broad hips. Women ought to stay at home; the way they were created indicates this, for they have broad hips and a wide fundament to sit upon, keep house and bear and raise children' [quoted in O'Faolain and Martines, 1973, p 209].

The so-called feminine virtues of irrationality, intuition, emotionality and passivity were extolled as the ideal characteristics of the woman. They would fit her for her natural supportive role of wife and mother, whilst her men folk got on with the rational and aggressive business of the market. This type of patriarchal ideology was used to justify depriving women in the propertied class of any power in decision making or of any role in the public arena of a market economy.

As time went on, the claim that 'women's place is in the home' began to be used to justify the gradual exclusion of women in the working class from economic activity or was used to induce feelings of guilt in those women whom economic necessity forced to participate in such activity. Whilst women in the bourgeois class were subordinate because of their lack of economic power and their separation from economic activity, women in the working class suffered a different kind of subordination in the 18th and 19th centuries. They were not prevented from working and, indeed, women and children were drawn into the factories at the beginning of the period, but gradually they were excluded from the more lucrative occupations and jobs began to be defined as 'men's work' or 'women's work', with men's work being better paid and women's work being seen as subordinate.

In his book, *The Political Theory of Possessive Individualism*, CB Macpherson (1962) constructs three models of society in an attempt to discover which would most closely correspond to Hobbes' concept of a society in which people are constantly striving each against the other. The book is an important contribution to an understanding of the essential characteristics of market capitalist societies. But, from a feminist perspective, it is marred by androcentrism, which was probably quite unconscious, but which is in itself instructive. Macpherson's first postulate for his model of a customary or status society is that:

'The productive and regulative work of the society is authoritatively allocated to groups, ranks, classes or persons. The allocation and performance are enforced by law or custom.'

In simple market societies and possessive market societies, he argues: 'There is no authoritative allocation of work' (Macpherson, 1962, p 49). In our view, both these statements demonstrate a blindness to the way in which the sexual division of labour means that work is allocated differentially to women and men in all types of society. This 'authoritative allocation' of work is sometimes achieved through custom and through the institution of marriage. In addition, as we shall suggest in a moment, the authoritative allocation of work to men and women (and, in some cases, the prohibition of women's access to particular kinds of work) has been achieved through law in the most possessive of market societies, for example, in England in the 19th and 20th centuries.

It is hard to find a society in which women's labour is 'free' in the sense in which Macpherson sees men's labour in a possessive market society and, in addition, it is clear that his 'individual', whose labour is alienable and who owns land and resources which are alienable, has to be a male individual (or, if it is a female, she must certainly be unmarried). In other words, we have in this book, which in all other respects provides an impeccable account of the requirements of different models of society, an example of the kind of androcentric theorising to which we drew attention in the last chapter.

But, let us return to the way in which the sexual division of labour, the institution of marriage and the law operated in 19th and 20th century England.

During the 19th century, high infant mortality began to be associated with women working in mines and factories and there was increasing alarm among capitalists who feared that the labour force, on which capitalist production depends, might not succeed in replacing itself. Protective legislation was hence passed to exclude women and children from some types of occupation. But, protection almost always has disadvantages for those who are, in theory, being protected and in this case protective legislation intensified the division into men's and women's work. Women's work in the mines and factories was regulated, but that did not mean that they were spared from doing heavy, arduous tasks provided that it was in the right conditions. Significantly enough, in the later 19th century, the largest number of women in paid employment were domestic servants in the homes of the bourgeoisie. This was almost exclusively women's work. It involved very long hours, was very poorly paid and it placed the woman in an intensely patriarchal environment. She was expected to live in the home of her employer who therefore had control over her waking and sleeping hours. Her obvious subordination was easily justified by the argument that she was under the protection of her master (a protection which often, in fact, involved sexual harassment) and that she was receiving a valuable apprenticeship in the kind of work which would best fit her for her future as a wife and mother. Thus, in the case of domestic service, women could be expected to work very long hours at very hard work without coming into conflict with the ideology of women's place being within the home.

This particular patriarchal ideology is one which persists to the present day, stressing the supposed fundamental differences in male and female character, which fit men for the hurly-burly of the market place and fit the woman to give socio-psychological support to other members of the family and to the old and sick, if she stays at home, and, if she ventures out into the world, encourages her into such jobs as nurse, primary school teacher or secretary, in all of which jobs she is expected to give personal service to the same groups for whom she is held responsible in the home, namely the old and sick, children and male superiors. It is not an ideology which is confined to married women but, nevertheless, the further justification for differential treatment of men and women is frequently related to marriage. For example, it is argued that girls should be taught cooking and needlework at school because they will need these skills when they get married. Or, it is argued that girls do not need as extensive an education as boys because they will only need to earn their livings for a short time and will then get married. In this way, because it was, and probably still is, expected that most women will marry, marriage casts its shadow both forwards and backwards over women's lives. It affects women's situation before they are married, after they have been married and even if they never get married at all.

Since the middle of the 18th century, marriage in this country has been a state regulated institution, a public law institution which regulates private rights between partners. People in our society are relatively free to choose their marriage partner but, once married, the state imposes a dominant and subordinate status on the partners. The man is held to be the head of the household, the woman is defined as his dependent. Marriage has never produced any legal disabilities for men, nor has it produced disabilities for them in their struggle for an economic wage. They have used it as an argument for a family wage which has further divided the labour force to the advantage of men. But, marriage does produce disabilities for women. It produced both obvious disadvantages such as those we have outlined and it still produces less obvious disadvantages in its effect on their relationship with the economic sphere.

The 18th century saw a very marked tightening up of control over marriage. In our world, in which our lives are carefully documented from birth to death, with certificates and registrations of all the main events and with details on the Inland Revenue, NHS and other computers, it is hard to grasp but, before 1753, because of the existence of formless marriages, consisting of promises only, it was not always clear who was married to whom and therefore who was the financial responsibility of whom, at least among those without property. After 1753, there was no longer any room for doubt about who was married to whom and who was, therefore, dependent on whom, even for those without property. In their book *Sexism and the Law*, Sachs and Hoff Wilson (1978) analyse 19th century cases in which the justifications for differential treatment of men and women are expressed both in terms of the supposed 'natural' attributes of the two sexes and in terms of the requirements of marriage. These were cases in which women in the bourgeois class were excluded from the professions and from professional training. According to the judges, women should be excluded from the harsh world of public affairs because they were possessed of peculiar refinement and delicacy. They should be excluded from the University because 'they have not the same power of intense labour as men have'. They should be spared the severe and incessant work which goes with a University education and besides, according to Lord Neaves, in a case in which women were attempting to gain access to Edinburgh University to study medicine:

'Much time must, or ought, to be given by women, to the acquisition of a knowledge of household affairs and family duties as well as to those ornamental parts of education which tend so much to social refinement and domestic happiness and the study necessary for mastering these must always form a serious distraction from severer pursuits, while there is little doubt that, in the public estimation, the want of these feminine arts and attractions in a woman would be ill supplied by such branches of knowledge as a University could bestow' [quoted in Sachs and Hoff Wilson, 1978, p 18].

Besides, 'gathering young men and women together in one institution might produce strange emulations and total idleness'. In these statements, the judges are expressing their view that women's and men's natures are fundamentally different. Women are delicate and refined and men are capable of intense labour in the harsh world of public affairs. But, we would argue that there are no grounds for believing in any fundamental difference between men and women, other than a very limited biological difference. Gender appropriate behaviour is socially constructed, as is so much else in social life. Girls and boys are taught their appropriate gender role within the family from a very early age, probably from birth. Indeed, some maternity hospitals have pink labels for the cribs of baby girls and blue for boys! There is a great deal of evidence that adults respond differently to girl or boy babies without even realising it and different behaviour is encouraged and rewarded and expected from girls and boys. Our biological sex is determined before birth, although there are instances where even that is more problematic than we are generally led to believe. But, our gender roles are learnt in the family and in the wider society. The issue of how much of our gendered character is due to nature and how much to nurture is still a live one, but we become suspicious when we find statements about women's nature being used to justify women's exclusion from certain areas of social life or from access to certain privileges. And that is what we see happening in the cases analysed by Sachs and Hoff Wilson and on many occasions before and since. Men and women may be excluded from certain occupations because of lack of ability but where that exclusion is justified simply on grounds of gender that is a sexist exclusion just as to exclude someone on the grounds of their race alone is racist.

The cases analysed by Sachs and Hoff Wilson provide a clear example of the way in which words such as 'Man' and 'Person' may be manipulated to further particular interests. The judges appealed to custom in their efforts to exclude women from certain areas of public and professional life; they also appealed to 'public estimation' of the appropriate roles and behaviour for women. Their arguments regarding the meaning of the word 'person' are extraordinarily devious. On the one hand, they argue that the 'uninterrupted usage' of centuries leads to the conclusion that the word 'persons' means 'male persons' and that if Parliament had intended women to be included in any specific context, Parliament would have made that clear. (We must, of course, remember that Parliament, at that time, consisted entirely of men elected by men.) But, in the case of *De Souza v Cobden* [1891] 1 QB 687, they try a different argument. A woman had been elected to the London County Council, unopposed, and she took her seat a year later, in accordance with a statutory provision that every election, not questioned within a year, would be good and valid. She was then prosecuted and convicted as 'a person who had acted in a corporate office without being qualified'. One of her grounds for appeal against her conviction was that if she was not qualified as a fit person to be a councillor, because she was a woman, by the same token, she could not be 'a person who had acted in a corporate office without being qualified' and that she was therefore exempt from the penalties. In the Court of Appeal, her argument was not accepted and as Sachs and Hoff Wilson say:

> 'The judges thus formally accepted a proposition that feminists had previously advanced as a campaigning point to demonstrate absurdity and unfairness, namely, that women were "persons" for the purposes of legal disabilities but "non-persons" for the purposes of legal rights' [Sachs and Hoff Wilson, 1978, p 27].

In his *The Law of the Constitution*, written in 1885, Dicey picked out 'Equality before the law' as one of the defining characteristics of the Rule of Law. He said that this meant that 'every man, whatever his rank or condition, is subject to the ordinary law and the jurisdiction of the ordinary tribunals'. But, if the judges are able to distinguish between men and women on the spurious grounds used in the cases analysed by Sachs and Hoff Wilson, is it really possible to make the sort of claims to equality and neutrality that Dicey and later writers like Hayek make for the Rule of Law? If women are not persons, what are they? And on what sort of neutral, general rule are the judges basing their decision?

We have argued that marriage deprived women of certain capacities. They could not own their own property until 1882 and they could not enter into contracts on their own account until 1935. Incidentally, this particular incapacity of married women to make contracts was used, in the 1913 case analysed by Sachs and Hoff Wilson, as an argument against allowing a woman to become a solicitor. What would happen, the judge asked, if they allowed an unmarried woman to become a solicitor and she then got married and was thus prevented from making contracts? In addition to these disabilities, until the 1940s, a marriage bar operated in the few occupations which were available for middle class women. This bar meant that women had to leave teaching and the civil service if they got married. They were also, until recently, following a judgment of the European Court of Justice, required to leave the armed forces on marriage. In these occupations, marriage and employment were seen as mutually exclusive. For unmarried bourgeois women, the poorly paid and often humiliating post of governess had been one of the very few opportunities for self-sufficiency of a very minimal kind in the 19th century. Jane Eyre is a typical example from fiction. It was an extremely oppressive occupation because the woman lived in her employer's house and had no independent life. An American teacher's contract from 1923 shows that life was also extremely circumscribed for them:

> 'This is an agreement between Miss X teacher, and the Board of Education of the ... school, whereby Miss X agrees to teach for a period of 8 months, beginning 1 September 1923. The Board of Education agrees to pay Miss X the sum of $75 per month. Miss X agrees:
>
> 1) Not to get married. This contract becomes null and void immediately if the teacher marries.
>
> 2) Not to keep company with men.

3) To be home between the hours of 8 pm and 6 am unless in attendance at a school function.

4) Not to leave town at any time without the permission of the chairman of the Board of Trustees.

5) Not to loiter downtown in ice cream stores.

6) Not to smoke cigarettes. This contract becomes null and void immediately if the teacher smokes cigarettes.

7) Not to drink beer, wine or whisky. This contract becomes null and void immediately.

8) Not to ride in a carriage or automobile with any man except her brother or father.

9) Not to dress in bright colours.

10) Not to dye her hair.

11) To wear at least two petticoats.

12) Not to wear dresses more than two inches above the ankles.

13) To keep the schoolroom clean.

    a) to sweep the floor at least once daily.

    b) to scrub the classroom floor at least once weekly with hot water and soap

    c) to clean the blackboard at least once daily.

    d) to start the fire at 7 am so that the room will be warm at 8 am when the children ..... arrive.

14) Not to use face powder, mascara or paint the lips.

Of course, contracts of employment for men are also frequently extremely exploitative, but it is the particular mixture of paternalistic protection and intrusiveness which makes these sorts of stipulations so offensive.

The cases analysed by Sachs and Hoff Wilson demonstrate the ways in which women could be discriminated against on the ground of their supposed gender attributes in the courts. But, as we have said, married women at least were not likely to find themselves in court very often in the 19th and early 20th centuries because of their inability to own property or to make contracts, which are the principle concerns of the civil law. It is often claimed that women have achieved formal equality before the law in the later 20th century. In other words, it is claimed that women's legal disabilities have now been abolished. Women, after all, have the vote and courts are now indifferent as to whether litigants or defendants are male or female. Evidence of differential sentencing policies in criminal cases and of sex-biased decisions in, for example, cases to decide with whom a child should live after divorce, cases concerned with the defence of provocation in murder or cases relating to matrimonial property throw some doubt on these claims but even if formal equality before the law were to be achieved at some point in the future would that result in substantive, that is actual, equality? We would argue that actual equality between men and women cannot be achieved until the relations of reproduction into which they enter to produce the next generation become non-hierarchical and the responsibility for children is genuinely shared. Without that revolution, men's jobs will continue to be better rewarded and women will continue to predominate in part time employment as they do at present. For the law to treat men and women as equal in that situation is analogous to its treating both rich and poor equally, when it comes to prohibiting sleeping on park benches or dining at the Ritz. Treating unequal people equally does little but reinforce the inequalities. Arguably, the only way to achieve substantive equality would be to treat unequal people unequally, that is to say, to discriminate positively in favour of the less advantaged, or to find ways of reducing disadvantages. But, that is not the method of the Rule of Law.

8   Men, Women, Work and Law

In the last chapter, we looked briefly at the ways in which married women suffered disadvantages. We want now to continue that discussion and to examine the relationship between married women, the world of paid employment and the Rule of Law. As we have seen, at least until the beginning of the 20th century, marriage created for the woman a special status, inferior to that of the unmarried woman and clearly inferior to that of her husband. She was a protected person, unable to own property and unable to make contracts. The 'neutral' framework of the Rule of Law did not include her and the ideology of freedom and equality did not affect her. How is the existence of this special status to be accounted for at a time when the Rule of Law was supposed to be in its purest form? What effect does the exclusion of such a large class of people from the realm of formal equality have upon the thesis, argued by many of the writers to whom we have referred in this book, that there is a close relationship between the Rule of Law and the demands of a full market economy? Does the retention of a special status for married women strengthen or undermine the argument about the connection between the Rule of Law and the market?

To try to answer those questions, we need to look in more detail at the history of the relationship between men, women and work and we need to stress the point that, whereas both men and women occupy dominant and subordinate *class* positions in capitalist societies, women in both classes are treated as subordinate to men in that class. In other words, women's position in society is determined not only by capitalism but also by the kinds of class and time specific patriarchal ideologies to which we have already referred.

In an article entitled 'The sexual division of labour and the subordination of women', Maureen Mackintosh (1981) examines the interconnection between Marxist and feminist analyses. She argues that a class analysis, alone, is not sufficient to explain the subordination of women in different societies, because women's situation is determined not only by their relationship with the form of economic organisation but also by their relationship with men. Patriarchal relations, in which men are dominant, are, as we have said, class specific and historically specific. By that, we mean that we must look at the way in which societies are actually organised, in order to produce food, shelter *and* children, before we can understand women's subordination. It is not enough, for example, to concentrate on the way in which production is organised in a capitalist society in order to understand women's situation. We must look at the whole of society and that includes the old, the sick, children and women, who may or may not be involved in the world of paid employment and we must take account of the socially constructed and class specific sexual division of labour operating at any particular time.

It is difficult to date the beginnings of capitalism. Its preconditions were probably the separation of the labourer from the land, the emergence of a class of 'free' landless labourers and the conditions for the accumulation of capital. These preconditions took time to develop but, by the mid-17th century, there were an estimated half a million workers who had been 'freed' from the soil and there was an emerging class of capitalists who were enabled to accumulate further capital by employing these 'freed' labourers in wage labour and were thus able in Macpherson's words 'to convert some of the power of others to their own use' (Macpherson, 1962, p 57) or, in Marxist terms, 'to appropriate their surplus labour'. In the transition period, there was a growing separation between work and home and between economic and domestic life.

Women in the dominant class in *pre*-capitalist society had a certain amount of power, of a managerial kind, in the day-to-day running of the manor, even though control over property belonged to their husbands. The manor was a production unit where a great deal of work and many workers needed to be organised. The lord of the manor was often away at court or at war and the task of managing the many concerns of the manor would fall to his wife. In the class of tradesmen and craftsmen, women had played an active part, both as partners to their husbands during marriage and as replacements for their husbands if they became widows. The list of trades in which women were engaged is impressive and includes wigmakers, bookbinders, hostelkeepers, hatters, goldsmiths, silkmakers, weavers, farriers, blacksmiths and parchment makers. Women were full members of guilds with the same privileges as men and they were able to obtain apprenticeships. In some towns, they were granted permission to trade, in their own right, as *femmes soles*. This meant that a married woman, with the consent of her husband, could trade and go to law and act independently of her husband, who could not be held responsible for her debts.

Restrictions on women guild members began to appear in the 15th century. At that time, women's membership of certain guilds was limited to the wives and daughters of male guild members and, in the 16th century, members of the weavers' guild, for example, were forbidden to teach their craft to *any* woman on pain of a fine of 20 shillings.

In some cases, the justification for the gradual exclusion of women from crafts and trades was industrial innovation. For example, the loom with several shuttles was introduced at an early stage in silk and worsted weaving. Fewer workers were needed to work the looms and it was argued that women lacked the necessary strength and should therefore be excluded. This argument about the supposed inferior physical strength of women as compared to men is a frequently recurring example of the kinds of patriarchal ideologies we have discussed. There are societies in which women do all the heavy work of lifting and carrying and digging. In such societies, the patriarchal ideology, which may exclude them from decision making, will be expressed in terms of their supposedly inferior brain power or lack of leadership qualities. Patriarchal ideologies are the means by which the subordination of women is legitimated. Although their incidence may be very widespread their actual content is time and culture specific. In other words, women have been relegated to a subordinate position in most societies that we know about, but the actual nature of their subordination and the actual content of the patriarchal ideologies which legitimate and reproduce their subordination will vary in different societies. Had the argument about the need for strength to operate the multi-shuttled loom been couched *merely* in terms of strength we would not classify it as a patriarchal ideology. Men and women with sufficient strength would be enabled to operate the looms and men and women without sufficient strength would not. But, where an argument for exclusion of certain groups from an occupation is based on the supposed *universal* characteristics of those groups, we are faced with a sexist or racist exclusion. The exclusion of women from silk and worsted weaving in the 16th century is a sexist exclusion of this kind which is why we are describing it as legitimated by a patriarchal ideology.

Women were thus gradually pushed out of some of the guilds but an even more serious threat to women's participation in the more lucrative forms of trade was the increasing capitalisation of those trades. With the development of capitalist enterprises, it became harder for women to gain or keep a foothold on their own account. In feudal society, land was the most valuable resource. There was no private property in land because, in theory, all the land in England belonged to the king, who merely gave to his tenants use rights in the land in return for certain services. This pattern was replicated throughout the feudal hierarchy, with direct producers or serfs also having *use* rights in plots of land in return for services to their immediate lord. With the transition to capitalism, capital became as important as land and land itself was becoming a marketable commodity, freely alienable – that is, an object to be bought and sold.

Control over money capital was in the hands of husbands rather than wives and any money capital built up by a woman before marriage became her husband's on marriage. Hence, an increase in the importance of capital meant a decline in the power of women to participate. At the same time, the guilds themselves were declining in the 16th century and statutes dissolving them and providing for further accumulation of wealth through money lending were passed in the latter half of the century. The market was beginning to be de-regulated. Women continued to work in a variety of occupations but they were losing some of the control which they had enjoyed and the work they did was beginning to be defined as less skilled. The successful craftsman began to separate his workshop from his home and his wife and daughter lost the opportunities for learning a trade. By the later 16th century, accumulated capital was taking over from land as the basis of economic power, and women in the emerging bourgeois class, were reduced, in the extreme case, to the producers of legitimate heirs or, if they had inherited some capital of their own, to a means by which men, through marriage, could accumulate more capital.

There had been no clear division between economic and domestic life on the feudal manor but, by the late 17th and early 18th centuries, the wives of the bourgeoisie were excluded from the market sectors of the economy. At the same time, the competitive, possessive, acquisitive ideology of the free market was becoming increasingly dominant and the market itself and the economic sphere were becoming elevated to the status of the centre of social life. In the bourgeois class, a clear sexual division developed, the effects of which have been felt in all classes to the present day and with that division into the domestic and the economic emerged new patriarchal ideologies, confirming the home as woman's 'natural' place.

The ideology of the economically dependent housewife, passive and nurturing, providing a safe haven at home to which her husband could return, to be cossetted, after his hectic day, dealing with the real business of the world, was an ideology specific to the bourgeoisie in the early years of the industrial revolution. In the growing class of landless labourers, men, women and children were all expected to contribute to the upkeep of the family. Women cottagers had enjoyed the same use rights in common land as had men and were able to eke out their subsistence by grazing livestock and gleaning and collecting firewood and so on. As these concrete status-related rights were gradually lost, women's chances of providing for themselves diminished and they became increasingly powerless. In some domestic industries, such as straw plaiting or lace making, women and children worked at piece-work rates, at home, whilst the men were engaged in agricultural labour. In these industries, women and children dealt directly with the merchants from whom they bought the raw materials they needed and to whom they sold the finished product. In other industries, such as textiles or mining, the work of the family members was more interdependent. Men worked, for example, as weavers or as face workers in the coal mines and were paid piece-work rates by the cloth merchant or mine owner. But, the weaver needed spinners and carders to prepare the yarn for him to weave and the coal-face worker needed people to carry the coal to the surface. They therefore had to pay other people to do these jobs for them, if they were unmarried; however, the married weaver or miner got his wife and children to perform these tasks for him. The man was paid by the capitalist according to the amount he had produced and he kept his wife and children on what he had received. The capitalist appropriated the surplus labour of men, women and children whilst dealing directly with the man alone. In this way, the married woman's surplus labour was appropriated by the capitalist whilst her labour was under the direct control of her husband. In these particular relations of production, we can see the potentially damaging effects of a sexual division of labour to women, where such a division is coupled with patriarchal ideologies. The man's job gained status because he was being paid. The woman's job, though equally demanding, was subsidiary to her husband's. She did not enter the labour market even in the disguise of a free and equal individual. She did not enter the labour market at all except as an appendage to her husband.

The nature of the dual oppression suffered by women in the mines in the early 19th century is summed up in the comment of one miner who said: 'I was obliged to get a woman early to avoid paying away all my profits' (quoted in Humphries, 1981, p 14). In other words, he would have had to pay a man three shillings and sixpence a day to do the work done by his wife. She received nothing but money to buy food for the whole family, which it was her responsibility to manage in such a way that the most important worker, that is to say, her husband, was kept as healthy as possible.

But, in fact, it became clear in the mid-19th century, that that task of managing to keep her husband, her children and herself fed and clothed on the portion of her husband's pay which he spared her was frequently an impossibility. Infant mortality was very high and employers began to be alarmed that the labour force might not succeed in replacing itself. Protective legislation was passed to exclude children from some types of work. As already observed, protection always has disadvantages for those who are in theory being protected. Women were prevented by the legislation from, for example, carrying coal to the surface but they were allowed to pick up the coal at the pithead or to load it on to canal boats. The division into men's work (seen as of primary importance) and women's work (seen as subsidiary) allows for differentiation in pay. So-called 'women's work' is less well paid even when it is done by men. And so-called 'men's work' is better rewarded even when done by women.

Part of the motivation behind the 19th century legislation to exclude women and children from the mines and to limit the hours they worked in the factories was a genuine alarm about the state of health and stamina of the labour force, but such alarm would have been unlikely to bring about changes in conditions if it had not coincided with changes in the way in which production was organised. The labour intensive early period of industrialisation was giving way to a period of increased mechanisation in which more and more capital was being invested in increasingly sophisticated machinery and the requirement was for a differently composed workforce. Throughout the 19th century, women were gradually excluded from various sectors of industry and one of the means of excluding them, rather than excluding men, was the propagation of the bourgeois patriarchal ideology of femininity which had, up until that time, been quite inappropriate to the working class. An example of the way in

111

which the ideology was expressed can be found in a report to the Royal Commission in 1843. Writing of the banks-women whose job it was to bank up coal at the pithead and load it into boats, one correspondent wrote:

'They drive coal carts, ride astride upon horses ... drink, swear, fight, smoke, whistle and sing and care for nobody ... Surely their circumstances are of a kind in which girls should never be placed?' [Humphries, 1981, p 28].

Such behaviour was shocking to bourgeois sensibilities and to bourgeois values, therefore, as it became less *necessary* to employ women in such work for practical reasons, bourgeois employers, almost inevitably male, became increasingly discriminating when it came to choosing men or women for particular types of work.

We can find a very good analysis of the way in which the sexual division of labour operated amongst weavers and spinners in the early 19th century in an article by William Lazonick (1978) called 'The subjection of labour to capitalism: the rise of the capitalist system'. He points out that, although the patriarchal argument about men's superior physical strength was used to exclude women from some areas of production, it had little basis in fact and men's ability to control others, an ability fostered by family relationships, was more crucial in the organisation of work than was any notional physical superiority. He suggests an explanation for the predominance of men in mule spinning, which has little to do with physical strength and much more to do with social relationships. He writes:

'Mule spinning from the 1790s (and indeed well into the 20th century in England) was operated on a subcontract basis, where the mule spinners were paid a piece-rate by the capitalist and in turn supervised (and usually paid) other workers, usually boys and girls, who functioned as piecers and cleaners. The productivity of spinning was dependent not only on the exertion of manual labour-power by the mule spinner, but also on his ability to keep the piecers and cleaners at work.

The maintenance of adequate levels of productivity usually meant beating and threatening the children (and here physical strength would be a factor, but in its supervisory application to other people, not in its technical application to machines), and in general it required that the children, whether out of fear or out of cultural adaptation, would respond to the authority of the mule spinner.

It should be noted that we are not here talking in most cases of a child responding to his or her actual father, or even his or her uncle, on the factory floor, but rather to an unrelated person who, nevertheless, was greatly aided in his job by the acculturation of children in general to the authority of the patriarch. It was the patriarchal tradition and practice of the pre-factory family which suited the adult male to perform this role of supervisor of labour much more effectively than the adult female' [Lazonick, 1978, p 9].

Lazonick continues:

'Women, along with children, were left to occupy the lower positions in the hierarchical structure of the cotton spinning factories. They were the supervised, not the supervisors.

And, in this capacity, their docility as well as their cheap labour-power were highly valued. The docility and powerlessness of working women, which had their origins in their subordination to men in the pre-capitalist and pre-factory family hierarchy, were now perpetuated by their subordination to men (overlookers) in the industrial capitalist enterprise, in turn reinforcing their subordinate position in the family in the era of industrial capitalism.

While mule spinners certainly sought to maintain male domination of the occupation, as evidenced by their exclusively male unions, it was not merely or even primarily the power of discriminatory unions which kept women out of the occupation of mule spinning. Rather, it was the hierarchical relations of capitalist production, which, by taking advantage of the "skill" of patriarchal authority, secured the occupation of mule spinning for the men.'

In her discussion of the 19th century protective legislation in the mines, Jane Humphries also gives a very clear account of the way in which work was organised between men, women and children and she explains why some mine owners resisted the exclusion of women whilst others welcomed it. She draws attention to the concern of the authorities for what they saw as the moral dangers of women working alongside men in the cramped conditions underground. The commissioners' accounts are full of a prurient kind of horror about what might be going on and in fact they pay much less attention to the *physical* dangers that men, women and children were exposed to, down the mines, than to the moral ones. Humphries argues that this was because the way in which men and women behaved towards each other in the mines posed a threat to the familial values of the commissioners themselves. It was hard to maintain an ideology of woman as the gentle, nurturing 'angel in the house', if she was to be found swearing and half-naked, hewing and carrying coal (Humphries, 1981, p 16).

Thus, women in both classes in an emerging and in a fully developed capitalist society were subordinate both to men and to capital. As reproducers of the next generation of capitalists and labourers they were oppressed by historically specific and class specific patriarchal ideologies. They were also excluded from full participation in the market and this, in our view, explains their exclusion from the ideology of the Rule of Law. Class inequality required the Rule of Law to defuse it. Sexual inequality was so well established through patriarchal ideologies that it did not require defusing. It seemed natural.

In 1870 and 1882, the Married Women's Property Acts were passed which, for the first time for some 10 centuries, gave married women control over their own capital and over their own earnings. Over the next decades, legislation gradually gave them equal guardianship rights, with their husbands, over their children and certain other legal disabilities were removed from them. However, we would argue, none of this legislation has succeeded in altering the dependent status of the wife and in fact social security law of the latter half of this century makes the wife's dependence explicit.

In his report which formed the basis of the welfare provisions in the 1940s, Beveridge said:

'The attitude of the housewife to gainful employment outside the home is not and *should* not be the same as that of the single woman. She has other duties.'

In other words, her primary task is to care for her home and family, to be dependent or at best semi-dependent on her husband. This dependent status of women is enshrined in social security law in the UK, most notoriously in the cohabitation rule which prohibits a woman from claiming benefit if she is living with a man because he should be supporting her and it is argued that to allow such a woman benefits would undermine the institution of marriage.

Divorce law is another area in which the dependence of women is reinforced, often by the patriarchal attitudes of the judges. In 1973, in *Wachtel v Wachtel*, Lord Denning said:

'When a marriage breaks up there will thence forward be two households instead of one. The husband will have to go out to work all day and must get some woman to look after the house – either a wife, if he remarries or a housekeeper, if he does not. He will also have to provide maintenance for the children. The wife will not usually have so much expense. She may go out to work herself, but she will not usually employ a housekeeper. She will do most of the housework herself, perhaps with some help. Or she may remarry in which case her new husband will provide for her. In any case, when there are two households the greater expense will , in most cases, fall on the husband' [*Wachtel v Wachtel* [1973] 1 All ER 829].

Since 1969, decisions about divorce itself, and about financial and residence arrangements for children after divorce, have been matters for enormous judicial discretion. This is an area of law where legal order has been replaced by a bureaucratic and regulatory form of law, in Unger's terms (Unger, 1976). The courts have powers to take all factors about a marriage into account and may make any of a wide variety of financial and residential arrangements. Discretion is therefore in the hands of the judges, who are frequently as patriarchal in their attitudes as Lord Denning.

In welfare law and family law, the broad paternalistic powers of the courts have been extended, in recent years, into new areas of domestic arrangements. The nuclear family, consisting of a married couple and their children, with the husband taking the primary responsibility for earning and the wife fulfilling the role of housewife has been seen as the basis of society by all governments in this century. For that reason, marriage has been encouraged and controlled. Control is now being extended to cohabiting relationships as well. Why might this be the case?

As we have seen, in the latter half of the 19th century concern was expressed that the next generation of workers was not being adequately reproduced. The commissioners appointed to inquire into conditions in the coal and ironstone mines in 1840 had produced a mass of shocking evidence and child mortality

114

was at a high level. Pressure was therefore exerted to exclude women and children from these industries. But, the relegation of women to the home cannot be explained solely in terms of the needs of capitalism. It was the object of struggle and thus presumably of choice, of the working class. It was open to working class organisations in the 1830s and 1840s to struggle for better conditions through other means. In textile districts, for example, the high level of women's employment and joint family income meant that practices such as eating shop-made pies and puddings and having the day care of infants and the washing and cleaning done by women who specialised in these jobs were common among the working class. Improved standards of home life do not necessarily involve more unpaid domestic labour. It appears, however, that the organisations of the working class colluded with the pressure from the bourgeoisie to intensify the sexual division of labour.

One male trade unionist at the 1877 Trade Union Congress expressed the view that:

'... men had the future of the country and their children to consider and it was their duty as men and as husbands to use their utmost efforts to bring about a condition of things, where their wives could be in their proper sphere at home, instead of being dragged into competition for livelihood against the great and strong men of the world' [Ramelson 1967, p 103].

Clearly, if women were to have the sole responsibility for housework and child care, both of which were demanding more time and energy as standards rose, families became more privatised and children were excluded from the workplace, then there was some substance in the argument that women would gain if they could be relieved of the double burden of wage work and domestic work. A family wage paid to the man should result in a higher standard of living for the family and a less arduous life for the wife. But, as 20th century feminists have perceived, any gains were in fact very partial and short term.

For the lowest paid workers, the family wage has never been a reality. It has always been necessary for wives to contribute to the family income, even if the ways in which they have achieved this were not immediately visible in the formal economy. Some wives of low paid workers have taken wage work in factories but many others have increased the family income by taking in boarders or cleaning or washing for wealthier families. Married women have engaged in a wide variety of jobs such as sewing, typing or baby minding, which are carried on within the home and are paid for informally and in cash and therefore never become part of official employment statistics. In other words, it seems likely that it has never been possible for the majority of working class families to manage on one income.

Attempts to secure a 'family wage' for men lead inevitably to an increase in the differential between men's and women's pay, which in turn leaves those many women who are working and who are in fact not supported by a man at a grave disadvantage. In addition, not all the men who are paid a 'family wage' in fact have a family to support.

At times of acute labour shortage in the 20th century, half-hearted attempts have been made by the state to socialise domestic labour in order to release more women for paid production. During the Second World War and in the immediate post-war period, for example, nurseries and creches were provided close to vital factories, and state-run canteens and restaurants were opened to provide cheap food for the families of workers. But, even when the need for women in the labour force was seen as most urgent, facilities for alternative child care were far from adequate.

In order to appreciate the value of the role-segregated family to developed capitalism, it may be useful to look at the characteristics of women's employment in our society. Women, both married and unmarried, are employed, to a large extent in the state sector, in nursing, teaching, cleaning and catering, and in clerical work and social work. In industry, they are concentrated in certain trades, in food and drink production, leather and shoe manufacture, textiles and tobacco and electronics. They are also heavily concentrated in the service industries. In addition, they are over-represented in the unskilled and semi-skilled sectors of those industries in which they are employed and in the junior rather than the senior positions in nursing teaching and the civil service.

Forty per cent of all women employed work part time and this proportion is much higher if married women alone are considered. The reason for the high participation of married women in part time work is the need to accommodate paid employment and family responsibilities. But, part time workers, whether male or female, suffer certain special disabilities. They are excluded from many fringe benefits enjoyed by full time workers. They experience more difficulty than other workers in attending union meetings and are therefore less involved in union affairs than are full time workers. They also have less job security than others and are less likely to gain promotion or additional training. The high proportion of married women in part time work suffer from all these disabilities and are therefore a particularly vulnerable section of the labour force. A segregated labour force is advantageous to capital because it provides some flexibility. As the composition of capital changes, the less skilled can be substituted for the more skilled in order to maintain profit levels. Married women, because of the assumptions about their dependence and about their responsibility for home and children, provide capital with a clearly defined, vulnerable labour force which can be recruited or dispensed with much more easily than can any other sector of the labour force. They have some of the characteristics of what Marx called the reserve army of labour, with the added advantage that their supposed dependence means that they move in and out of the labour market rather than constituting merely a reserve army, ready to be drawn in.

The allocation of the primary responsibility for the physical welfare of the male worker and his children to women has contributed to the relatively weak position of women in the labour market, to their concentration in certain sectors, their predominance in part time work, their low level of unionisation and their low average wage. The patriarchal ideology which stresses the supposed differences in the male and female character, the instrumentality of the male and the nurturance of the female, serves to perpetuate the division. 'Man's nature' fits him for the market whilst 'Woman's nature' fits her to take care of other members of the family. It has also been pointed out that the socialisation of girls in the family conceals the fact that the qualities which they bring to paid employment are skills learnt during socialisation rather than natural attributes of women. Because nimble fingers or an ability to relate to small children, a deferential manner or a sympathetic attitude are seen as part of women's nature it is not considered necessary to reward their acquisition in the same way as the skills learnt by young men in apprenticeships and training are rewarded. Because women are concentrated in these particular sectors of industry, the effects of such potentially reforming measures as the Equal Pay Act 1970 or the Sex Discrimination Act 1975 have been minimal. Broadly speaking, women and men are not in competition for the same jobs and it is therefore possible for the gross inequality between women's and men's pay to continue.

Patriarchal ideologies and the particular socialisation of girls in the family, coupled with a marked lack of enthusiasm on the part of the state for the socialisation of domestic labour, go some way towards explaining women's weak position in the labour market. But, do they provide sufficient explanation for the apparent reluctance of individual capitalists, as distinct from the capitalist state, to maximise profits by substituting lower paid female workers for higher paid men? Many employers were bitterly opposed to the introduction and implementation of the protective factory legislation in the 19th century. Women represented for them a cheap and satisfactory labour force. But, it seems that the general interests of capital as a whole, as expressed in state policies, lay in prioritising the male breadwinner, and that the state has consistently fostered this idea. And, in the end, it was state interests which prevailed.

Opposition to the substitution of women for men has also come from male trade unionists, who have systematically struggled against what they perceived as 'deskilling' and who are, in periods of economic crisis, intent on protecting full time jobs as against part time jobs which in effect, of course, means protecting men's jobs as against women's jobs. The patriarchal ideology which extolled women's place in the home began to be internalised by the working class, or at any rate by the skilled sections of the male working class in the late 19th century. During the First World War, the introduction of large numbers of women and unskilled men into munitions factories was the occasion for widespread militancy. The Government's attempts to recruit more women for industry were seen as a threat to the privileged position of craftsmen already threatened by the introduction of more and more sophisticated machinery. The engineering unions struggled against the employment of 'cheap labour' and argued that jobs in engineering should be the preserve of men and should be returned to men as soon as the immediate emergency conditions of wartime were over.

In the capital intensive, high technology industries in which male workers predominate, wages constitute a lower percentage of total production costs than they do in the labour intensive sectors or in those industries, such as the service industries, which have expanded most rapidly in the last 40 years and in which women are largely employed in this country. In the capital intensive sector, men's jobs are in the process of being deskilled and the labour force is being reduced. The substitution of women for men, even if it could be achieved against union opposition, would not increase profits appreciably. However, it is clear that where they *can* avoid union militancy and where a high labour input is required, capitalists are keen on employing women rather than men, at lower wages. And, that is what has been happening in recent years as western capital has penetrated third world countries.

Women are employed in world market factories in these countries at very low wages and for long hours thus producing a considerable reduction in the cost of labour over similar operations in the west and consequently increasing profits. The so-called 'free trade zones' in these countries are characterised by many of the same social ills as were experienced by workers in 19th century Britain. Child mortality is high and even infanticide is not infrequent and women work compulsory overtime to the detriment of their health. Their socialisation in the family means that these women provide a docile, efficient, non-organised labour force.

Thus, in the Third World, women reduce labour costs to the capitalists by working in extremely exploitative conditions in the labour intensive industries, whilst in the West women reduce the cost of the reproduction of labour by the work which they do in the home and also provide a particular type of workforce, imbued with skills, which are not recognised as skills because they are seen as the natural attributes of women. Women's special role, in and out of the labour market, can be explained in part by their socialisation in the home. But, central to that socialisation is the expectation that women will marry and will be financially dependent on a man and subordinate to him. In this way, the institution of marriage reduces women's opportunities in the labour market because it limits their expectations and horizons. Employment is regarded as merely a prelude to marriage and, even when a career is contemplated, it is likely to be a career which will be able to accommodate family responsibilities.

Attempts to procure a family wage for men, which are based on the concept of the dependent family and on the requirements of marriage, are detrimental to single women, to unsupported working mothers and to all women who work, in that they give preference to the male wage which may or may not, in reality, be supporting dependents. Women's subordinate position in the labour market and their relegation to, and concentration in, particular sectors of the economy are the results rather than the cause of the marriage contract. Women are exploited within marriage and because of marriage, but because marriage legitimates the inequalities in the labour market it may still, in fact, provide women with better economic prospects than they may achieve by remaining single. In other words, from the woman's point of view, marriage tends to create the conditions for its own continuation and encourages entry into a second marriage if a particular union comes to an end.

The dependence assumed in marriage is extended beyond marriage by custody arrangements and maintenance provisions on divorce and, as can be demonstrated, the courts have tended to use the almost unlimited discretion conferred on them to reinforce the stereotypical view of sex roles and the sexual division of labour within the family. Women have tended to get custody of children on divorce and maintenance for themselves and the children. The court's normal practice of identifying the 'best interests of the child' with having a mother to look after the child's daily needs and the preference given to 'good' mothers over fathers in custody disputes as a consequence, have increased the power of mothers within the family. But, at the same time, the effect of the court's apparent bias in favour of women in these disputes has been to reinforce the ideology of the importance of the 'mothering role'. In the majority of custody cases, children are already living with the mother and the court merely gives its sanction to a de facto arrangement but in doing so it further legitimates the sexual division of labour between parents, reinforcing the view that motherhood is the natural sphere of women.

What are the implications of our argument for women's position in any kind of society in the future? We would argue that in most societies women's fertility has been the object of control and the extent of that control has varied according to class and historical conditions. Under early capitalism, control over women's fertility was exercised through marriage and through punitive application of the Poor Law. Within marriage, a woman was subject to her husband's authority and any children she bore were his property. During the last 100 years, this situation has been modified and women have gradually achieved formal equality in rights over children and some measure of control over their own fertility in that, for example, in 1979, it was established, in the courts, that a woman does not require her husband's permission to have an abortion.

The contemporary campaign to liberalise abortion law has claimed that a woman has a right to choose whether or not to have a child. Women, it is argued, should be granted control over their bodies rather than being subject to the decisions of a male dominated medical profession or of their husbands. Advances in contraceptive techniques and increased availability of contraception and abortion have made 'a woman's right to choose' a realisable objective. Following our argument that women's oppression is connected with the perceived need for the group or for individual men to control the fertility of women does this increasing control over their own bodies enjoyed by women herald a decline in oppression? It should obviously be pointed out that like any other so-called 'human right' the right of a woman to choose not to have children is contingent on the demands of society. In a capitalist society, it is contingent on the demand for labour and for controllers of capital. There is at present, in Britain, no perceived shortage of labour and therefore any fall in the birth rate will not immediately activate state intervention. However, the potential for state intervention is always present in the shape of modifications in abortion law, changes in welfare benefits or increased provision for child-care facilities and we may be sure that these mechanisms would be activated if it were thought necessary.

In the state socialist societies of eastern Europe, state interference in biological reproduction was fairly overt. This was because the particular type of economic organisation adopted by these states required a quantitative expansion of the labour force which could not be met by immigration. Initially, women were drawn into industry in large numbers but because there was no corresponding socialisation of domestic labour or child care facilities there was an inevitable fall in the birth rate as women's dual roles as producers and reproducers came into conflict with each other. Consequently, pro-natalist policies were adopted in Czechoslovakia and in the former Soviet Union. These included improvements in nursery facilities and maternity leave and benefits. In the Soviet Union, the official attitude to abortion underwent rapid changes during the 50 years following the revolution being at one time legalised, then prohibited and then made legal again. Likewise, the availability of contraceptives and the resources allocated to their development and production varied according to state policies.

In state socialist societies, the right of a woman to choose whether or not to have children was clearly subject to collective or state decisions about priorities and about the perceived need for expanding or contracting production. The concept of an individual right, even over one's own body, is more appropriate to a bourgeois ideology of private citizens protecting themselves against state interference than it is to an ideology of collectivism.

In market societies, human rights might be seen as contingent on the needs of capital, but the dominant ideology which legitimates the system is one of individual possessors of basic human rights. In a socialist or communist society, collective decision making and planning would be essential and individual rights would be explicitly subordinate to the perceived general interest. What are the implications of this for the liberation of women? Given that the birth rate would inevitably be a matter of state or collective planning and given that control over the birth rate in the absence of a universal system of production of test-tube babies means control over women's fertility, and given the connection between control over women's fertility and their subordination, is women's subordination an inevitability in a socialist society? It may be argued that *all* members of such a society would be subject to planning and that therefore the situation of women would be no different from that of men, but it seems clear that control over fertility, either by encouraging or inhibiting births is a qualitatively different kind of control from control over, for example, the work people do or the conditions of life they enjoy and to that extent we would argue that women would inevitably be the *objects* of planning in such societies. They would be the people who were planned.

It may also be argued that women would play an equal part in the planning and decision making and that therefore their subordination would be mediated. Certainly, ideally that would be the case though in our view it would not alter the fact that women's fertility would be controlled by the planners in a way in which men's sexuality would not but, in any case, an analysis of European state socialist societies shows that women have a long way to go before they can be said to have achieved equality in decision making in any society.

The experience of state socialist societies has shown that writers such as Engels were over optimistic when they thought that women's oppression would end with their incorporation into the productive labour force. Without a corresponding socialisation of domestic labour and child care facilities women's entry into the labour force merely creates, for them, a double burden which may well depress their potential. If societies (or those with power within them) perceive a need for a high birth rate, then this can only be achieved by biological engineering in the laboratory or by the spreading of the responsibility for bearing and rearing children more evenly throughout society, by socialising child-care and by involving both men and women in its organisation. Any other solution threatens to perpetuate the oppression of women.

What we are arguing then is that women's subordination takes class specific forms in different societies at different times. It is related to their role in the family and to their role in the sphere of production and those dual roles are interdependent and socially constructed. Men seek control over women in order to secure control over their labour and children. In a capitalist society, the state and law are not only capitalist but also patriarchal, but patriarchal relations of reproduction and the patriarchal ideologies which emerge with them and then reinforce them are not exclusive to capitalism. For women, there are two forms of domination, class and gender and, in this society, marriage is the crucial *legal* expression of women's subordination. Through marriage and legislation and through the operation of discretion in the courts, women's dependence and therefore subordination is continually being reproduced.

9   The Wider Implications of the Rule of Law

As we suggested in Chapter 3, the purpose of the ethnographic material was to highlight the role and method of law in Western society. Even so, there is a danger that the conclusion might be reached that what is primarily illustrated is that different societies have different ways of maintaining order and resolving disputes, which in turn simply reflects different ways of understanding the world. This might, perhaps, be qualified by the knowledge that the way in which 'justice' is dispensed and indeed the 'justice' itself which *is* dispensed will almost certainly reflect the interests of those with power within any society, rather than the interests of the powerless. In a limited sense, this is correct but it also has to be realised that, in contradiction of the quotation from Dickens, the position is not simply that 'we do as we do' while they 'must do as they do'. When we considered ethnographic examples, we did not of course presume to make value judgments about the way in which other societies organised their dispute resolution or rule making because the intention was to illustrate that, for us, law is only an aspect and mechanism in the creation and maintenance of order, and also that not every society feels the need for law, which we often assume to be a universal need. The implicit, and sometimes explicit, argument was that a 'Rule of Law society' will be a society in which the basic unit is the individual and in which, in disputes which become legal, the antagonists will relate to each other in a way which makes estrangement upon resolution almost inevitable.

This centrality of the individual is also manifest in the Rule of Law attribution of formal individual equality before the law. Unlike the Nuer, for instance, we do not perceive ourselves as first and foremost *social* beings (members of society), but rather as individuals whose goals and ambitions are to be found in individual achievement, even if this is secured at the expense of fellow members of society. We have also argued that this ideological perception of individual separateness affects other perceptions and, in particular, when we discussed property, we found that the idea of absolute rights over land or things also reflected and reinforced the notion of separateness. In our society, men and women of property have no obligations to men and women of poverty; and charity, though it might receive approval, is not obligatory and the poor enjoy no rights, by reason of that status, against the rich.

Another reflection of our emphasis upon individualism is to be found in the mechanism of the free market, notwithstanding such controls as do exist. Within the free market, there is of course formal equality again and each person may, to her peril or benefit, enter into contracts and will in turn be equally liable for any damage suffered because of breach. It is of the essence of the market that individuals are free to make individual choices and to enter into such bargains as they choose.

Although until now we have avoided comparing the merits of the law way of seeing the world with other ways, it is at this point necessary to consider the wider international implications of this perspective. We will argue that, in spite of our way of using ethnography, it is not finally possible simply to adopt the Dickensian relativist position which isolates our way of understanding rules and dispute resolution from those of other peoples. The impossibility is caused only indirectly, but nevertheless necessarily, by our legal world. That it is so is because the economies of the rich and largely Western (though including Japan) states have come to affect every corner of the world, no matter how remote, how picturesque or how 'primitive', whether land or sea, or inhabited or uninhabited. No matter wherever, our legal perception of the world affects. Our argument is that other peoples cannot simply do things the way in which they might wish because of the dominance of the Western economic system, the Western concept of law and consequently our dominance in the ability to define issues.

To exemplify the inter-relationship of the law and economy and to sustain our argument is nowhere easier than in an examination of so-called Third World debt. If we are able to apply once more the cartographical question about map drawing, we will quickly see the partisan nature of the 'debt map'. This is a debt map which not only allows, but insists upon, a continuing and massive and almost unbelievable transfer of wealth from the poorest countries to the richest. The cartographical question becomes:

'How have the richest nations in the world been able to devise a way of portraying the world which makes it seem inevitable (and indeed sometimes even makes it seem just) that such a transfer should take place?'

Our suggestion is that it is the law way of perceiving the world which is central in the creation of that map.

We have already seen that a major role for law in our society lies in its legitimation of the unequal distribution of wealth, and we saw that property exists because of the legal guarantee of rights over things and land. But, in providing those guarantees to all individuals and in treating all individuals formally equally, the law also makes it ordinary that the rich should be protected in their riches and the poor in their poverty. So ordinary and so commonsensical has our property regime become that, as we saw, it is often difficult to think of it as anything other than natural.

Of course, it can be argued, and it usually is, that the typical Western property regime (that is, our way of defining and distributing property) receives overwhelming support from the populace residing in such states. Polls, politics and politicians constantly confirm public approval of the capitalist way of dealing with the world, together with its understanding of property ownership and distribution. Within most such states there is a consensus even between government and opposition that there is indeed no alternative to the comparatively free market, the capitalist economy and the drive for efficiency and growth; even though there may be differences about the details. While the hegemony of those assumptions is ever expanding, this is not yet common sense which is universal and, in particular, many so-called Third World citizens would hesitate before endorsement. But, while this might be accepted, it might still be fairly asked of what relevance a discussion of Third World poverty and Third World debt can be to a consideration of the law way of perceiving the world.

The answer is to be found in the mechanisms by which the poorest countries and the poorest citizens of the poorest countries are kept in poverty. These are the mechanisms which give the affluent West the ability to be able to define the international rules in accordance with which the Third World must play the 'game'. And it is here that Western conceptions of law are absolutely crucial as we will exemplify by reference to the phenomenon of Third World debt. It is because of four vital legal concepts, intrinsically connected with the Rule of Law, that the West has been able to maintain a facade of rectitude and morality while absorbing much of the Third World's scarce resources. These concepts are property, contract, debt and legal personality. Before directing attention to these key concepts, however, some facts about Third World debt are necessary.

When in 1990 the World Bank reported that 1989 was the seventh successive year in which the net flow of money was from the so-called developing nations to the developed (that is, there was a transfer of wealth from the poor countries to the rich), it probably came as no surprise. What one might have been surprised by however was that the indebtedness of the poorer countries actually increased substantially over that seven years. Thus, not only was there a net transfer of wealth from poor to rich, but, at the end of the seven years, more was owed than at the beginning. In the words of the World Bank (1989, p 158):

'Most of the debt burdened countries saw little improvement in their external financing situation in 1988–89. Net transfers from these countries increased over previous years and debt indicators did not show a reduction in the burden that external debt imposes on these countries' economies.'

And, indeed, the total amount owed by the developing countries rose to a figure of which it is almost impossible to conceive. It rose to US $1,189 billion. And it rose to that from $1,165 the year before. When the debt crisis (as it is often called) really began to overwhelm the poor countries in 1982, the debt owed by those states was a 'mere' $753 billion. So, in spite of a significant, if not invariable, transfer of wealth from the poor to the rich, their indebtedness was well on the way to doubling and, by the end of 1992, had reached, according to the World Bank (World Bank, 1993, p 31), $1,662,000,000,000!

Since the first edition of this book, there has been no amelioration of the problem. Now the total amount owed by developing countries is $2,465,100,000,000. From 1990, the debt has grown by 70%. Although strong sentiment has been expressed by ordinary people in the developed world, and although the G8 countries have resolved to provide some help, few consider that any real improvement will result.

What does this mean for debtor countries? Most clearly, it means that much needed income from exports is diverted from such expenditure as health, education, welfare and infrastructural investment to service these debts (that is, pay interest, and in some cases repay capital as loans fall due). The percentage of export earnings is sometimes extraordinary, especially when one remembers the critical poverty experienced by so many poor citizens of so many poor states. Some of the very poorest states are paying almost 40% of their export receipts – Nicaragua must pay 39%, Brazil 38%, while Guinea Bissau with 80% of its population assessed as living in absolute poverty is called upon to divert 67% of its export earning and Sierra Leone 60%. At the same time, most of these states have seen their terms of trade deteriorate significantly. Thus, the price they receive for their exports has declined, while the price they pay for imports has increased. Primary commodities in particular have declined in value (or rather in price) over the last 15 years.

Developing countries as a whole reduced the percentage of their gross national product spent on education between 1985 and 1995 from 4.1% to 3.8%, while industrial countries allocated 5.2% of a hugely greater budget. Many such countries must export ever more and import less, in order merely to stand still in their economic plight. How, we must ask, did that happen and for whose advantage?

The problem is one that has very substantially arisen after the Second World War in what many wish to call the 'age of development'. There was a belief in the postwar world, current at least in the West, but also often elsewhere, that salvation for poorer countries lay in 'development'. In a famous speech, President Truman in 1948 outlined the problems of poor nations and promised to solve them. Unfortunately, perhaps, the subsequent definitions of 'under development' requiring development for salvation were almost exclusively in purely economic terms and, even then, in the crudest possible economic terms. A country's poverty or affluence was simply defined by consideration of its Gross Domestic Product per inhabitant. If this was below a rather arbitrary amount, the country was to be regarded as 'underdeveloped' and in need of development. It is fair to add that this view was also held by many leaders of newly decolonised countries who saw the future in terms of emulating the success and power of industrialised nations. The combination of industrial goals on the part of the underdeveloped and a wish to profitably place capital by the industrialised states, proved irresistible and the apparent goal was to make economically poorer countries more like wealthy nations. The problems inherent in these goals are now well appreciated but it is sufficient for the moment to observe that there has been shown to be very little correlation between Gross Domestic Product and anything else.

However, in order to finance such developments, debts were of course incurred. Such borrowing is not inherently unwise particularly if the money borrowed is used to increase the quality of life of the citizens in a sustainable way. Nevertheless, in the 1970s, the seeds of a future debt crisis were sown in abundance. The decision of the Organisation of Petroleum Exporting Countries to dramatically and, effectively, substantially raise the price of oil (a decision which was not unjustifiable) led to very large quantities of money becoming available to be loaned. The oil rich nations suddenly found themselves in possession of more dollars than they could absorb or use in their own states. They thus tended to deposit their surplus 'petro-dollars' (in fact indistinguishable from other dollars) into European and American banks which in turn were obviously concerned to lend out dollars so that profits could be made through the money which was thus loaned. Needless to say, it was also very much in the interest of the industrialised countries that the money was loaned to developing countries, who could then be expected to purchase from the 'developed' states thus stimulating *their* economies. The sums of money thus available were extraordinarily large and they presented substantial problems to the would-be lending banks in that much of the money which was deposited by OPEC countries was put on comparatively short term deposit. Short term loans with no guarantee of refinancing are not always easy to make because borrowers want the security of knowing that loans will not suddenly and inconveniently be called in. On the other hand, a cardinal rule of banking was that one thing no bank should do was to 'borrow short and lend long', that is, money which was on short term deposit could not be relied upon to enable long term loans as a subsequent withdrawal of the deposit could prove disastrous.

The banks overcame this dilemma with the aid of a legal device. Within the loan contract was a provision for a flexible rate of interest to be paid by the borrower. This was not traditionally a common practice although it has become normal now, even on ordinary domestic loans, mortgages and credit cards. The insertion of such a variable interest clause by the banks enabled long term loans from short term deposits, since bankers knew that they would always be able to demand the current rate of interest from their borrowers which in turn meant that they would always, if necessary, be able to borrow the money to cover their loans. This was an important change in bank policy which contributed to the subsequent crisis in bank lending policy.

A second dramatic change in bank lending policy which was true both of European and US banks was that, when lending to states or to private enterprise where those loans were guaranteed by governments, the banks effectively gave up appraisal of the viability of the project for which the loan was required. This was probably because of a widespread, if unjustified, belief among the banks that countries do not become bankrupt and similarly cannot default on loans. In one notable interview, the then manager of the Midland Bank, Sir Kit McMahon, when speaking about Third World debt observed that, whenever it was suggested in his bank that he might write off some of these debts, he always received letters from British borrowers arguing that if there was some writing off of loans to be done, then it should be done first for British borrowers. The inference was that there is a parallel between a loan to a sad old man in Surrey and a loan to a poor nation. The crucial point he fails to mention is that the initial criterion for lending was very different because of the loan proposal appraisal – or lack of it.

Thus, the risk of lending money to the Third World was often simply unassessed or under assessed. It was, however, often even more irresponsible than this in that banks often made no effort to distinguish between loans which were required for different sorts of projects. They did not distinguish between loans for military spending, loans for absurd prestige projects, loans for inappropriate industrialisation or anything else. Nor yet, on many occasions, did banks concern themselves to ensure that the money was used for the project for which it was loaned. If a loan was government guaranteed, this, it was thought, was sufficient. The only mitigation of responsibility is that the banks were themselves under pressure to lend the money to be able to obtain a return on the money they held on deposit. Yet, a further criticism is that many banks failed to distinguish between the regimes to whom they lent, being as prepared to loan to oppressive military dictators renowned for their abuse of human rights as to democratic regimes. Some lenders indeed preferred the former, believing them to possess a stability which democratic regimes might not!

Yet another problem (for the states which became indebted) was that, incredible though it may at first seem, much of the money that was loaned never actually left the lending bank! As Susan George points out, having agreed a loan, almost instantaneously, and sometimes *actually* instantaneously, a large percentage of that loan went straight back to the bank from which it had been borrowed as deposits (George, 1989, p 19). This happened partly because corruption allowed officials to absorb a percentage of the loans anyway, but partly also because companies in the Third World who borrowed money from the banks of the developed states often preferred to leave the loan deposited in First World currency in First World banks rather than repatriating it. Apart from such companies, one need not look beyond ex-President Ceaucesceau of Romania, ex-President Marcos in the Phillipines, ex-President Somoza in Nicaragua, ex-President Noriega in Panama, ex-President Duvalier in Haiti or ex-President Mobutu in Zaire to imagine the fate of many loans. It is reported that on one remarkable occasion 'Baby Doc' Duvalier obtained for Haiti a loan of $22 million from the International Monetary Fund and within three days had deposited $20 million into a foreign bank in his own personal name. President Mobutu, the plight of whose country has already been remarked, had 'acquired' personal wealth in Western banks and states estimated at between four and six *billion* dollars. Little of it has been traced since his death.

What we see, then, is the ability of political leaders and their families and followers to transfer money to rich Western banks. Amazingly, it is estimated that between 1983 and 1985 70% of all new loans to Latin America debtor countries simply returned to the lending rich countries. Supposedly, between 1976 and 1981, of the $272 billion borrowed by Latin America, 8.4% actually arrived in the borrowing state!

As to the purpose of the loans, a significant proportion of those purposes simply beggar belief – from the nuclear power station in the Phillipines built in spite of the fact that it was situated on an earthquake fault line and close to active volcanoes which (hopefully) can never be commissioned, (Adams, 1991, p 124); to prestige and useless buildings (palaces and cathedrals); to arms and armaments, not least, to Iraq; and all the way through to projects necessarily destructive both of the environment and also necessarily destructive of the way of life and the very ability to live, for significant numbers of people in those countries.

Yet, when all is said and done, it was seemingly anticipated both by borrowers and lenders at the time the loans were made, that they would be repaid. This was, at least with hindsight, inherently unlikely, but the possibility of repayment was greatly decreased, even for those few countries which had borrowed comparatively wisely, by changing and unforeseen external circumstances – changes largely generated by the affluent states. In particular, the collapse in commodity prices, which were effectively set by importing states with their commodity futures markets, and a collapse naturally to the advantage of the commodity importing countries (that is, those industrialised and rich) was devastating and greatly increased the likelihood that debt could not continue to be serviced. What were the debtor countries to do? What they were effectively forced to do was to enter into agreements with the International Monetary Fund, after 'negotiation'.

The World Bank and the International Monetary Fund (IMF) both contribute to a reply to the 'Who drew that map?' question. Like the United Nations, the World Bank and the IMF were created at the end of Second World War in order, it was said, to prevent a repetition of the world economic crises of the 1920s and 1930s. But, neither the World Bank nor the IMF had anything nearly as unacceptably democratic as 'one member, one vote'. The power in each organisation was given quite explicitly to the wealthy countries, with the US having an explicitly dominant role. Indeed, so explicit was the dominant role of the US that the headquarters of both organisations are in Washington where they can maintain constant contact with the US Government.

The main points of the new economic order (free world trade) represented by these organisations were to be fixed rates of exchange and equal treatment for trading partners. It was recognised that sometimes problems arose when countries suffered balance of payments difficulties and this was one of the reasons for the existence of the IMF. Interestingly, at the meeting which set up the IMF, the British delegate, JM Keynes, argued for a system whereby balance of payments problems should become the concern of both debtor *and* creditor nation. He considered that the problem of balance of payments deficits and difficulties was not a problem or matter of concern only for the debtor nation, but also for creditor countries. The US view however (which reflected its view that it would be a creditor nation for the foreseeable future) which prevailed was that the problem of balance of payments 'adjustment' was a problem to be resolved by debtor nations alone.

The US plan acknowledged the need to grant debtor countries loans to finance the debts and to prevent them from setting up trade barriers. Without the IMF to make loans, the fear was that where countries suffered severe and substantial balance of payments problems their logical response would be to increase import tariffs and/or decrease imports which would severely hinder free world trade. Thus, the IMF was to be a credit granting organisation, but with the power and duty to force the debtor nation into 'balance of payments discipline'. This was to be achieved by the acceptance by the debtor country of a 'balance of payments orientated policy'. While the World Bank was to be responsible for long term project related development investment, the IMF was to be responsible for short term balance of payments difficulties, but, without IMF membership, a state could not belong to the World Bank and, without conformity to IMF rules, no development aid would be forthcoming from the World Bank.

Voting power within these organisations belongs explicitly to those states with economic power. Because of the strength of the US after the Second World War, it received a quota of 20% which actually allowed it to prevent any substantial reallocation of power. As any change in the quota system required 85% of the votes, the 20% held by the US amounted to a power to veto.

What then does the IMF do? What it does is, seen from one point of view, extremely subtle and, from another, utterly absurd. When a country's government finds itself with very substantial debts and continuing balance of payments problems, if it is to be granted credits by the IMF, it must consult with the IMF and may well be required to adopt an 'austerity programme' or, as the IMF itself euphemistically puts it, it may be required to 'practise adjustment'. What does such an IMF restructuring involve? One author has summarised the process as follows:

'When Third World countries get into serious financial difficulties as many do, the International Monetary Fund "rescues" them. It assists in rescheduling debt payments and organising new loans to get a country over a crisis period, but in the process it insists on changes in economic policies. This restructuring or stabilisation is designed "to get the economy going again" in conventional terms, which mainly means cutting spending and increasing export earnings in order to start paying off the debt.

The standard IMF rescue package includes reducing government spending on welfare and subsidies on food and housing, holding down or cutting wages, giving the green light to free enterprise, encouraging foreign investment, deflating and restricting credit and devaluing the currency thus making exports more competitive. All these measures impose increased hardships on the poor. They redistribute wealth and opportunities to the rich who have capital to invest, because the point of the exercise is to encourage them to generate more economic activity – especially exports' [Trainer, 1989, p 103].

130

Because it is a basic tenet of IMF programmes that local consumption should be discouraged to enable external consumption (that is, exports), recovery of the economy involves directing resources to export production to the rich world and, at the same time, charging less for export items through devaluation. Production capacity is thus directed to securing profits from exports rather than satisfying local demand.

Similarly, the recent move towards 'debt for equity swaps' (debts may be exchanged in return for a share in the capital assets of a state – 'Equity' here is not to be confused with its meaning of 'justice'!) and also the IMF's pressure for privatisation both help to transfer the ownership of the more productive capacity to foreign banks and corporations. Local firms may also suffer because measures such as restricting credit can devastate small businesses. On the other hand, transnational corporations are then in a strong position to move in and exploit these business opportunities. Such measures may in one sense succeed in 'getting an economy going' (although this is doubtful), but, even if this is the case, the cost will be borne by those least able to afford it. The costs of these stabilisation programmes are enormous. In fact, the protests which these policies have evoked from poor people who have seen food prices rise and their welfare and subsidies cut led to the term 'IMF riots'. In so far as there is a resulting stimulus to the economy, it is mainly effective in increasing exports and making foreign investment more attractive and so the package is a delight to importers and consumers in rich countries and to transnational corporations, but it produces the very opposite of development in the interests of the people of the Third World.

Thus, the result is that while states must 'practise adjustment' in IMF terms or lose the status that enables them to borrow in order to survive and pay for essential imports, the adjustment is essentially paid for by the poorest section of the population who lose subsidies which may have made the purchase of food, education and services possible. So, the very subtle point about the debts of poor nations is that the very poorest people who obtained no benefit whatsoever from the loans which were made to their governments are now called upon by the IMF to make the sacrifices that make their country's debts repayable. Even more incredibly, these same people not only often obtained no benefit, but their condition actually deteriorated *because* the loans were made, in that the industrialisation which they often facilitated made peasant existence ever more precarious. There is a relevant story told about the Scottish philosopher. Supposedly, once when he was asked whether he believed in baptism his reply was 'Believe in it? – I've seen it done!'

But why is this about law and the law way of seeing the world? First and foremost, it is because it is the legal instrument of contract which makes Third World debt possible. It is law which crystallises an agreement between two parties and insists upon performance of the promises or damages in lieu. Traditionally, notions of Rule of Law and freedom of contract focus upon the formal equality of the contracting parties and the freedom to make contracts whether beneficial or harmful, rather than looking at the substantive inequality of the parties which forces the poor into unsatisfactory and sometimes manifestly unjust bargains.

Should a country's government wish to deny a debt, that is, if it wants to default, the result of such default would be an inability to obtain credit for essential imports. The very idea of contract is in many ways central to the Rule of Law way of viewing the world. It is also, of course, at the core of capitalism. It is because contracts are binding that the market economy can survive. At the same time, however, just as all are equal in their ability to contract, not all are equal in their bargaining power.

A common response to Third World debt, at least in rich nations, is the argument that, if money was borrowed pursuant to contract, then the borrower should obviously repay as agreed. In fact, at first sight, this seems almost a truism and it remains the position of most bankers and politicians. It is a position very much easier to maintain with regard to debts incurred within the rich nations than with Third World debt. What distinguishes the latter is that very often great encouragement and even inducement was given by would be lenders to persuade potential borrowers to enter into loan contracts. It was also not uncommon for agents to be paid commission for money they were able to place by way of loan and those agents, of course, incurred no liability regardless of the result.

A second important legal feature of Third World debt is that contracts for the lending of money have undergone significant change in form, especially since the Second World War. While a central feature of contract law was, and supposedly still is, that contracts would only be enforced if the terms and conditions were certain and clear (contracts could and still can be declared void for uncertainty), this historically meant that, when banks or building societies lent money, they lent for a fixed term at a fixed rate of interest. Each party to the contract was thus taking a chance on the future prevailing rate of interest. If it rose above the level at which the loan was made, the bank stood to lose; if it fell, then the borrower was the loser. Such contracts are now rare indeed. Legal ingenuity enabled the insertion of clauses by which one party alone could unilaterally alter some of the terms of the contract and, in particular, the rate of interest to be paid. Dramatically high international interest rates have been quite devastating to poor nations, while only increasing the rate of return for the lender. Ironically, but not surprisingly, the interest paid by the Third World already greatly exceeds the sums borrowed anyway even though the principal remains outstanding.

A further feature which has to do with law of these international debts is concerned with commodity pricing. Ex-President Nyerere of Tanzania tells the story of waking up one morning when he was President to hear that overnight the price of cotton had actually halved. Yet, as he also points out, the international producers of primary produce have no ability to be able to determine the price of their produce; the very price with which they hope to repay the loans. Rather, the prices for many commodities are fixed in the commodity markets in the West, where commodity futures traders fix, through speculation, the price of commodities to be delivered in the future. Obviously, the price of cotton had halved because of a belief, for whatever reason, that there was a potential excess of supply over demand for cotton.

But, while we have seen that the lenders had provided themselves with a variable contract tied to external circumstances, the borrowers enjoyed no comparable benefit. Any international collapse in the prices their exports brought in did nothing to alter their obligations under the loan agreements. Inequitable though this might seem, it is made much more so by the difference between trade in primary produce and trade in manufactured goods. Although we supposedly live in a time of free trade, there is in fact a very clear distinction between free trade concerned with manufactured goods and free trade in commodities. The last GATT agreement establishing the World Trade Organisation has not resolved this problem for primary commodity producers. The rich countries remain determined to protect with import restriction and internal and export subsidies in support of their own farmers and primary producers. To be able to produce the cheapest food in the world by no means guarantees a market. There is no free world trade in sugar, meat, rice or wheat.

At the same time, these difficulties for poor countries have in turn been aggravated by IMF policies aimed at forcing indebted countries to develop their exports at the expense of internal demand. As different states attempted to increase their exports of produce, so demand for those products was satisfied and so the price fell. Thus, it was possible to export more and yet receive a lower price. If Zambia is an extreme example, seeing its price for its copper exports halve and then halve again, it is certainly not the only example.

If all this seems rather remote from a discussion of law, it is not. It is related intimately to our earlier consideration of law as a system by which the social world is translated. What we see here is that the law way of seeing Third World debt in terms of contractual debts is not only desperately misleading but the consequences of accepting the translation can be utterly tragic. To see the problem as one of contractual debt is to accept a translated social problem as *really* existing as a legal problem. It is to mistake the translation for the reality. If the legal translation of the problem into contractual debt is translated back into the social reality, the problem is very different. The problem then changes from how the poor states are to repay their debts, to a problem of scarce resources being taken from people in abject and complete poverty and often starvation, in order to further enrich those who already enjoy greater material wealth than is imaginable or even desired by most people. Thus, the central point is that the law way of seeing intimately and directly affects even those who do not share its perspective, in a way which at once disables them and vindicates us.

Even so, the device of contract could not in itself have led to quite the injustices that it has but for another peculiarly legal concept, the concept of the legal person. At law, human beings are not the only 'persons' who have the ability to enter into contracts. Under law, other entities such as companies, local authorities and indeed states are all legal persons with contracting ability. What this means, for instance, is that if a company enters into a contract then if, even before the contract is due for performance, there is a complete change of shareholders, directors and even the entire personnel of the company, the company will remain bound by the contracts into which it has entered. It is this device of legal personality which legitimates a quite strange social reality.

As we have said, and again this distinguishes loans made to states from domestic loans, states borrowed as legal persons (or sometimes in that capacity guaranteed such loans). When it became difficult to service or repay the loans, the true effect of IMF 'advice' was essentially to exact repayment from the poorest people by removing subsidies and 'suppressing internal demand', which is a euphemism for making things too expensive for the poor to buy, so that it is the poorest who suffer most, so that repayment may be made. (In fact, repayment is much less encouraged than the continuing paying of interest.) The social reality of what is occurring is as incredible as it is outrageous. What is really happening is that, where loans which were often irresponsibly made, to borrowers who irresponsibly absorbed, wasted or stole the money, are not being serviced, then others who saw not a cent of the loan are called upon to repay. How is it that this situation is not universally regarded as completely absurd? The answer lies of course in our ability to make statements such as 'Nicaragua borrowed the money therefore Nicaragua must repay it'. Obviously 'Nicaragua' did not borrow the money, rather some people within the Nicaraguan Government or dictatorship borrowed it, under the cloak of the legal personality of the state.

Pursuing the example of Nicaragua makes the point even clearer because under the Sandinista regime which overthrew one of the world's most atrocious dictators, General Somoza, some 50% of its entire export receipts were required to service 'Nicaragua's' debt. These debts had been incurred by General Somoza and as one author (George, 1988, p 13) aptly says:

'Some outright thefts like those of Somoza in Nicaragua will never be punished and their victims will never be compensated. On the contrary, the victims will be expected to continue to reimburse the ill-gotten gains of their predecessors and this under increasingly difficult economic conditions imposed upon them by hostile and powerful neighbours. Somoza pocketed most of the international loans meant for the reconstruction of Nicaragua after the 1972 earthquake and continued to steal from his country right up to the moment he was forced out in 1979. When he fled the country, he left $3 million in the treasury. Nicaragua's debt is now $4 billion – three quarters of which was contracted under the Somoza regime.'

Thus, money borrowed by Somoza was not only smuggled out of the country but was also used to pay and arm the very people, the army, who oppressed the people so viciously. Even now, the poor of Nicaragua are making sacrifices to pay off those whose loans made oppression and poverty possible. This remains the case even though the electorate finally did as the US wished and voted in a government prepared to adopt free market, non-socialist policies.

This extraordinary situation applies to many other states as well. The people effectively called upon to repay the debts of Iraq incurred for military spending under Saddam Hussain again are the people who received no gain and much pain from the expenditure. If anything, the position in South Africa is even more incredible. The apartheid regime was largely supported through the activity of international finance. These loans were made to a state which was an international pariah and in which the majority of its people were disenfranchised because of the colour of their skin. Yet, the loans remain repayable and, if the IMF is to have its way, the poor must once more shoulder the burden. East European states too, having joined the IMF, were called upon to continue to service loans taken out by the old so-called communist regimes. (Of course, it should be observed that loans from the World Bank and the IMF are very much a minority of the total 'owed' but because of the conditions which apply to these loans they have a significance beyond their percentage. As a matter of interest, while South Africa owes nearly one third of its 'debt' to the World Bank and the IMF, sub-Saharan Africa 'owes' slightly less than one fifth of its 'debt' to those bodies.)

Although it is difficult, and perhaps inappropriate, to keep moral indignation out of a discussion about Third World debt, the legal points which come from it are surely neutral. Not only is this a classic example of the law's ability to redefine through translation in that one discovers that, in simply applying legal terminology in an apparently neutral way, the reality of the phenomenon translated has been transformed, and this is no less true of law in international trade than it is in domestic law; but, even more importantly, in the context of this chapter, it illustrates the extent to which the law way of understanding the world has imposed itself on every state regardless of the ideologies of the people within it. Had this chapter been about international debt rather than law, it would have been appropriate to offer further illustration of the effect of the activities of the World Bank and the IMF and to have made some suggestions about what might be done. For us, however, it is the fact of the translation and its effects which need to be understood and what is done with the evidence must be left to the reader. The effect of the legal translation has been accurately summarised by Fidel Castro when he observed in 1985:

> 'We are caught up in the Third World War, an economic war, it is an undeclared war, over the extortionate interest rates of the debt. The corpses are piling up but the aggressors maintain that the war does not exist; that the dead are alive and healthy' [quoted in Branford and Kucinski, 1988, p 1].

*An earlier version of this chapter is to be found in Mansell (1991).

10 Legitimation, Sovereignty and Globalisation

Astute readers might well have observed something of a paradox in the book so far. On the one hand, we have suggested that underpinning the Rule of Law is the legitimating phenomenon 'democracy'. It is democracy that provides authority and legitimacy for the actions of law making governments in countries operating within the Rule of Law. On the other hand, in the last chapter, we saw that democratic choices of populations – at least in heavily indebted states – are greatly constrained. The 'reality' of the indebtedness seems to make the election of a government not committed to the economic policies dictated by the International Monetary Fund either unthinkable or even suicidal. Dire threats both explicit and implicit hang over the heads of governments unwilling to follow the prescribed course of economic action.

Such constraints upon the electorate of indebted states are, however, reflected also in almost all states not directly dictated to by international financial organisations. Thus, in many states, including Western European and North American, there has been a tendency for mainstream political parties to become increasingly less differentiated – at least in economic policies. Even parties which traditionally described themselves as 'left' have, in fighting elections (often successfully), abandoned to a very considerable extent both goals of equality (or limited inequality) and the goal of a pivotal role for the state in allocating resources. Any debate about the desirability of a command economy as opposed to a demand economy (central planning rather than the very alive hand of the market), common sense dictates, is an argument which has been resolved.

Similarly, it is also common sense that a high tax economy is not an economy which will be able to compete with low tax economies. High taxation leads to capital flight and thus there has also been a large measure of acceptance that states cannot afford to maintain welfare systems which need high taxation. It is rational (or at least common sense) that individuals should provide for life's vicissitudes whether through insurance or otherwise, but it is irrational for the state to do this for all.

The effect of such seismic shifts in perception caused largely by the globalisation of the world economy has been to significantly remove economics from politics. If all the major parties of democratic states accept in essence the principles which are pursued by the International Monetary Fund, and if, because of the consensus, parties disagreeing are seen as being beyond the pale, then the idea of democratic control over the economy is redundant. This view receives some explicit recognition by those states which have ceded independence to state or union banks which in effect are able to set monetary policy without reference to governments.

Yet, here is a further paradox (apparently). While democracy comes to be substantively about less and less, the international community has become more and more insistent that democratic government is the only internationally acceptable form. Not only do we have the phenomenon of 'conditionality' by which aid from rich to poor states is made conditional upon progress towards a democratic form of government but we also have immensely respected legal articles arguing that there is an emerging human right to democracy. Such a paradox requires consideration.

We shall first consider this development by outlining the argument in a truly seminal article in international law – Thomas Franck's 'The emerging right to democratic governance' published in the 1992 *American Journal of International Law* (Franck, 1992) – and will then discuss the significance of the constraints upon the governance and will end by attempting to assess the meaning and importance of the insights provided.

Franck's article is of course very much a product of his time. The Cold War was nearly over, there had been unusual international coherence over Iraq's invasion of Kuwait and President Yeltsin of the Russian Republic had recently defeated an attempt to re-establish non-democratic government. In addition, there had been a united response to the overthrow of the elected government of Haiti – both the United Nations General Assembly and the Organisation of American States had unanimously called for the restoration of constitutional government. This was perhaps the high water mark for those who were sympathetic to the idea that a new world order was being created. If these expectations have been frustrated it remains true that that emphasis upon democratic governance has survived and this is the importance of Franck's argument.

By 'democratic governance', Franck has in mind two related aspects. The first is the argument that governments derive 'their just powers from the consent of the governed' (as the US Declaration of Independence has it) and the second and related aspect of this concept is that a nation earns ' separate and equal status' in the community of states by demonstrating 'a decent respect to the opinions of mankind'. Thus, democratic governance is not only a fully enfranchised constituency with one vote for each adult but also it requires consent and consent for governance which is clearly limited – that is, limited to governing in conformity with the most basic norms of international law. According to Franck, the international community of states is moving to an acceptance that *only* democracy validates governance. Other models, whether 'guided' democracy in the guise of modernism or dictated governments attempting to use scientific knowledge, are rapidly succumbing, leading to the 'almost complete triumph of the democratic notions of Hume, Locke, Jefferson and Madison – in Latin America, Africa, Eastern Europe and, to a lesser extent,

Asia' (1992, p 49). This is an argument he repeats in his 1995 classic *Fairness in International Law and Institutions* (Franck, 1995). In a paean to the American Declaration of Independence, he states:

'For 200 years, these two notions – that the right to govern depends on governments having met both the democratic entitlement of the governed and also the standards of the community of states – have remained a radical vision. This radicalism, while not yet fully encapsulated in law, is now rapidly becoming a normative rule of the international system. The "opinions of mankind" have begun in earnest to require that governments, as a prerequisite to membership in the community of nations, derive "their just powers from the consent of the governed". Increasingly, governments recognise that their legitimacy depends upon meeting normative expectations of the community of states. Democracy is thus on the way to becoming a global entitlement, one which may be promoted and protected by collective international processes.'

And, in the original article in terms which should remind the reader of Mr Podsnap in the first chapter of this book, he adds:

'These lucky few nations (that is, Western democracies) have succeeded in evolving their own legitimate means of validating the process by which the people choose those they entrust with the exercise of power'

and they have made a bargain of the social compact by which they have:

'... surrendered control over the nation's validation process to various others: national electoral commissions, judges, an inquisitive press and, above all, the citizenry acting at the ballot box ... In many nations, unfortunately, no such bargain was struck' [Franck, 1993, p 50].

Franck then proceeds to develop his thesis by considering the history and content of the right to self-determination and its democratic content and the concept of determinacy by which he means the clarity, precision and unambiguity of rules. Determinacy, he suggests, is necessary to persuade states to comply with rules even when it is not in their short term interests so to do. Precision, it is argued, leads to the acceptance by states of rules as rules and the value of compliance for that reason. As Karl Llewellyn might have said, clarity and precision aid the necessary 'felt rightness' about the rules, and compliance with the rules becomes an obligation in itself (although the difficulty of states having such feelings should not be underestimated). Evidence of the operation of this phenomenon is well expressed in DP Moynihan's *On the Law of Nations* (Moynihan, 1990) where he condemns unequivocally the Reagan regime's attempts to destabilise Sandinista Nicaragua not because he did not want the regime removed but because the actions taken were indefensible in international law. His argument there is that short term gains bought through non-compliance with rules invariably weaken the system of international law to the very great detriment of the US.

As to self-determination, Franck teases out the developing emphasis not only upon the consent of the governed but also with what he sees to be necessarily accompanying attributes – particularly freedom of expression and an emphasis upon plebiscites and free elections in the developing United Nations practice. Of great, if ironic (as we shall see) significance was the United Nations' assistance in supervising elections in Nicaragua in 1990 and in overseeing elections in Haiti in 1991.

The argument is then developed that the freedom of democratic states is necessarily constrained notwithstanding Article 2(7) of the United Nations Charter which provides that the UN Organisation shall not interfere in matters 'essentially within the domestic jurisdiction of states'. It is constrained first and foremost by the basic standards accepted by the international community through Conventions, Declarations and Covenants recognising basic human rights. It is constrained also by the reality, he suggests, of the problem arising from self-determination denied, which leads to the flight of 'hordes of refugees, placing onerous economic, social and political strains on the neighbouring states of refuge'. His examples are Bangladesh, Eritrea and Southern Sudan (though significantly not Israel).

Further, Franck argues that, while many considered self-determination to be primarily concerned with decolonisation, since that process has been almost completed, the concept has actually retained its vigour, as may be demonstrated both by the withdrawal by the Soviet Union of its forces from Eastern Europe and the Baltic states and more recently by the break up of the former republic of Yugoslavia.

It should be observed in passing that Franck's enthusiasm for such self-determination rather glibly avoids crucial difficulties with the concept. Because decolonisation was about liberating colonies, the basic principle came to be accepted that self-determination did not legitimate minorities *within* a colony. The principle of *uti possidetis* was to be applied and the import of this is that colonial boundaries could only be changed by the consent of states which emerged. In essence, the principle of *uti possidetis*, while intended to prevent the fragmentation of emerging states, led to a confirmation of colonial injustices. The effect of the principle was that colonial boundaries – especially in Africa – which had been drawn for the convenience of colonial powers (often with a vague map and a ruler) became sacrosanct. The result of the application of this principle led both to disaffected but substantial minorities who might have hoped for independence (such as the Ibo people of Nigeria) and to borders which cut through ethnic communities as, for example, in the boundary between Somalia and Ethiopia. The justice of established borders is often difficult to defend and limits to rights of secession do little to help.

That notwithstanding, Franck's basic argument holds. It is possible to perceive a pattern in the international community, moving towards recognition of constitutional government, concerning itself with the rights enumerated in international human rights documents and especially the International Covenant of Civil and Political Rights.

For the clearest evidence of development in this direction, Franck, as has been said, uses the example of Haiti. It is worth considering this example in some detail although the points to be made could, with modification, apply to the other examples he provides such as Nicaragua or Panama. Haiti was, as is observed, the first instance in which the United Nations, acting at the request of a national government (the so-called Haitian Transitional Government) 'intervened in the electoral process solely to validate the legitimacy of the outcome'. The General Assembly created a United Nations Observer Group for the Verification of the Elections in Haiti in 1990 and authorised it to do more than merely oversee the ballot. Essentially, it involved itself in a civil education programme promoting the importance of elected authorities, both national and regional. When the election was held in December 1990, Bertrand Aristide, a former priest and a proclaimed promoter of the interests of the poor, was elected president with more than 65% of the vote. His government, elected after the United Nations sponsored crash course in electoral fairness, lasted only until 30 September 1991 when there was a military coup replacing Aristide with General Raoul Cedras as head of state. The United Nations, in what can be, and was by some members, seen as intervention in the internal affairs of a member state immediately expressed its disapproval. Several UN states – especially China and Cuba – objected vehemently, arguing that elections should never be regarded as a matter affecting international peace and security. Because of China's opposition, the Security Council was unable to act. The General Assembly, however, passed by consensus a resolution which 'strongly condemns both the attempted illegal replacement of the constitutional President of Haiti and the use of violence, military coercion and the violation of human rights in that country' and demanded the immediate restoration of the legitimate government and appealed both to UN member states and to members of the Organisation of American States to isolate Haiti diplomatically and economically. (The dilemma for Cuba in particular was acute, obviously preferring as it did an Aristide government to a Cedras regime. The prospect of US direct intervention in the internal affairs of a Central American state persuaded Cuba that this was the worse spectre – even though they would have suspected some US complicity in the Cedras coup.)

As is now well known, the international pressure upon the military regime built up, finally under US leadership, so that General Cedras was persuaded to opt for exile and the Aristide government was duly reinstated. On the face of it (and this is the extent to which Franck analyses the saga), here was the international community intervening altruistically and promoting the recognition of a right to democratic governance. Those familiar with the exploits of the US in Central America might be more hesitant in accepting the story as described. They would be correct in their hesitancy.

In the early stages of Aristide's exile, he received little US support. There was an effort indeed within the US by government officials to portray Aristide as mentally unstable and economically highly suspect (Chomsky, 1993). His attempts in his brief period in power to help his impoverished constituency and to promote their interests at the expense of the wealthy minority was viewed as dangerously left wing by the US. Much of Aristide's brief attempts at reform had been intended to reverse the policies promoted by the USAID and the World Bank, which had in 1981 prescribed expansion of private enterprise and minimisation of 'social objectives' – policies which of course increased poverty and reduced expenditure on both health and education. The result was a decline of 56% in Haiti's (already desperately low) level of wages in the 1980s.

Further, evidence suggests that the US chose to exert its irresistible pressure for the return of Aristide only when Haitian refugees provided a most unwelcome problem. Some 40,000 refugees fled the Cedras regime for the US. Twenty seven thousand were forcibly repatriated by the US State Department but there was much adverse publicity. The easiest resolution of the difficulty was Aristide's restoration so that would-be economic immigrants would have no human rights justification for fleeing to a rich neighbour. All of this, however, might be overlooked but for the quite extraordinary conditions upon which the US insisted in return for its help. Aristide was returned to power on condition that he stand for no further term as president and, even more significantly, that economic policies be adopted which essentially reflected those required by the IMF – an export-driven trade and investment policy intended to open Haiti to both foreign investment and imports. Thus, according to Chomsky (Chomsky, 1999, p 108), a state once almost self-sufficient in rice production now imports some 50% of its requirements. There is an effective prohibition upon providing subsidies for electricity, fuel, water or food for the Haitian poor.

The result of this triumph for democratic governance observed by Franck is that when parliamentary elections were held in Haiti in April 1997 with economic policy no longer contentious, the turn-out of the voting constituency was 5%! With remarkable hubris, the Christian Science Monitor headlined its story reporting this fact 'Democracy in Practice: Did Haiti Fail US Hope?' (Chomsky, 1999, p 109). In fairness to Franck, he did not of course know what was to happen but if he had, only two lines of argument sustaining his thesis would be possible. He might argue that low turn-outs in themselves reflect the fact that the government enjoys the consent and confidence of the governed or he might argue that Haiti is atypical. The first, though arguable, ignores reasons which studies have suggested for voter apathy – much less contentment than alienation or a feeling of hopelessness and a refusal to believe that voting can effect change. JK Galbraith's *The Culture of Contentment* clearly evidences this (Galbraith, 1992).

As to the suggestion that Haiti might be atypical, the evidence is rather that it is absolutely typical. When the US Senate passed the remarkable so-called Helms Burton Act designed to further isolate Cuba in the international community, the Act not only provided remarkable provisions designed to dissuade non-US companies from doing business with Cuba, but more importantly for our purposes (and less reported) provided the criteria which required fulfilment before the US would accept democratic credentials and drop its trade boycott and embargo. Included in these were a government without either Fidel or Raoul Castro (specified by name) to be explicitly committed to free market principles! Thus, for the US Senate, the idea of democratic governance without an irrevocable commitment to liberal capitalism is inconceivable.

Again, the argument might be made that the US Senate does not represent the world community. In answer to this, one needs not only to recognise the economic might of the US but also to examine its wider influence. At the time of writing, the bombing of Kosovo by NATO has just ceased. It began when the Yugoslavian Government refused to accept the so-called Interim Agreement for Peace and Self-Government in Kosovo, which was drafted at Rambouillet in France. Consistently with Franck's argument, the draft agreement laid down detailed provisions for the conduct and supervision of free and fair elections. An obligation was to be placed on the parties to the agreement to ensure an open and free political environment, with free media effectively accountable to registered political parties and candidates and available to voters throughout Kosovo. For those concerned with democratic governance, these provisions seem necessary and unexceptional. Or at least they do until Chapter 4 of the draft Interim Agreement is considered. This concerns itself with economic issues, and Article 1(i) states 'The economy of Kosovo shall function in accordance with free market principles'. Quite how this is necessarily reconcilable with free and fair elections is not explained. Article 1(6) goes on apparently innocuously to state:

'Federal and other authorities shall within their respective powers and responsibilities ensure the free movement of persons, goods, services and capital to Kosovo, including from international sources. They shall, in particular, allow access to Kosovo without discrimination for persons delivering such goods and services.'

It is not necessary to have a particular view of the propriety of the NATO intervention to recognise the remarkable constraint which is here intended to operate irrevocably upon any Kosovon Government.

Such examples confirm the view that in so far as the Franck thesis correctly describes the emerging acceptance of democratic governance, it is governance inherently directed towards liberal capitalism and free markets. Fukuyama's thesis in *The End of History and the Last Man* (Fukuyama, 1992) seems sustained in its view that inevitably this form of political and economic organisation is irresistible and irrevocable. We shall critically consider that sentiment in due course.

Such explicit constraints upon democratic governance are not however the only ones. Globalisation and the marked increase in international treaties by which states voluntarily agree to limit their sovereignty have been remarkable features of the second half of the 20th century. The previous chapter considered just how the International Monetary Fund dictates economic policies. Here, however, a little more needs to be said about the World Trade Organisation and the constraints that it effects over national policies. It should of course be immediately observed that states which have joined the World Trade Organisation did so voluntarily, although it must also be remembered that, while a state has no will, those who represent it often represent particular and usually affluent interests.

The World Trade Organisation (WTO), as most will know, is a body charged with administering the General Agreement on Tariff and Trade and is concerned with the promotion of free trade. While there are many points to be made in other contexts concerning the fairness of the results promoted by the WTO, this is not the objective here. Rather, what we want to do is to suggest just how the WTO constrains national policies. That it does so with regard to trade and tariff is obvious but less obvious is the clear effect upon democratic governance.

Recently within Europe, two issues have arisen which illustrate the problem perfectly. European citizens have overwhelmingly rejected the idea of genetically modified food crops. Such has been the consumer resistance in the United Kingdom that all major supermarkets have resolved not simply to ensure that products containing genetically modified ingredients are labelled as such, but rather to phase out the use of such ingredients entirely. The resistance to their use is no doubt stimulated by fear induced by the cattle infection Bovine Spongiform Encephalopathy (BSE) and the related new variant Creutzfeldt-Jakob disease in humans. Although much of government and many scientists have attempted to reassure a sceptical public, this has been markedly unsuccessful. Whether the scepticism is justified or not remains a moot point but most people seem to have internalised what is known as the precautionary principle of law – viz, the greater the possible harm the greater the reason for extreme caution. More explicitly:

> '... one understanding of the principle is that substances or activities which might be detrimental to the environment should be regulated even in the *absence* of conclusive evidence of their harmfulness; lack of full scientific evidence should not be used as a reason for postponing measures to prevent environmental degradation' [Holder, 1997, p 123].

Such evidence as there is does at the very least call into question the justification for genetically modified food crops. If democratic governance is about governing with consent, the European public has made it abundantly clear that it does not approve. Recognising this raises the question as to quite why the UK Government, in particular, remains so enthusiastic. Part of the answer may lie in the interests of British companies which have spent heavily on development and research in this area. But, because so much of the technology is owned by very few (and foreign) companies, this seems unlikely.

The much more probable explanation lies in the fear of European governments of the WTO and its procedures for resolving disputes.

This also applies to the second contemporary issue awaiting resolution. Much American beef is produced with the assistance of Bovine Somatotropin (BST), a growth hormone that not only promotes growth when injected into the animal at frequent intervals, but also increases lactation from cows by some 12–15%. The US authorities have been persuaded that scientific studies do not evidence any harm to humans from this practice. Considerable research in Europe has failed to provide conclusive evidence either way, but again there is little doubt that the importation both of BST produced beef and the hormone itself for injection into European cattle is resisted by European voters. It is probable that this resistance would not be overcome regardless of safety evidence. Gratuitous use of such injections in order to produce more of a product of which there is already a surplus – certainly at least for Europe – does not seem manifestly sensible. As with genetically modified crops, there is widespread concern about what seems to be a needless interference with natural processes and with incalculable results. A Greenpeace survey (a MORI poll) found 74% of the public were worried about contamination by genetically modified crops – a worry which will only be strengthened by a report from the John Innes Centre in Norwich (a report commissioned by the Ministry of Agriculture, Fisheries and Food) which concluded in essence that, because of the inability to confine genetically modified crops, their co-existence with organic food and farming was not possible and a choice would have to be made between them. This, of course, is because of the unintended dispersal of pollen and seeds and because of the impossibility of measuring the impact of such crops upon the environment without actually testing this. Such tests might themselves irrevocably alter the environment. The Director of the Soil Association in making this point observed: 'Farm scale trial plots are rather like letting a rat with bubonic plague out into the environment and then seeing what happens' ((1999) *The Independent*, 18 June).

Although our views on these two issues are probably plain, this is, for the sake of this argument, unimportant. What is important is that a substantial majority of the public, 'crass and ignorant' though they may be, withholds its consent from these developments. European governments, however, find themselves confronted by international obligations within the WTO which may force them either to accept these imports or pay enormous 'compensation' to would-be US exporters whose products are not accepted.

This is not the place for an extended discussion of the means by which the WTO resolves disputes, but some points are relevant. The first is that, in developments since the Second World War, there has been a consistent attempt to further liberalise trade and to bring down barriers which impede this goal. At the same time, as we observed in passing in the last chapter, this liberalisation has been selective and has greatly favoured the developed world. Restraints on

145

imports from the poor world, particularly but not exclusively agricultural, have tended to give the lie to free trade. There are also studies which suggest that disguised protectionism and indirect subsidies further qualify the goal (Chomsky, 1999, p 65). This notwithstanding, the accepted wisdom of the move to liberalisation may be seen to some extent in the new provisions by which international trade disputes are resolved within the WTO. While considerable emphasis is placed upon the need to resolve disputes through such mechanisms as consultation, good offices, conciliation and mediation, should all these fail, there is now the means for authoritative adjudication which must be accepted. Thus, there has been an increasing legalisation of the process. The 1994 Dispute Settlement Understanding provided for a Dispute Settlement Body to oversee and organise the resolution to disputes. What is crucially important for our argument is that governments party to GATT now must accept a decision which might well be unacceptable to their constituents. In effect, the Dispute Settlement Body is responsible for constituting a (supposedly) neutral panel of experts who consider whether a party is in breach of its obligations. There is the right of an appeal to an Appellate Body consisting of seven individuals who must be 'persons of recognised authority with demonstrated expertise in law, international trade and the subject matter of the overseeing agreements generally' (Article 17(3)).

Again, the strength of such a process with its ability to insist upon the implementation of rulings and recommendations is obvious, but so too are the problems. At the time of writing, Europe is coming under ever-increasing pressure from the US to comply with rulings that the impediment to the US beef and hormone imports is a breach of WTO obligations. Because there is provision for the award of compensation or the suspension of concessions, a government flouts such rulings at its peril. The so-called emerging right to democratic governance must be qualified once more.

There is yet a further major constraint upon democratic governance and this comes from corporate power. It is said that of the 100 largest economic entities in the world only half are states. The others, of course, are corporations (or even individuals such as Bill Gates of Microsoft) whose financial might states can ignore at their peril. Such is the power to stimulate or break the economies of nations that few governments will be able to resist the largest corporations, and the smallest states in terms of economy will be the most constrained.

A recent exemplification of this phenomenon (though there is a myriad of such examples) has concerned the activities of Michael Ashcroft, a man with dual citizenship of Belize and the UK who, according to *The Times* ((1999) 11 June) is not only paying to the British Conservative Party £360,000 per month but has also been able to influence politics in Belize to the direct benefit of the holding company of which he is chairman and chief executive. He also, incidentally, obtained appointment as the permanent representative of Belize at the United Nations in New York. The Government of Belize (until defeat in 1998) believes that it lost the election because of the intervention of Mr Ashcroft's company. The ousted prime minister claimed that he had attracted the ire of Mr Ashcroft because his government had attempted to modify offshore legislation passed by a previous government in 1990 under which the subsidiaries of the holding company were given exemption from income tax until 2020. In the words of *The Times* report:

> 'The opposition ... said it was alarmed by his power. We respect his status as a businessman, but we are very concerned at his growing ability to actually control the economy. In a small country like ours, it does not take very much, especially when you own the largest bank in the country. We are pretty much hostage to his needs.'

The government he helped to elect admitted that the economic power Mr Ashcroft wields was potentially dangerous but this had been balanced against the need to bring prosperity.

This is an unusually frank admission of the influence of companies and individuals yet in some ways it is of less concern than the activities of the largest corporations whose influences are often difficult to prove. Another article from *The Times* ((1999) 12 May) by Michael Pinto-Duschinsky provides evidence for this argument. The article considers the activities of Deutsche Bank and its ability to influence events to suit its own interests rather than those of the public. Deutsche Bank has assets of some £400,000,000,000 (that is, four hundred billion pounds). Deutsche Bank is one of the very largest German corporations and comfortably in the world's 100 largest yet; as is pointed out, it does not gain influence by political donation or party support. In a sense, such a large multinational corporation has to be above politics since it will be intent upon retaining influence regardless of which political party governs any particular country where it has interests. The influence is exercised not even by lobbying, but simply by the often implied, but sometimes explicit, threat to move capital, investments, factories and jobs to other states. Pinto-Duschinsky suggests that it was just such influence which ensured the sacking of Oskar Lafontaine from his post as Germany's Finance Minister. Lafontaine was seen by corporations as over committed to welfare spending. Significantly, since his ousting, the German Chancellor Gerhard Schroeder has announced major reductions in such spending – reductions which would even have been unlikely had Chancellor Kohl been re-elected. The June 1999 budget was the most austere in Germany's postwar history, cutting both welfare expenditure and corporation tax. It is even suggested that when one sees the ease with which retiring cabinet ministers and senior civil servants translate into senior posts in corporations that onlookers should anticipate a high level of co-operation, because of the promise of highly rewarded future employment. Such promises need not be explicit.

What exercised the author of this article was the means adopted by Deutsche Bank to resist the claims of Holocaust survivors. The victims maintain that

Deutsche Bank's role in actively assisting the Holocaust is provable and that reparations should be payable. The suggestion is made that both the German and US Governments have been coerced to provide support for Deutsche Bank's resistance to these claims – support which, in the case of the German Government, even includes plans to invalidate the victims' lawyers by portraying them as avaricious (offensively referred to in the German Chancellery documents as the 'Shylock motive').

Although this might be thought to be an isolated example, it is unique only in its particular facts. So intimate is the relationship between a state's largest investors and its government, and so accepted is the view that the interests between the two coincide, that the fact that one is the result of 'democratic governance' and the other financial muscle is scarcely noticed. Intimate though the relationship is, it is seldom transparent.

Even less readily observable by, or understandable to, the voting constituencies of states are the problems and constraints posed by international monetary transactions. The threat of withdrawal of capital or transfer of enterprises has some physical reality which may be grasped, but speculative transactions in currency are rather difficult to comprehend. The magnitude of the phenomenon of international monetary transactions is as awesome as it is opaque. It is also a comparatively modern development. As is observed in *World Guide* (1999, p 69), whereas, in 1975, 80% of currency transactions (the process whereby one currency is traded for another) were concerned with business transactions in the real economy – that is, concerned with purchasing or selling goods internationally or investing or whatever; by 1997, these transactions amounted to only 2.5% with the other 97.5% of the speculative kind – that is currency bought and sold by currency traders speculatively. And the sums of money traded are extraordinary. 'At a time when the annual value of all the world's exports amounts to $3 trillion, on a normal [sic] day's trading, the world's capital markets move $1.3 trillion, more than the total gold and foreign currency reserves of all the members of the IMF' (Ireland, 1997, p 279).

Whether this speculation is in any sense rational is beyond the scope of this book and the matter is still the subject of great debate. Either way, the speculation necessarily constrains any government's policies since, if it is seen to be beyond the orthodox, the national currency is likely to come under speculative attack. In one IMF study, a suggestion of what might lead to and sustain a speculative attack makes this point clear:

'A speculative attack on a fixed or arranged exchange rate is a sudden and massive restructuring of portfolios in which market participants attempt to reap gains or prevent losses from an expected change in the exchange rate regime. It was once thought by economists that speculative attacks were market pathologies that would not be present or possible in healthy markets. Recent research has considered that *a speculative attack is a market's rational response to a perceived inconsistency in economic policies*. In this research, a country tries to sustain a fixed exchange rate using a limited quantity of reserves and pursues other higher priority objectives such as inflation objectives that might be inconsistent with the fixed exchange rate. Private market participants – called speculators – who recognise the policy inconsistency and the limited availability of resources come to realise that the fixed exchange rate cannot be sustained. In foreseeing the unsustainability of policies, market participants anticipate profits and losses and enter into foreign exchange transactions that ultimately hasten the collapse of the exchange rate regime' [Solomon, 1999, p 157].

As an argument, it has to be said that this analysis conceals more than it reveals. If it is the case that this is simply a rational market response to objectively pathological policies, we certainly need to consider further just what amounts to a perceived inconsistency in economic policies. What it almost certainly means in practice is a government pursuing policies at variance with those regarded as orthodox by the IMF – particularly state spending upon welfare or subsidies. Yet again, democratic governance, regardless of the voting constituency, must follow policies which try to make a national currency invulnerable to currency speculators (or 'private market participants').

An important way of encompassing what we have argued so far is to place the discussion within an analysis of state sovereignty. What should have become clear is that since 1945 changes in the meaning of sovereignty is one of the most remarkable features of the second half of the 20th century. It is specifically to this subject and the allied topic of globalisation that this chapter now turns.

The traditional view of sovereignty is usually traced back to the Treaty of Westphalia of 1648. This is slightly arbitrary but nevertheless convenient. In the words of one author:

'... the Peace of Westphalia of 1648 [is] one of the most important points demarking the mediaeval from the modern period in Europe's development. Like all such historical benchmarks, Westphalia is in some respects more a convenient reference point than the source of a fully formed new normative system. Some elements that characterise the modern world, separating us from the Middle Ages, were well established long before 1648; others did not emerge until many years after. Still, the Peace of Westphalia created at least the foundations of a new European system – one that would not become truly a world system until the second half of the 20th century – out of the ruins of the political structures and the idealised rationale for them that had existed more or less unchanged in Europe for the preceding 1,000 years' [Miller, 1990, p 20].

As we shall see, although that quotation is not inaccurate, its assertion about the second half of the 20th century will require qualification. The Treaty of Westphalia (at the risk of over simplifying) may be said to have 'created the basis for a *decentralised system of sovereign and equal nation states*' (Miller, 1990, p 21). The reaction to the Thirty Years War which had devastated Europe was a move to enable separate states to co-exist with a reciprocal prohibition upon interference with the internal affairs of other states. In other words, the foundations were laid for a state to enjoy unlimited power over its own territory without interference. Implicitly, there was the recognition that destructive wars could only be avoided by recognition of this principle. Needless to say, the theory did not hold sway entirely and there were many subsequent interventions and wars notwithstanding. Nevertheless, the theory has continued in its importance and such wars and interventions as there have been have been arguably fewer than might otherwise have been the case.

The other manifestation of state sovereignty has been the concept of sovereign equality. Because each sovereign (whether a prince or parliament) has absolute power within its own state, it follows that there cannot be relationships of dominance and subordination between states – although of course there may be economic hegemony, the interference can never be direct. We observed in the previous chapter how this formal equality is reinforced in the UN Charter, providing as it does for one vote for each state in the United Nations General Assembly. We have also mentioned Article 2(7) of the Charter which is the other manifestation of the Westphalian order in providing that the UN Organisation shall not interfere in matters 'essentially within the domestic jurisdiction of states'.

But, while the UN Charter seemed to reinforce the Westphalian order, in asserting rights for the Security Council in particular, it also laid the ground for a considerable modification of that system. Both World Wars had provided clear evidence of the limitations and the need for some reassessment. The rise of fascism in Europe and the view that that should be a matter only for each state (so strong was this view in the 1930s that the UK forbore to protest against German mistreatment of its citizens arguing that this would be an unwarranted intrusion into the domestic affairs of another state) was seen to have led to the European conflagration and Holocaust. Thus, the aftermath of the war provided a UN Charter which allocated power to the Security Council – the US, China, USSR (now Russia), France and the UK, that is, the world powers of 1945 – to intervene even militarily in situations which it judged to threaten world peace. Such provisions obviously contained the potential to directly constrain and restrain individual states. While initially it was assumed that threats to peace would only occur in inter-state disputes this is no longer the case as may be evidenced by UN intervention in Somalia, belatedly in Rwanda and, to a lesser extent (because the action was never formally approved by the Security Council), by the North Atlantic Treaty Organisation's intervention in Kosovo. These examples were only the latest manifestation of very considerable changes accelerated by the end of the Cold War.

Most importantly, Article 2(7) of the Charter had become almost unrecognisable in the way it had come to be interpreted particularly after the signing of the two UN Covenants on Human Rights, signed in 1966 and now in force, with most of the world's states parties to them. In the face of Soviet and Chinese opposition, it became clear that international discussion of a state's internal policies which were breaches of human rights could not be prevented. While the exact import of Article 2(7) remains a matter of contention as we saw with the debate over intervention in Cuba, almost all states have been forced to accept that human rights abuses and in particular genocide cannot now be argued as matters essentially within the domestic jurisdiction of a state.

No case better illustrates the post Westphalian notion of sovereignty than the currently ongoing saga concerning General Pinochet, sometime dictator (and torturer) of Chile. At last, the recognition that the principle violators of human rights are sovereigns themselves has resulted in international action. The limitations of sovereign immunity (the doctrine by which heads of states were immune from foreign jurisdiction) have been accepted and any who are responsible for genocide, crimes against humanity or war crimes may well have lost such immunity. The coming years will determine whether dictators responsible for such deeds may be brought to trial in other states under their laws which give effect to internationally accepted human rights obligations. Those already vulnerable and living in exile include Alfredo Stroessner of Paraguay now living in Brazil, Hissein Habre of Chad now in Senegal, Idi Amin of Uganda now in Saudi Arabia, 'Baby Doc' Duvalier of Haiti now in France, Raoul Cedras of Haiti now in Panama and Mengistu Heile Mariam of Ethiopia now in Zimbabwe.

Even more significantly, following the formation of two *ad hoc* international criminal tribunals concerned with atrocities in the former Yugoslavia and Rwanda, we have the development of an International Criminal Court which is intended to concern itself with those responsible for human rights abuses both international and domestic. Only seven UN members (including the US, China and Iraq) voted against the creation of the court which will (hopefully) positively limit sovereignty in the interests of citizens.

These are (in our view) positive constraints on sovereignty and they are under pinned by contemporary concepts of human rights. At the same time, however, it is necessary to remember two points. The foundations of UN human rights activity is to be found within the Universal Declaration which is both time and space specific. In particular, as Michael Ignatieff points out, the Declaration was 'a comprehensive attempt to outlaw the kind of jurisprudence which the Nazis had used to pervert the Rule of Law in Germany' (Ignatieff, 1999, p 58). 'The declaration may still be a child of the Enlightenment, but it was written when faith in the Enlightenment faced its deepest crisis of confidence.' The paradox was that the Declaration represented an attempted secular assertion of ' the natural rights of man'.

The second point is that there does seem to be a clear relationship between the doctrine of individual human rights and the world of liberal capitalism. The stress upon the rights of individuals relates directly to the sort of policies espoused by the IMF and the US, in which an inherent part of freedom is the freedom to exploit. It is reminiscent of Lenin's diatribe against these rights of free speech and other basic human rights because, he argued, they were a blatant sham. They made no sense when placed beside rights over private property because they could only be exercised in a meaningful way by those who had access to capital in order to use the rights. Or again, to quote Ignatieff, he observes:

'As the global market economy polarised traditional societies and moralities and drew every corner of the planet into a single economic machine, human rights emerged as the secular creed that the new global middle class needed in order to justify their domination of the new cosmopolitan order.'

The case is put most explicitly in an essay in a book he is reviewing (Anderson, 1998, p 115) where the author states:

'Given the class interest of the internationalist class carrying out this [human rights] agenda the claim to universalism is a sham. The universalism is mere globalism and a globalism, moreover, whose key terms are established by capital.'

It is important to remember this when we explicitly consider globalisation itself. The apparently positive features such as human rights protection have to be balanced against the economic realities of globalisation. Earlier in this chapter, we saw the manifestations of globalisation in apparently committing almost all states to uniform economic policies. Such has been their dominance that many writers argue that globalisation is best understood in terms which make this reality clear. *World Guide* (1999) is not untypical when it suggests that globalisation is really a euphemism for 'transnationalisation' by which is meant 'the unfettered expansion of transnational corporations into the world economy' (*World Guide*, 1999, p 63). Thus, the most important features of globalisation are concerned with increasing liberalisation of capital and trade flows and a minimising of restrictions to aid this process.

To readers of *The End of History and the Last Man*, these notions will be familiar. The (sophisticated) argument there, with which we disagree, is that liberal democracy and market orientated economic order are progressively becoming the only viable option for modern societies. The disagreement arises over the content both of 'liberal democracy' and the inevitability of market orientated economic order. It is difficult to reject the view that Fukuyama falls into the error of ethnocentricity. What, he argues, is inevitable and final happens to coincide with the very situation within the US in which he is living. In many ways, also significantly, his views coincide with the current US Treasury secretary Lawrence Summers. An interview with him reported in *The Guardian* ((1999) 16 June) is well worth summarising. The Summers thesis is that the US and the rest of the world's interest coincide. He believes both in totally free and open markets and in the freedom of capital to move freely around the world. While accepting that this is obviously in the interests of the US, he argues that it is in fact in the interests of all. As to the problem of the difficulties posed by constituencies who vote for decent labour standards, social welfare and environmental protection only to see capital flee to less taxed and regulated economies, Summers sees this as a global problem. The interview continues:

'As capital becomes more mobile than labour there are concerns that companies will exploit that greater mobility by playing off competing jurisdictions against one another. The fear is that we will find ourselves in a race to the bottom – a bottom in which governments cannot promote fair taxes, uphold fair labour standards or protect the environment. That is not the world we want to build.'

But, quite how we are to avoid it remains unspecified. The interview continues:

'Summers thinks free capital mobility is good and he calls this "integration". He also recognises that individuals are concerned that governments should help improve their welfare through welfare rights, social insurance and environmental protection. He calls this "insurance" or "public purpose". Finally, he accepts that people like to elect their own government and have a say in things like their taxes. He calls this "sovereignty".

The problem, he believes is that while it is easy to have any two out of the three (integration, insurance, sovereignty) it is very hard to have all three at the same time. The answer, Summers believes, is to make other countries see that what is good for the US is also good for them – in his own words, "to finesse sovereignty problems by highlighting the national benefits of internationally congenial behaviour". Other countries should understand that it is in their interests to have financial, social and other systems just like those in the US ...'

Summers then goes on to advocate the extension of internationalisation to labour standards, environmental standards and finally tax regimes and social welfare provision. This, the author states, is seen to be the modern version of the 'civilizing mission' of the 19th century colonial powers. After hearing Summers advocate a greater opening of domestic financial markets to foreign providers of financial services, the interviewer (Chang Noi) presciently and pertinently concludes:

'The old colonial powers argued that small countries should surrender their sovereignty in return for the benefits of "civilization". The language has changed from "civilisation" to "good governance", but the message remains the same.'

(These are very frank views expressed by Summers and indeed, as an economist, he has a remarkable reputation for frankness. When Chief Economist of the World Bank, he once wrote in 1992 a paper for the Bank suggesting that it made economic sense to export pollution from the developed to the underdeveloped world. Because life expectancy is already low in the latter countries, fewer people would die of the pollution because they would be dead from other causes before the pollution affected them! 'The economic logic' he said 'behind dumping a load of toxic waste in the lowest wage country is impeccable and we should face up to that'. Indeed, we should – even if it means reconsidering 'economic logic'! (Chomsky, 1993, p 107).

This would be an appropriate point to finish this chapter. The notion of 'good governance' and the implications undreamt of by Franck, together with the consequent 'democratic deficit', are, hopefully, clear. But, globalisation and the arguments which have led to politics no longer being concerned with economics require one final addendum. For those familiar with a Marxian approach, this is related to the concept of alienation. Globalisation has removed major problems from anything resembling the 'local'. So large do these problems appear that feelings of powerlessness are everywhere to be seen – or, if not seen, heard. Such feelings are aggravated by the impression that crucial areas for decision making such as the environment, threats to health, nuclear power and weapons, the arms trade, to name but a few, are not appropriate for political debate. This is in part because of the economic consensus but at least as much because so many policies have the air of inevitability about them, as presented. The internalisation of Mrs Thatcher's mantra – 'There is no alternative' – by even the government which replaced her seems finally (at least, as evidenced by the June 1999 European elections) to have persuaded the electorate that there is little to be voted for or even against. If this is true for the affluent states, it is even more so for the poor, forced by debt, the International Monetary Fund and corporate power to hopelessly pursue 'democratic governance' to the benefit of the very few.

All that is required now is to appraise the significance of what we have argued. If democratic governance is increasingly seen to be the only truly legitimate form of government and is yet constrained by 'economic reality', what does this suggest about our legitimation of law? We think that it says both a little and a great deal. It says little because, as we saw earlier, legitimating worlds are simply that. They are the means by which we justify what is done. They do not have to be true, or even virtuous; it is enough that they perform the task of justification. That is the dispassionate appraisal of legitimating worlds.

The passionate perspective however cannot avoid seeking to analyse the exercise of power which legitimating worlds both disguise and justify. The question for the sociologist of law, if not for the philosopher of law, is who benefits from such a legitimation and who suffers because of it? Because these are not only factual questions, but questions the answers to which have political implications, the next chapter will address these issues explicitly.

11   Equality and the Rule of Law

At this point, it is necessary to return to the concept of the Rule of Law and its relationship to particular forms of economic organisation and, in turn, its relationship to a market way of understanding the world. The Rule of Law, as we have suggested, rests upon a central proposition, namely, that in essence all human beings are equal. Thus, as *essentially* equal individuals, it makes sense to have laws which apply to us all equally. That we are rich or poor, male or female, black or white is less significant than that we are individuals equal in our 'humaness'. This idea of essential equality is not unproblematic and it is often used to validate a very particular conception of the equal human nature that we are supposed to possess. We have argued already that what is distinctive about liberal capitalist society is its great emphasis upon individuality and private property (the two are clearly interrelated) and yet most of us, most of the time, do not see this as anything other than entirely natural. For us, the essence of human nature is to be found in assumptions which, without strong evidence, seem self-evident. Within Western capitalism, one finds such assumptions about human nature as the natural desire to compete, the naturalness of male aggression, the natural distinction between maleness (aggression), and femaleness (maternalism), the natural desire to accumulate wealth and to be ambitious. Yet, all of these assumptions are not merely functional for the continuance of our particular way of organising the world, they are also the very attitudes which distinguish us from others. And, as we saw, early anthropologists (see especially the example of the description of the Eskimo) were only too ready to declare defective those societies where other assumptions about human nature prevailed. Whereas for many peoples co-operation seems much more 'natural' than competition; caring for people in the society more 'natural' than ignoring or even exploiting them; and ensuring that everybody in the community had sufficient resources to live on and no-one more than he or she could use, more 'natural' than individual goals to obtain more resources than could ever be consumed – our ideology means most of us think the opposite. This, however, is less interesting than the fact that so many accept this individualist perspective as simply 'human nature', and as such almost of unquestionable truth.

Yet, the effect of this assumption of the quality of human nature makes lots of exercises of power much easier. For us, the very wealthy have only done what was natural, while the very poor have either had bad luck or were simply not clever enough to compete. Thus, while wealth brings no obligation, poverty carries no claims or rights and this in turn legitimates a system in which, while all are equal before the law, the affluent are protected in their wealth and the poor in their poverty. And because those with wealth are successful and those without are unsuccessful in achieving the equally desired goal (that is, wealth), it makes sense to assume that our essential human nature is identical. And, here, we return to a vital feature of the Rule of Law, equality before the law.

A useful description of the virtues of the Rule of Law is to be found in Friedrich von Hayek's book *The Road to Serfdom* (1976). Hayek's ideas have been of great importance to conservative philosophy in Britain as governed by Margaret Thatcher. His intention in *The Road to Serfdom* is to counter the view that the Rule of Law validates a less than just society and suffers in comparison with the legal systems where, rather than being constantly concerned to curb official powers, law is concerned with social engineering, that is, deciding issues through central planning in order to pursue economic and social goals. Not insignificantly he takes as his starting text the quotation from Karl Mannheim pointing out that the phenomenon of the Rule of Law is unique to a particular form of economic organisation – liberal competitive capitalism. In Mannheim's words:

> 'Recent studies in the sociology of law once more confirm that the fundamental principle of formal law by which every case must be judged according to general rational precepts, [laws] which must have as few exceptions as possible and are based on logical subsumptions, obtains only for the liberal competitive phase of capitalism' [quoted in Hayek, 1976, p 54].

Hayek never denies the proposition but wants to argue that regardless of its uniqueness only the Rule of Law guarantees a 'free country' as opposed to states governed by arbitrary government. (Of course, writing as he was in 1944, by 'arbitrary government', he was referring primarily to totalitarianism in Fascist or Communist states.)

The essence of what Hayek sees as central to government by the Rule of Law (as government 'by law rather than by men' [!]) is 'that the government in all its actions is bound by rules fixed and announced beforehand' (Hayek, 1976, p 54), thus allowing individuals to plan their lives accordingly. This is contrasted with economic planning of the collectivist kind where, as Hayek says, because:

> '... it [the state] must provide for the actual needs of people as they arise and then choose deliberately between them [it] must constantly decide questions which cannot be answered by formal principles only, and in making these decisions it must set up distinctions of merit between the needs of different people' [Hayek, 1976, p 55].

To Hayek, such state actions are abhorrent because they circumscribe individual choice by dictating in particular cases. This is unacceptable state intervention. Furthermore, it is only with the Rule of Law that individuals can plan and take decisions which they are best able to take, without fear of state interference. Thus, the clearer and more explicit are powers given by government and the less discretion that is permitted of bureaucrats, the greater the certainty of the limitation of government interference, and thus the greater is the certainty within which individuals can take decisions. Hayek, along with many contemporary conservatives, regards this as the very basis for individual freedom. He regards with equanimity the fact that (as he expressly acknowledges) the necessary result of this:

'... is that formal equality before the law is in conflict, and in fact incompatible, with any activity of the government deliberately aiming at material or substantive equality of different people, and that any policy aiming at a substantive ideal of distributive justice must lead to the destruction of the Rule of Law.'

This he accepts because, 'for the law to produce the same result for different people, it is necessary to treat them differently' and this is incompatible with his understanding of the Rule of Law (Hayek, 1976, p 59). While this may not be an illogical point of view, it might affect the value we place upon the Rule of Law when so defined.

What is very clearly at the heart of Hayek's thesis is the centrality of the individual and the separateness of the individual from other individuals. His views argue that what is in the interests of individuals is, by definition almost, in the interest of society and the freedom of the individual to pursue his or her own interest which is of paramount importance. Nevertheless, it will no doubt have been observed that the freedom to which Hayek constantly refers is economic freedom and the freedom of the market place. This is the freedom to buy and sell and here there is formal equality regardless of substantive inequality. This he contrasts with the sort of freedom which was espoused by the socialists:

'The coming of socialism was to be the leap from the realm of necessity to the realm of freedom. It was to bring "economic freedom", without which the political freedom already gained "was not worth having". Only socialism was capable of effecting the consummation of the age long struggle for freedom in which the attainment of political freedom was but a first step.

The subtle change in meaning to which the word freedom was subjected in order that this argument should sound plausible is important. To the great apostles of political freedom the word had meant freedom from coercion, freedom from the arbitrary power of other men, release from ties which left the individual no choice but obedience to the orders of a superior to whom he was attached. The new freedom promised, however, was to be freedom from necessity, release from the compulsion of the circumstances which inevitably limit the range of choice of all of us, although for some very much more than for others. Before man could be truly free, the "despotism of physical want" had to be broken, the "restraints of the economic system" relaxed.

Freedom, in this sense, is, of course, merely another name for power or wealth. Yet, although the promises of this new freedom were often coupled with irresponsible promises of a great increase in material wealth in a socialist society, it was not from such an absolute conquest of the niggardliness of nature that economic freedom was expected. What the promise really amounted to was that the great existing disparities in the range of choice of different people were to disappear. The demand for the new freedom was thus only another name for the old demand for an equal distribution of wealth. But, the new name gave the socialists another word in common with the liberals and they exploited it to the full. And although the word was used in a different sense by the two groups, few people noticed this and still fewer asked themselves whether the two kinds of freedom promised really could be combined' [Hayek, 1976, p 19].

That is a quotation of great significance. The argument Hayek is making is that 'freedom', which has usually in the past been identified exclusively as (for mainstream philosophers and politicians) civil and political freedoms which were to be regarded as necessary irrespective of wealth, has been hijacked as a concept by those who argue that without substantive rather than formal equality there can be no real freedom. Reading Hayek, one could be forgiven for thinking that such 'socialist' ideas are a recent invention of an aggressive group who were intent on giving 'bourgeois' freedoms a bad name!

In fact, nothing could be further from the truth. It is correct that philosophers in the 17th and 18th century particularly were concerned when they spoke of the 'Rights of Man' with, primarily, individual civil liberties (for men of property) rather than with substantive equality; but, it is equally incontrovertible that, while the philosophical aristocrats were debating the need for political rights, the common people were often demanding food, work, or an end to the worst abuses of power and privilege. Such demands are not necessarily incompatible but there has been a constant, if sometimes, indirect tension between the two.

For various reasons, the history of those who thought freedom should begin with a solid meal is much less accessible than the history of published and articulate treatises on political rights. A central reason is that those whose first demand was for bread were often illiterate and also unreported. Any history of an understanding of freedom and rights must, in contradistinction to Hayek's view, bear in mind what JFC Harrison observes in the opening paragraph of his book *The Common People:*

'For the last 1,000 years or more at least 70% and sometimes as many as 90% of the population have been ordinary (common) people who had to work to make a living and who were ruled by a small minority who lived off the labour of the majority. Most history is concerned with this minority, who owned most of the wealth, exercised supreme power, and made all important decisions in the country. When the common people appear in history at all they are not central but only in the background, almost like characters off-stage' [1984, p 13].

The history of arguments about freedom and rights always mentions the articulate (and wealthy!) thinkers but seldom alludes to the popular feeling, or indeed to the activities of the rebellious as creating the conditions in which ideas are formulated. Partly, as we said, this is because of the illiteracy of those demanding what they saw as social justice, but it is also because in so far as their motives were recorded they were written by people who wrote about them rather than with them.

At any rate, what Hayek saw was surely rather disingenuous given the extensive 19th and 20th century consideration of economic demands. The contrast between Hayek's arguments and those made by Marx in his *Economic and Philosophical Manuscripts* of 1844 could not be more stark. While they are addressing many of the same questions, so different are their approaches that it is 'bialogue' rather than 'dialogue' which best captures the contrast. Whereas Hayek makes unexamined assumptions about the naturalness of competition, Marx attempted to understand what concepts such as competition and private property might imply (Sayers, 1998). Although Marx was writing 100 years earlier than Hayek, and although in the present political climate it might seem irrelevant to refer to Marx rather than Hayek alone there are good reasons for doing so. And for those who argue that Marx's consideration of labour is now irrelevant it is important to remember that if European labour has to some extent and in some ways escaped from the conditions Marx analysed, many in the so-called Third World have not.

Marx's thesis in the *Economic and Philosophical Manuscripts of 1844* (1977) essentially calls into question the availability of the individual freedom which Hayek takes for granted. Marx makes the point that to have freedom while forced to work desperately long hours in order to physically survive does in itself make a nonsense of such conceptions of freedom. Who are these individuals of whom Hayek speaks, who require minimal interference if they are to fulfil their individual potential? For Marx, they are the owners of capital, rather than the 'slaves of industry'. His argument is that the worker's freedom is lost, first, in the economic necessity to sell his or her labour in return for the means of subsistence, and, secondly, in the worker's alienation from the very things that the sold labour creates – that which the worker creates belongs to the purchaser of his or her sold labour not to the worker. For many if not for most workers, work time is almost literally lost time; it is simply the activity the worker performs of necessity in order to survive. The limited other time at the worker's disposal is the only time in which he (usually) or she can be human. This effectively in Marx's argument dehumanises people, preventing them either fulfilling themselves by participating in the non-animal aspects of life as in the amity of society, or in the creation of useful and beautiful things, for example. If the central feature of the worker's life is sold labour power such organisation of labour estranges man from nature, for which he has little time, and from himself because the central point of life is separate from what the worker could and would wish to do. This in turn leaves him with an individual life to lead and an individual struggle to survive. Existence is centred on individualism rather than on social being (Marx, 1977, pp 66–80).

As we said, if that picture of life does not seem a fair description now for the life of a European worker, in the international world of work, it is still surely largely accurate. What Hayek ignores then is that to treat unequal people equally brings benefit if at all only to those whose life is not already dictated by economic necessity.

A more challenging defence of the Rule of Law is to be found in the writings of EP Thompson who defends it in spite of perceived limitations. He observed:

'I am insisting only upon an obvious point – that there is a difference between arbitrary power and the Rule of Law. But, the Rule of Law itself, the imposing of effective inhibitions upon power and the defence of the citizen from power's all-intrusive claims, seems to me to be an unqualified human good' [Thompson, 1977, p 266].

And he goes on to make the point that, because the Rule of Law finally constrained those in whose interests it operated in that they too became unable to act in an arbitrarily oppressive way, it prevented, at least on occasions, bloodshed and misery. Further, in espousing the virtue of justice blindfold, people came to internalise a value more substantial and more substantive than might otherwise have been the case.

These are interesting arguments from an eminent historian but they should not be accepted without qualification. There is, of course, no necessary causal link between the Rule of Law and the restraint of the powerful. Apartheid South Africa always claimed to be a Rule of Law state even while 4.5 million white people ruled 28 million disenfranchised black people and also owned 87% of the land. Apartheid South Africa also executed more people than any comparable state (in fact, no other state was comparable) and yet, because of the appearance of safeguards for defendants, was able to claim that this practice too was consistent with the Rule of Law. Certainly, in some ways, it was the Rule of Law ideology which provided the clothes with which the state attempted to hide the nakedness of government aggression.

A second qualification which we have argued, and this applies no less to Thompson than to Hayek, is that the assumption that we either have the Rule of Law or we have secret police, arbitrary government, and a lack of accountability is a false choice. We have been at pains to make it clear not only that the Rule of Law is not inherently superior or inferior to other methods of government, but also that it is clear that it has a special relationship with a particular form of economic organisation, namely liberal capitalism.

A further qualification of Thompson's proposition needs to be made. In a book written in 1971, Frank Parkin argued that Eastern Europe offered much more scope for, and the possibility of, significant change than did liberal capitalist states. Events have borne out his prediction even if not with the results he might have foreseen. To illustrate his argument, Parkin quotes from Steinbeck's novel, *The Grapes of Wrath*, a novel set in the US in the economic depression of the 1930s. In the extract, a tenant farmer whose shack is about to be bulldozed on the instructions of the new landowners threatens to shoot the driver of the tractor. The tractor driver protests:

'"It's not me. There's nothing I can do. I'll lose my job if I don't do it. And look – suppose you kill me? They'll just hang you, but long before you're hung there'll be another guy on the tractor, and he'll bump the house down. You're not killing the right guy."

"That's so", the tenant said. "Who gave you orders? I'll go after him. He's the one to kill."

"You're wrong. He got his orders from the bank. The bank told him 'Clear those people out or it's your job.'"

"Well, there's a president of the bank. There's a board of directors. I'll fill up the magazine of the rifle and go into the bank."

The driver said: "Fellow was telling me the bank gets orders from the east. The orders were: 'Make the land show a profit or we'll close you up.'"

"But where does it stop? Who can we shoot? I don't aim to starve to death before I kill the man that's starving me."

"I don't know. Maybe there's nobody to shoot. Maybe the thing isn't men at all. Maybe, like you said, the property's doing it. Anyway, I told you my orders"' [quoted in Parkin, 1971, pp 162–63].

As Parkin points out, in a command system of the kind Hayek fears, there is much less of a problem about whom to shoot (or in our terms at whose door complaints should be laid). In a market based Rule of Law system, it is precisely because it is so diffuse in its operation and so opaque in its political design, in that the market seems neutral, that it is difficult to attach responsibility. Parkin's argument is very perceptive and it does to some extent explain why recent changes occurred in Eastern Europe even if it does not explain the particular changes which did in fact occur. Changes came at least in part, first, because the people apparently responsible for political and economic problems were highly visible, but, secondly, and importantly for the argument that follows, the legitimating ideology of Marxist-Leninism did not match the lived reality of those to whom it was supposed to be relevant. If the official values of socialist society in East Europe laid heavy emphasis upon equality and classlessness, then any move towards large scale inequality and privilege was obviously going to lead to serious tension. And that point is no less true because the people have chosen not only to shoot their commanders, literally in the case of Romania, and figuratively elsewhere, but also to junk the legitimating ideology which had been so obviously betrayed. It can also be surmised that cynicism with such explicit ideology (or propaganda as some would argue) has made East Europeans much more sympathetic to ways of organising society where ideology is well hidden by the free market.

What then is the significance of the comparative invisibility of our legitimating economic ideology? How has it happened, how is it maintained and with what effect? We suggest that there is a central and crucial feature which renders our legitimating economic ideology much less explicit but no less important. It is concerned with the perception of the market and the construction of market relations.

Any market which is not exclusively concerned with barter requires what might be described as a system of 'numeracising' or 'mathematising' of things. A market requires ways of evaluating that which is for sale. This is done by attributing to things a value, in terms of money numbers, at which they will attract customers. This is not simply a matter of *pricing* goods. It is first concerned with translating the meaning of goods into numbers and it does this by defining goods in terms of money value. In thinking about goods in numerical terms, we are actually translating things into numbers and the fact that these numbers are money is a separate point. We are evaluating things in quantitative terms. André Gorz, in his book *Critique of Economic Reason*, explains the significance of this translation in a way which not only questions fundamental assumptions of many economics courses but also is of relevance to the Rule of Law. His argument is that this process of numeracising and mathematising is often inappropriate but always coercive. A quotation is illustrative (1989, p 107):

'Men, therefore, may prefer to use money as a yardstick even in efforts which do not have the aim of making additions to a society's stock of utility. Even when the aim is to add to solidarity, collective effectiveness, or societal authenticity, men, once committed to rationalisation, deployed a variety of cost-benefit analyses to measure their performance ... A whole host of social problems from urban renewal to delinquency-prevention projects remain a mess in part because of the use of money for ends that money alone cannot serve.'

His argument, then, is that economic rationality is both extended to cover areas to which it is quite unsuited but also that this mathematised way of thinking, 'colonises' our minds and mutilates the 'relational fabric on which social integration, education and individual socialisation depend', or, put rather more simply, once we have mathematised problems, the rules of capitalist economics take over and the results come to appear inevitable and value free.

An example is appropriate. If, for instance, we knew that in London there were 10,000 homeless people and that economists had calculated that the cost of providing housing was around £30,000 per person, then the calculation about homelessness becomes an obvious one. Having performed it, we are then able to ask 'rational' questions about whether the necessary expenditure might not be spent more usefully (or more profitably) elsewhere. To some extent, at least once we have such figures, we no longer need to see or hear the homeless because we have 'the measure of the problem'. The point is better brought out in a poem entitled 'Commonsense' by Alan Brownjohn (Brownjohn, 1988, pp 20–21) viz:

'An agricultural labourer, who has
A wife and four children, receives 20s a week
3/4 buys food, and the members of the family
Have three meals a day.
How much is that per person per meal?
From Pitman's Common Sense Arithmetic, 1917

A gardener, paid 24s a week, is
Fined 1/3 if he comes to work late.
At the end of 26 weeks, he receives
£30.5.3. How
Often was he late?
From Pitman's Common Sense Arithmetic, 1917

A milk dealer buys milk at 3d a quart. He
Dilutes it with 3% water and sells
124 gallons of the mixture at
4d per quart. How much of his profit is made by
Adulterating the milk?
From Pitman's Common Sense Arithmetic, 1917

The table printed below gives the number
Of paupers in the United Kingdom, and
The total cost of poor relief.
Find the average number
Of paupers per 10,000 people.
From Pitman's Common Sense Arithmetic, 1917

An army had to march to the relief of
A besieged town, 500 miles away, which
Had telegraphed that it could hold out for 18 days.
The army made forced marches at the rate of 18
Miles a day. Would it be there in time?
From Pitman's Common Sense Arithmetic, 1917

Out of an army of 28,000 men,
15% were
Killed, 25% were
Wounded. Calculate
how many men there were left to fight.
From Pitman's Common Sense Arithmetic, 1917

These sums are offered to
That host of young people in our Elementary Schools, who
Are so ardently desirous of setting
Foot upon the first rung of the
Educational ladder ...
From Pitman's Common Sense Arithmetic, 1917

Many economics students would probably wish to take issue with this
example arguing that if the data is correct then we are at least in a position to
calculate cost and take *rational* decisions. Gorz's argument, however, is that there

are some social problems and questions which though they may be amenable to rational solution are often dehumanised and impersonalised by the very mathematising process. It is that process which creates the formal equality of individuals wonderfully. If we speak of 10,000 homeless people, each is equal to each and all of the others. There is an obvious relationship between liberalism and the principle of utility and formal equality in that each unit in any number is formally equal. It is not mere coincidence that the Royal Statistical Society was formed and quickly became important in the 1830s along with the rise of liberalism. The belief was that problems required measurement before they could be resolved.

We also see the limits in this process of mathematising in the economist's need to quantify that which is scarcely quantifiable, a need which can lead to quite extraordinary processes. Very often, the quantification of quality is even argued to be both rational and value free. Works of art are worth the price which the market places upon them and their value is no more and no less than the price obtainable in the open market. Humankind's natural heritage or environmental 'wealth' is very often deemed worthy of protection only where the 'price' to be paid for this is less than the (quantifiable) benefits which might ensue.

It is this felt need to quantify in order to become 'official' which has driven much of the action of the government of the UK from the 1980s to the present. Unfortunately, many would argue, the actions of many professional people, are by definition, not terribly easy to usefully quantify. Nevertheless, the people who had generally and traditionally been trusted to fulfil their paid professional roles fell to be 'evaluated' (a word with numerical overtones) whether teachers, social workers, doctors, probation officers or police officers. At first sight, this process seems eminently sensible, until, however, the task is faced of defining the criteria against which people are to be judged. The problem is twofold. Where people are employed to think a good deal, there is no way of ensuring that their thoughts are directed to the job, and, secondly, unless the appraiser or evaluator spends all and every day with teachers, police officer's or doctors, it is impossible to assess their activities. Granted that problem, the resolution has been found in a crude process of quantification which many argue disguises more than it reveals. Attention is focussed upon those things which can be quantified; written plans and record keeping for teachers, 'clear-up' rates for police, numbers of patients treated for doctors and hospitals, and for university teachers a count of research publications. In each case, that which is judged is either peripheral to the main purpose of the job, as in teaching, or focuses upon but one aspect of a job for other professionals. The result may be confidently predicted – those who are deemed successful and ready for promotion will be those best at that which is measured rather than at the job itself.

Again, we see clearly that, in quantifying problems in order to resolve them, we translate a social reality into a statistical world and, in so doing, just as when we translate into the legal world, the resolvable problem is not identical to that which has been translated. Furthermore, the translation affects the very way in which we perceive and a mathematised world fits easily within the liberal philosophy and the formal equalities demanded by the Rule of Law.

This is not to suggest that quantification as such is not valuable. It clearly is. It is rather to argue, first, that to mathematise a problem may be to predetermine an outcome, because the problem is at least perceived as objective, and, secondly, that there is often an attempt to quantify (at all costs one might say!) phenomena which are arguably inherently unquantifiable. A dominant theme in Robert Pirsig's seminal novel *Zen and the Art of Motorcycle Maintenance* (1974) is the clash between understanding qualitatively and understanding quantitatively. Pirsig, who writes brilliantly of pre-Socratic philosophy, posits the view that, until Socrates, the world had been understood by the Greeks in two competing but equal ways, first, through logic and, secondly, through what he calls 'quality' or through understanding which while not illogical is equally not logical. It is Pirsig's view that, after Socrates, and because of Socrates, the world of logic colonised the world of quality and achieved dominance, greatly diminishing the appreciation of non-logical understanding. We still do have non-logical ways of communicating and understanding, most clearly in the arts where we learn from novels, painting, poetry, sculpture or whatever by a means to which logic is irrelevant, but for Pirsig this artistic understanding is often overwhelmed by the logical world of facts and deductive inference.

Habermas, of whom Gorz writes, took the view that this dominant economic rationality leads to an irresistible dynamic which in turn leads to a dominance of economic and administrative subsystems – all de-personalised but all powerful in their ability to place constraints upon our ability to see social problems as 'quality problems' rather than as logical problems.

What interests Gorz, and is of relevance to this chapter, is how it is that economic rationalism achieved ideological dominance. He argues that counting and calculation become necessary in a time when human activities become directed not merely to simply living but to producing for a market. It is when this becomes the dominant goal that everything must be calculated to ensure profitability. As long as profit is the goal, then many choices become obvious, rational and necessary. If one is to compete and continue to compete in the market there is no alternative but to become 'efficient' in order to do at least as well as competitors. This economic rationality according to Gorz is necessary when (a) work is not simply for personal consumption and (b) the production is for exchange on a *free* market in that any agreement on price or the limitation of competition prevents economic rationality from being the only way to determine what needs to be done.

Equally crucially, as he makes clear, any 'self-limiting of needs' such as a decision that one is satisfied with less than might be made by way of profit, also defeats the imperative of economic rationality. In economic terms, to strive for less than one could achieve is irrational and to be satisfied with less than is obtainable makes counting, calculation and mathematical prediction at best of marginal use. It is Gorz's argument that when people are able and free to decide their level of need and their level of effort, economic rationality ceases to dominate and may indeed be quite irrelevant. To exemplify this proposition Gorz uses Weber's example to suggest that if workers are able to choose freely how much work to do they choose to do that amount which satisfies what they perceive to be their needs. If people are obtaining what they deem to be sufficient for their needs, there can be no purpose in further work (unless it is pleasurable). Fortunately, at least for the system of capitalism, this satisfaction is seldom seen to be achieved, except for a small minority, for two very clear reasons. The first is that we are socialised to believe that our needs are infinite and the second is that wages are kept at a level which generally prevents workers from working less. The old trade union slogan to the effect that when one wishes the rich to work harder they must be paid more, while when the poor require persuasion to work harder they must be paid less, is not irrelevant. And our needs are also greatly aggravated by the consumer society in which we exist, and by our separateness either as nuclear families or individuals which dictates a needless repetition of goods. Individual ownership of commodities from televisions to books, which could easily serve many more people, dictates duplication. It is not difficult to formulate the argument that a great deal of the antipathy incurred by gypsy communities, by the hippy communities of the past, and by the new age travellers of today, has its origin in the fact that, while not working in the disciplined way which capitalism seems to require, and while not a part of the wage economy, they yet appear able to live lives of feckless enjoyment. The very fact that this is facilitated by communal living which eschews many consumer goods, and shares and recycles others, is implicitly perceived as a threat to what Gorz describes as economic rationality or indeed the foundation of capitalism itself. Gorz would argue that accounting, the discipline at the very basis of economic rationality, simply falls apart if people limit their needs in order to limit their work. 'Accounting is familiar with categories of "more" and of "less" but doesn't know that of "enough"' (Gorz, 1989, p 112). More particularly, he argues that capitalism can take no account of the 'sufficient'. Because economic rationality demanded the maximum input from workers, this had to be calculated as profitability rather than the satisfaction of needs; profitability is calculable, satisfaction is not. Even better, as he points out (Gorz, 1989, p 113):

> 'What is important here is that the "spirit of capitalism" severed the link between work and need. The goal of work was no longer the satisfaction of felt needs, and effort was no longer matched to the level of satisfaction to be attained. The rationalising passion became autonomous with respect to all determinate goals. In place of the certainty of experience that "enough is enough" it gave rise to an objective measure of the efficiency of effort and of its success: the size of profits. Success was no longer therefore a matter for personal assessment and a question of the "quality of life", it was measurable by the amount of

money earned, by accumulated wealth. Quantification gave rise to an indisputable criterion and a hierarchical scale which had no need of validation by any authority, any norm, any scale of values. Efficiency was measurable and, through it, an individual's ability and virtue: more was better than less, those who succeed in earning more are better than those who earn less.'

And, he adds, because no quantity is the greatest possible so no success is so great that a greater success cannot be imagined. The significance of these propositions is not difficult to discover. Each year in the UK, *The Sunday Times* publishes a list and thumbnail sketch of the 200 wealthiest people in Britain. Wealthy they may be, satisfied they were certainly not. For most of us not on the list (and this in itself is a major reason as to why we never *will* be on the list), there is something of a puzzle as to what continues to drive those with such wealth to want to accumulate more. After all, even if, as is almost undeniable, the *chance* of a satisfactory life may be greater for the possessor of £1 million rather than the possessor of a mere £1,000, the difference between possessing £1 million and £100 million seems, at least to the outsider, pretty marginal. Yet, as a generalisation, it can be asserted that the 200 wealthiest wanted more! Perhaps, the most invalidating observation which can be made by the impecunious is that many of the 200 seem to be, *except in money terms,* in a state of dire poverty. They seem to have been deluded into money fetishism, unable any longer to understand that money, as such, is meaningless unless converted into something desirable. (The only immediate exception to such an explanation which springs readily to mind is the Walt Disney comic character, Scrooge McDuck, who did at least savour the perverted pleasure of swimming in his swimming pool full of gold coins!)

At the same time, as this urge for ever more was required to cajole workers into rationally working away their lives, they needed also to be persuaded that they continue to have needs which can be satisfied by expenditure made possible by hard work. But, if this were the dynamic of capitalism, its needs began to pervade morality. Not only did work come to be perceived as a moral good in itself but words associated with this philosophy took on the same value. On the one hand, we have a description by Norman Lewis in *The Missionaries* (1988) of the missionaries in the verdant and abundant South Sea Island of Mourea, actually having the plentiful bread fruit trees (the source of food for an almost work free community) cut down, in order to force the natives to work in order to eat, for the good of their souls. On the other, most of us find it difficult to think of development, of growth, or of efficiency as being anything other than incontestable 'goods'. Even a concept such as progress seems unanswerable as a desired goal. Yet, 'growth', 'development' and 'efficiency' all lead to the idea that good may be measured quantitatively. In Gorz's words (1989, p 121):

'Quantitative measurement as a substitute for rational value judgment confers supreme moral security and intellectual comfort: the Good becomes measurable and calculable;

decisions and moral judgments can follow from the implementation of a procedure of impersonal, objective, quantifying calculation and individual subjects do not have to shoulder the burden [of decision making] anxiously and uncertainly.'

Gorz is not arguing that quantitative measurement has no place, but rather that the process of numeracising problems may not be at all appropriate, and even where it is relevant that we should be careful that we control the statistics rather than being controlled by them. It remains true that in many ways a person who knows a family which is homeless knows much more about homelessness than does the expert who knows the extent of the problem. Thus, of course, as with law, the social phenomenon translated into a specialist world takes on a different character.

But, what law and statistics have in common is their ability to ascribe formal equality to the unequal. Each has its part to play in creating and maintaining the apparent objectivity of economic rationality in particular by reinforcing the conditions necessary for the operation of the market. For Gorz, a central feature of the history of capitalism has been the struggle to determine within which limits economic rationality and the market must operate.

Conclusion

We conclude the main body of this book by returning to the common sense of law. If there has been a central thesis to this book it has been that the common sense of law both reveals and conceals exercises of power. The argument has been that law, like any other system of power allocation and dispute resolution, plays a central part in reinforcing the particular social reality in which it exists. That it can do this while using only very limited amounts of physical force is a tribute to its ability to disguise political acts as politically neutral. The implications of this realisation are far-reaching but individual readers will reach their own conclusions. There is, we hope, no necessary conclusion to be drawn although we also hope that a suspicion of authority may seem appropriate. If our political views are transparent (as indeed they are), we would repeat our argument that all law books are political regardless of whether their authors consider them so. To us, an increase in suspicion directed towards hallowed institutions (an increase deplored by the Conservative Government and, perhaps, even more so by 'New Labour') seems entirely healthy. If the result is 'institutional cynicism' – cynicism directed towards institutions such as government, royalty, church and law – that seems an excellent starting point from which to move towards a world with very different, and significantly more humane, values than often capitalism presents, and a world in which all individuals may find fulfilment as an integral part of the society in which they live. The 'reality' of the present world hides from us the invalidity of the 'there is no alternative' proposition.

12 Reconsiderations

Introduction

The central theme of this book has been that we are constrained and dominated by what we do not put into question and criticise, both about the world in general, and about law in particular. Thus, it seems appropriate that this book should end by putting itself in question and, in particular, its claim to provide an account of law which is in some sense better than the picture of law it criticises, namely, the common sense of the Rule of Law. Arguably, to fail to do this would be to evade the argument that all the book is doing is replacing one dominating reality with another, and that argument may be seen as the disabling paranoia of the left on which the 20th century is ending. Therefore, just as the pages of this book have sought to show where some of the dominant ideas of, and about, law have come from, and has thereby sought to evaluate them, so in these reconsiderations we will comment on the origins of the basic critical ideas that inform this book and thereby seek to evaluate them.

Perhaps, the most basic idea of this book, and the one that lies not only in, but behind its pages, is the idea of big ideas; the idea that big ideas answering big questions can illuminate the world, and thereby contribute to changing it for the better. Thus, the pages of this book have been animated by the presence of a number of such big ideas, responding to such big questions as whether the law is necessary, how social realities arise, and what part law plays in the subordination of women.

It may be observed that the central presence of such big ideas in this book reflects the fact that, when the lectures out of which this book arose were first delivered in the early 1970s, big ideas were very much in fashion. Thus, at that time, students and academics seemed to be both drawn to the big questions, of the 'what is law, or capitalism, or whatever, really about?' kind, and equally confident that it was possible to find big and revealing answers, in the form of relatively simple, but widely embracing generalisations. Paradigmatic of this enthusiasm for the revelatory big idea was the interest, shared by among others many lawyers, in sociology, particularly in the form of an interest in the classical social theorists, such as Marx, Durkheim and Weber, and in Marx most particularly. Thus, Berger and Luckmann's *The Social Construction of Reality*, which has of course strongly informed this book, and which was first published in 1967, very much fitted this pattern, in that it offered to reveal and throw light on a great deal, indeed virtually the whole social world, on the basis of a few fairly simple big ideas drawn from the sociology of knowledge particularly as it had been developed by Karl Mannheim (1936).

At the millennium, by contrast, such big ideas can look distinctly unfashionable (of course, we are of the view that fashion should always be treated with scepticism!). Further, not only have particular big ideas, such as those of sociology and Marxism, become dramatically less popular, but the very idea of posing big questions about the nature of law and justice and seeking big answers to them has itself been seriously questioned and criticised, not only intellectually and academically, but also in terms of whether it is a useful political strategy. While a very large number of factors have no doubt contributed to this questioning of the big idea, one might single out three in particular.

First, and most obviously, would be the dramatic and highly conspicuous collapse of Eastern European and Soviet style socialism, symbolised by the dismantling of the Berlin Wall in 1989. While this event can be read in many ways, certainly the way it has been dominantly interpreted in the West, is as a victory of capitalism over Marxist socialism, leaving liberal capitalism as the only contender left in the ring. Moreover, many have interpreted, indeed celebrated, the failure of Eastern European socialism not just as proof of the failure of a particular big idea, the Socialist big idea, but as proof of the folly in believing in the possibility of any big ideas to realise progress. Certainly, this is the interpretation that has been seized upon by much of the political right.

Secondly, over the last two decades, across almost the entire academic and intellectual world, there has spread a deep loss of faith and confidence in the possibility of truth and reason. Thus, under a host of labels, such as post-modernism, post-structuralism, and post-Marxism, the twin beliefs, now identified with modernity, that it was possible through reason to discover universal truths behind the appearances of the world, and that such truth was on the side of progress, have been themselves progressively discarded. We will return later to consider in more detail that post-modern position. However, suffice it to say at this stage that it clearly leads academics away from posing big questions towards more particular, more modest, and more local questions and concerns.

Thirdly, for students as well as academics, big ideas today seem to hold out considerably less interest and attraction than they did. While the visible failure of socialism and the post-modern doubts about truth and reason may contribute to this, such a lack of interest probably results mainly from the demands of reality, in the form of the realities of the market, which both swallow the space for big ideas and undermine their relevance. To anticipate a conclusion, it is a paradox that in the world to which the big ideas of this book may be seen to most clearly apply, namely, our contemporary world in which the constraints of reality in the form of the market realities are most overwhelming, there appears to be no place for those big ideas.

Against the recognition that big ideas today may appear out of fashion, we want in these reconsiderations, in the spirit of self-criticism indicated earlier, to do three things: first, to draw out, so that we may more clearly recognise them, the big ideas presented in the preceding chapters, as well as both making explicit some of the underlying ideas on which they depend, and briefly expanding upon what may be thought to be a somewhat underdeveloped aspect of those ideas, namely, the relation between the Rule of Law and market capitalism; secondly, to suggest some criticisms both of those particular ideas, and of the idea of big ideas generally, particularly against the background of two of the historical factors we have mentioned, the failure of eastern European socialism and the theory of post-modernism; finally, by way of conclusion, we will consider what role big ideas might have today, in our market dominated world, both in general and in particular for our understanding of law.

The big ideas

In the preceding chapters, the recurring metaphor which has been deployed in relation to law has been that of law as an interpretation or translation, of law as a process which translates from a primary reality to a secondary reality or from a world of everyday talk and experience to a world constituted by specialist knowledges and languages. Most importantly, it has been argued that, despite appearances to the contrary, this interpretation or translation is not politically neutral, but rather is political in the sense that it serves the interests of some over others, thereby revealing it as a mechanism of power. Thus, one of the key arguments has been that, beyond the obvious and visible force of the law, the hidden and, hence, more insidious power of the law is to be found in the way the legal interpretation of the world comes to be taken for granted as natural, necessary and right, and as such taken as neutral as between different interests.

On this basis, the task for a critical introduction to law has then been to uncover the hidden politics of law, by showing that the legal interpretation of the world, as a world of rules, individual rights and private property, etc, far from being natural, necessary and right, as it appears in common sense, is in reality respectively, artificial, historically and culturally contingent, and the embodiment of only a particular version of right, namely that of formal equality before the law. The ultimate political thrust being that, if one shows that the legal interpretation of the world is not a necessary one, but is merely an historically and culturally contingent one, it becomes possible to envisage alternatives to the law form of order, based on alternative and more attractive views of social relations than that which is encoded in the law, namely, the view that social relations are relations between competitive and distrusting strangers.

In pursuing this task, a number of critical ideas have informed this book. First, through the devise of introducing comparative ethnographic materials on order maintenance and dispute resolution, the book has sought to demonstrate that both order, and the ways of maintaining it, are relative, in order to establish the relativity of our form of law and our form of order. Secondly, principally through the writings of Berger and Luckmann, the book has employed as one of its central critical themes the idea that by showing how realities are socially constructed we are that much less constrained by them, just as we are less in awe of the conjurer when we know how he does his tricks. Thirdly, there has been the idea that a critical approach involves criticising knowledge and received understandings in terms of the interests which are served by such knowledges or understandings being held, for example, the received understanding or common sense that private property is natural, or that 'a woman's place is in the home'.

It should be noted that none of these three ideas in themselves directly reveal a substantive value preference for or against anything, for example, for or against the Rule of Law, private property or the position of women. The most that is apparently being asserted by arguing for these ideas is that by understanding where knowledges, and in particular common sense knowledges, come from, how they are maintained, and what interests they serve, or in short to understand how knowledges operate as forms of power, the better then are we placed to resist their power. Indeed, the apparent value neutrality of Berger and Luckmann's account of social reality, in particular, is demonstrated by the fact that it can be used to inform quite different political positions. Thus, while it draws heavily upon and informs Marxist literature, it can also be used to defend a deeply conservative right wing position. This is, we should note, the position for which one of its authors, Peter Berger, vigorously argues today (Berger, 1987).

However, while a value agnosticism may be consistent with demonstrating cultural relativism, showing where knowledges and received understandings come from, and what interests they serve, this is clearly not the position of the authors of this book. Indeed, what for us gives ideas like those of social constructionism, political bite is precisely that they provide some leverage on the established structures of power, and they do so because such ideas reveal the dominant understandings as in some sense flawed or at least partial. In other words, to reveal that knowledge or received understandings are ideological, in the sense that they reflect certain interests, facilitate certain forms of power or legitimise certain social practices, only becomes politically interesting if it is premised on the possibility of non, or at least less, ideological forms of knowledge. Certainly, this possibility is the premise of the tradition of ideology critique, which is the tradition which centrally informs this book, and which runs from the 18th century continental Enlightenment, principally through Marx and Marxist writings, to the present day.

Now, the central device of ideology critique, most explicit perhaps in this book in the chapters on patriarchal ideologies and the position of women, is a dichotomy, a dichotomy which may be expressed in various ways, for example, between ideology and reality, appearance or map and reality, surface and foundations, false and true consciousness, perceived and real interests, form and content, etc, in which the first term of each pair is presented as an imperfect representation or version of the latter, that is to say, as a false picture of some sort of true or truer reality. To mention just a few examples, we have already encountered, the appearance of marriage as a means of protecting women and children when it is argued that in reality it might rather be seen to provide men with a family, contractual ideas concealing the realities of inequality of bargaining power in relation to third world debts, or the ideology of formal equality masking the reality of social inequalities.

Different versions of ideology critique, or theories of ideology, differ not only in what each takes as the measure of the true or real but also in how the true or real is conceived as relating to the false or merely apparent. Thus, at its crudest, the apparent may be presented simply as the product of the more or less conscious manipulation of the powerful seeking to conceal their true interests, while in more sophisticated versions of Marxism for example, the apparent is conceived as the historically necessary form in which social relations of production appear at a particular stage of historical development. Thus, according to the Soviet Marxist jurist Pashukanis, who became very influential in the West in the early 1970s, when big ideas were, as we noted, so fashionable, the reality of capitalism as a way of organising production ensured that social relations appeared in the form of relations between legal subjects with equal rights and duties, typically mediated through the institution of contract (Pashukanis, 1978).

The preceding chapters, while eschewing explicitly adopting any particular theory of ideology, nevertheless arguably implicitly do adopt one in so far as they clearly reveal a preference for the social or the collective, in some sense or another, as the reality from which the ideological translation which is law, and which is heavy with individualism, arises. Thus, there is clearly a preference for seeing problems in their full social context as more real, or at least more complete than the way they appear in the law. Equally, there is a clear preference for treating social justice in the sense of outcomes as real justice, while the formal equality of individuals before the law is primarily presented as the means of concealing fundamental inequalities, that is to say as ideological. Indeed, the central concepts of translation, and of a primary and secondary reality distinction, are ultimately metaphors which rely for their effectiveness on an unspoken assumption that the social is more real than the individuals and individualism that the law constructs, that the social problem or issue, not the legal version of it, is the real problem or issue, and possibly that, for example, social and collective ownership of land is more original and natural than the legal artifice of private property.

Indeed, one might suggest that the central dichotomy on which these chapters work is that of the social and the individual, and that the essential method, revealed, for example, in the reliance on the psychiatric examples of RD Laing, whose views were so influential in the early 1970s, as well of course as in the reliance on Berger and Luckmann, is that of showing the social intelligibility of the individual and of individual phenomena. Thus, for example, Laing and others, looking at the psychiatric process and literature, sought to show how the behaviour and symptoms that were often traditionally treated as signs of the madness of individuals frequently become socially intelligible when considered in the larger context of family or society, just as Berger and Luckmann sought to identify the social origins of our individual experience in order to make it intelligible, and just as Durkheim had earlier sought to explain individual life in terms of the collective life, and Marx had sought an explanation of the forms of consciousness in terms of 'social being' (Durkheim, 1984; Sayers, 1998).

These, then, are the main big ideas in the preceding chapters, which to summarise, are those of an ideology critique, operating primarily through seeking explanations in terms of the social, of the common sense of law, as a means thereby of making the political in law explicit and thereby resisting its hidden forms of power. While in subsequent sections we will offer some critical thoughts on these big ideas, and of the idea of ideology critique in particular, it is important, in order to demonstrate the potential of such a critique in relation to law to briefly indicate at least one way in which it can be and has been more fully developed.

While the previous chapters have repeatedly asserted a close connection between the Rule of Law and market capitalism, indeed the chapter on the exclusion of women from the Rule of Law explicitly assumes this connection, they do not perhaps present as strong a case as can be made out for this connection. Thus, while Andre Gorz's critique of economic rationality, which appears as the main vehicle for establishing this connection, can be used to show how both law and the mathematisation typical of market capitalism similarly treat people as abstract equal units, this may be seen as a mere gloss on the arguments of the classical social theorists, and Marx in particular, which seek a linkage between the Rule of Law and market capitalism. Put in its most straightforward form, the argument, expressed in the language of ideology critique, is that if the Rule of Law is to be seen as an ideology it should also be seen as in some sense the necessary ideology of market capitalism.

While there is much evidence to suggest that the dominance of the Rule of Law ideology and a full market capitalist economy historically arose together, different traditions and authors theorise differently about what makes the relationship between them necessary. However, one recurring theme in many such accounts is the recognition of the importance of the fact, mentioned at the very outset of this book, namely that in Rule of Law societies such as ours, law appears as a distinct, self sufficient and autonomous bit of the world, which is more or less separated from the everyday world. This separation of law from society, which was reflected in the metaphors of primary and secondary realities and of translation, is as was noted the basis of the possibility of studying and learning of law, as in traditional forms of legal education, in isolation from both society and value considerations, such as those of justice.

In relation to this phenomenon of the autonomy of law in capitalism Max Weber, the German sociologist, argued that under capitalism a distinct form of legal rationality came to dominate, which he called 'formal logical rationality' (Rheinstein, 1966). This, he argued, was distinctive in that it involved conceiving of legal thought as constituting a complete and self-sufficient system, rather than law being merely a means of implementing purposes or values external to the law, such as political goals or religious values. In short, based on such rationality, law became not just a means but an end in itself. The crucial significance of this was that while legal orders had previously sought to acquire legitimacy from external sources, such as from the Gods or other versions of so-called natural law, in the type of law which came to prevail under capitalism (Rule of Law type law), law became increasingly its own legitimation or, put differently, law came of age in so far as it no longer depended on external sources to give it validity. Most simply, this meant that just because a rule was a Rule of Law, in the sense of being a properly enacted part of the law, this was treated as making the rule rightful and therefore as constituting a sufficient reason for obeying it.

This idea of law, as quite separate from morality and other values, is usually described, in contradistinction to natural law, as legal positivism, for it takes the view that law is merely posited, and is to be obeyed simply because it is posited or put into place in the right way. What is important to stress is that this type of law demands our obedience in a quite distinct, and distinctly modern way. Thus, while natural law, which claims legitimacy through its origins, for example in the heavens, demands our obedience precisely because it contains particular values, in the legal positivism characteristic of the Rule of Law type of law, it is precisely because the law claims to exclude all particular values, and therefore to be neutral between them, that it demands our obedience. Put more succinctly, law in the Rule of Law form establishes its identity by excluding ideas of substantive justice, and it does so by equating justice with the idea of rules, and identifying it 'with the administration of justice and the requirement and guarantees of legal procedure' (Douzinas et al, 1994). Thus, one might suggest that the fundamental basis of law's appearance as a neutral translation, and as an autonomous entity independent of, for example, politics, rests upon the acceptance of the idea that justice can be reduced to and identified with rules independent of their content. That is, of course, the Rule of Law version of justice.

The earlier chapters of this book have amply demonstrated the deficiencies of that Rule of Law version of justice, principally by showing that applying the same rule to different and unequal people (and rules by their nature imply at least a degree of general application), produces and reproduces inequality. Therefore, the 'big' question that may be asked concerns how this has arisen. How does this Rule of Law version of justice come, as the evidence suggests it does, to be the dominant received common sense in market capitalist societies. The standard or official answer to this question is that rules, which necessarily, at least in principle, treat people equivalently, appear good under market capitalism because it is under capitalism that we have at last recognised what was always and universally true but hitherto unrecognised, namely that as the American Declaration of Independence puts it 'that it is a self-evident truth that all men are created equal'. In short, the argument is that it is just to treat people equivalently because they are in fact equal.

An alternative and less counterfactual explanation, and one which builds on a Marxist theory of ideology, is that rules as a device for treating people equally, that is to say, as equivalents, come to appear right and just, and hence a source of legitimacy in capitalism, precisely because capitalism practically works on the basis of equivalent exchange, in so far as commodities exchange in the market for their equivalent. Thus, just as everyone, whether rich or poor, man or women, black or white, pays the same price for commodities in the marketplace, so in a world which is organised on the basis of market exchange justice will appear in the form of everyone paying the same price by being treated as equivalent, whatever their real differences. In other words, justice will appear in the form of rules.

What underpins this sort of account, we should note, is a theory of ideology which argues that the knowledges and ideas that we have about the world, in this case, our ideas of justice, primarily reflect the practical or material realities, which in this case are those of the market. This view, that Rule of Law justice is merely the practically adequate expression of market exchange, spans much of the political spectrum, for, albeit leading to very different conclusions, it is held by Marx and Hayek (Hayek, 1973 and 1976). Arguably, in the case of both authors, it leads, since it is based on the denial that justice is ever anything more than an expression of the underlying social relations, to a denial that justice is a critical tool for law or anything else. Indeed, more generally, one might note that, while some would argue that an ideology critique, such as that offered in this book, is inadequate if it fails to specify how, and on what basis, particular ideologies, such as that of the Rule of Law arise, theories of ideology which are too deterministic may leave no space for social criticism rather than social explanation.

Finally, having characterised the approach of this book as ideology critique and indicated how that can be and has been developed, it remains in this section to note how much the ideology critique that is presented here shares with that of which it offers a critique, namely the Rule of Law. Broadly, both the Rule of Law idea and the critique of it presented in this book adopt the Enlightenment or modernist view that reason can be used to criticise and resist unjustified power. Thus, historically, the Rule of Law ideas, particularly as they were expressed in the constitutional developments of the 17th and 18th centuries in England and elsewhere, emerged to challenge the legitimacy of traditional distributions of power, or in short to subject power to a test of reason. Thus, the essential modern meaning of the Rule of Law is that no exercise of state or other power is to be treated as legitimate unless it can be positively justified in terms of legal rules. Put differently, the Rule of Law sought the control of power by making the powers of the powerful explicit. This is the basic idea of constitutionalism. Similarly, we would suggest the critique of law that has been presented in this book seeks to control and resist power by making its exercise explicit, in this case by making explicit the hidden politics of law.

Further, not only do the Rule of Law and the critique of it presented in this book share a faith in the capacity of reason to control power but both adopt a similar idea of power, namely, that of power as something which people have or possess. Hence, they both deploy the same view of what the problem of power is, albeit directed to very different targets, namely that the problem of power is who has got it, how it is distributed and whether that distribution can be justified. For the defenders of the Rule of Law, power is sufficiently justified if it is justified in terms of existing rules; by contrast, the critique of the Rule of Law in this book demands a more substantive or real justification of power. It is in this belief in the ability of reason to resist power, which is the very hallmark of modernity, that the critique of law as ideology developed in this book reveals a common cause with the Rule of Law.

Criticising the 'big' ideas

This section will consider some criticisms of three of the particular big ideas advanced in this book, namely those of social constructionism, the relation of power and knowledge, and social justice, before turning to the contemporary unease with big ideas in general.

Social constructionism

In so far as Berger and Luckmann's social constructionism, on which this book has so heavily relied, is seen as an invitation to adopt a sceptical attitude to received understandings, then it is surely valuable. However, as a specific theory it is open to a number of major criticisms.

First, it should be noted that although Berger and Luckmann's theorising can be seen as making an important contribution to our understanding of how social order and stability is maintained in the absence of specific control mechanisms, such as law (in the form of actual or threatened force), yet in the final analysis their account answers the question of where social order comes from in terms of making certain assumptions about the very thing the thrust of the book seeks to deny, namely a universal human nature. Thus, for Berger and Luckmann, it is human nature to fear and abhor uncertainty and to seek an economy of psychological effort. Consequently, they argue that people in effect impose order on themselves by closing down the almost infinite possibilities which are theoretically open, and by accepting the order presented to them as the only possibility they thereby constitute it as reality. This approach may be questioned, not only because of its questionable assumptions about human nature – is it not equally human nature to seek freedom and innovation? – but also because, and as a consequence of those assumptions, it is unable to account for social change as opposed to social stability. Further, it can be argued that their analysis fails to account for the fact that societies differ in the degree of orderliness they display. This suggests that the universal human nature on which they rely may not be so universal after all.

Secondly, it can be argued that the social construction of reality explains too little, in that it fails to account for why particular versions of order and reality, rather than others, prevail in particular societies. Thus, for example, why in market capitalist societies does order appear in the legal form of rules, rights and property, etc? While one might reply that that was not their task, it nevertheless might be suggested that reliance on Berger and Luckmann sometimes involves a sleight of hand, in that it is tempting to think that in understanding *how* the common sense of law is maintained we know *why* that is the common sense. Certainly, as indicated earlier, social construction theory, arguably, only becomes politically interesting when linked to theories which do attempt to link dominant knowledges to particular social or other conditions.

Thirdly, and the other side of the coin of the argument that it explains too little is the argument that the social construction of reality, like the sociology of knowledge generally explains too much. Put differently, the theory that 'The social habitat of the thinker determines a whole system of opinions and theories which appear to him as unquestionably true or self evident' (Popper, 1945, 2, p 367) is a theory of such generality and adaptability that it cannot be falsified, rather, one might suggest, like the Azande witchcraft beliefs. Thus, while we might agree with Popper that the popularity of the ideas of the sociology of knowledge lies in 'The ease with which they can be applied, and in the satisfaction which they confer on those who see through things and the follies of the unenlightened' (Popper, 1945, 2, p 369) being popular does not, unless one adopts a purely consensual theory of truth (that is to say, one that equates truth with that on which there is a consensus), make them true. For those who would argue for a stronger theory of truth, the sociology of knowledge, by revealing all forms of knowledge, without considering the merits of their separate claims to truth, as equally capable of being explained in terms of their social origins, creates the danger that it tends to destroy the basis of rational discussion, for it tends to explain everything away. Grossly overstating it, the argument is that social constructionism while appearing to explain everything may end up explaining nothing.

Power and knowledge

Central to this book is the argument that that which passes for knowledge of reality, that is, that is knowledge of how things 'necessarily and naturally' are, is a means of exercising power over those who accept that knowledge or, in short, that such knowledge is a constraining, limiting or negative form of power. Now, while that view, expressed as a critique of the dogmas and prejudices and superstitions of the past, was a central message of the 18th century Enlightenment, equally, of course, was the contrary message that knowledge could be a constraint on power and a means of freeing people, literally from ignorance. What reconciled these two views of knowledge, in which knowledge could appear as both a means of power and as a constraint on power, was of course a distinction between true and false knowledge. Thus, while false knowledge constrained, true knowledge liberated, and it liberated precisely because its truth was the guarantee or warranty that it was not a form of power (Macintyre, 1985).

Though we have already noted how the sociology of knowledge tends to obliterate that distinction between false and true knowledges, by treating both as capable of being socially explained in the same way, the critique of common sense knowledge as a form of hidden power, one of the key messages of this book, crucially depends on the belief that one can identify a form of knowledge which is not also a form of power. Thus, to reveal that certain ways of knowing the world, for example, through legal concepts and categories like property and individual rights, is an exercise of power because it achieves results contrary to the apparent interests of certain groups, precisely because they do not realise that it is against their interests, is to claim to have knowledge of what people's true interests are (see Lukes, 1974). More than anything else, perhaps, it was on this claim that the world was until recently split; between liberals on the one hand who resisted the idea that we can question the revealed preferences of individuals as an expression of their true interests, and on the other hand those, principally socialists, who sometimes claimed that they had a more or less privileged, scientific and disinterested understanding of what people's real interests were; the basis of this claim of disinterestedness resting on the claim that their understanding represented the interests of humanity as such, or of a universal human interest. In the failure of Eastern European 'socialism', we can arguably see the failure of probably the most ambitious claim to have discovered such a powerfree, because disinterested, form of knowledge, and one which had in consequence the capacity to reveal how other forms of knowledge operated as forms of power.

Of course, long before the Berlin Wall came down, many contemporary thinkers, often drawing on Nietzsche, had rejected both the idea that there was such a thing as humanity, or a universal human interest, or a 'we' who could be dominated or liberated, and had accepted that there was therefore no form of knowledge that escaped from also being a form of power. Most influentially, the French scholar Michel Foucault has argued, beyond social constructionism, that since knowledges constitute reality, if all forms of knowledge are also forms of power, then reality is always and everywhere an effect of power (Foucault, 1980). Thus, contrary to the view of power which, as mentioned earlier, is shared by both the liberal defenders and the socialist critics of the Rule of Law that power is a negative constraining force and that in consequence the problem of power is about who possesses it. Foucault saw power as a positively constituting force. If, then, such things as the individual, natural rights and freedoms, humanity, the social, and all other grounding realities for different political positions were merely the effects of power/knowledges, then a critique of power in terms of them, such as liberalism and socialism had in different ways attempted, was simply not possible.

At the centre of this book has been the argument that, compared to the legal interpretation of the world, there is a less artificial or at least less limited or primary reality, and a more human way of living which is social and collective, and that this is reflected, for example, in more contextual forms of dispute resolution and in a more social idea of justice. The worrying thought that Foucault's writing engenders is how to argue for this if that too is merely an effect of power, in particular, if as has been argued, the idea or category of the social is seen to be merely the product of a particular form of discourse that emerged at a particular time in history.

Social justice

In opposition to the liberal position that the individual is morally as well as ontologically prior to the social, this book has indicated a clear preference for an idea of social justice, as opposed to an individual conception of justice, just as it has indicated a clear preference for the primacy of the social reality over the reality of legal individuals. Further, it might be suggested that the idea of social justice has been the single most important critical idea which has been used, not only in this book, but much more generally, to resist and question the form of justice embodied in the Rule of Law. Thus, against the Rule of Law version of justice, which essentially equates justice with fair play, in the form of everyone playing by the same game rules, social justice sees justice in terms of results or outcomes, and is concerned, with whether those outcomes, usually seen in terms of the relative distribution of wealth and power, can be justified in terms of merit, desert or some other criterion.

While there are clearly many on the left, including the authors of this book who still believe that the idea of social justice is a meaningful one, in recent years the very notion of social justice has come under very heavy criticism, particularly from the political right, whether Conservative of Labour. This has been significantly fuelled by the ability of such critics to point to what has been done in the name social justice in the 'socialist' regimes of Eastern Europe and the former Soviet Union. Hayek, for example, who has long been in the forefront of the campaign against social justice, argues that social justice is a dangerous myth, a myth because it has no agreed meaning or content, and dangerous precisely because, since it has no agreed meaning, it becomes the label under which those in power can impose on others their view of what is in the social good (Hayek, 1960 and 1976). This is, we should note, essentially the same criticism that this book has made about Rule of Law justice, namely, that it presents particular interests as universal interests. Thus, argues Hayek, rather than being the means of criticising and controlling unjustified power, social justice becomes, particularly in state socialist systems operating on the basis of command economies, a dominating mechanism of power.

Additionally, Hayek argues that it is particularly inappropriate to judge market outcomes, such as who becomes rich and who poor, in terms of social justice, since in market based societies such outcomes are not planned or intended, and in Hayek's view the term justice can only be properly applied to intentional or deliberate actions. Furthermore, claims Hayek, the realisation of social justice involves continual interference with the spontaneous order of the market with the consequent destruction of individual freedom and economic success, both of which are so evident in the former 'socialist' regimes of Eastern Europe.

However, one interprets the story of the collapse of those regimes, it is difficult to resist the conclusion that their fall was among other things, apparently, a major defeat for the idea that social justice could be the central organising principle of a society, rather than being a more or less marginal qualification on a spontaneous order operating under a set of general rules of fair play. This certainly seems the view of the Social Justice Commission in its report (Commission on Social Justice, 1994). (Here, however, it should be admitted that the authors are in disagreement. Another perspective is that the idea of social justice being a central organising principle of East European states is ludicrous. As we argue elsewhere, it was actually a manifestly inadequate legitimation of a political world characterised by repression and inequality.)

The idea of big ideas

While the primacy of social explanations and of social justice might have been the most obvious and immediate casualties of the fall of Eastern European socialism, many would see that fall as just a further stage in a much larger defeat, namely, the defeat of modernity, identified in this context with the ideas that we have both reason enough to understand the world, and to realise its improvement through conscious planning (Bauman, 1992). Though liberal critics, such as Popper (1945, 1) and Hayek (1944 and 1960), long railed against the destruction of the open society and its spontaneous orders by the ambitious social engineering that characterised modernity, it was only in the 1970s, as both

181

in the East and the West the failure of the planned society became increasingly undeniable, that the movement against treating the world as something to be organised by deliberate reason really gained momentum. In the worldwide move to the right which followed, the real casualty of the fall of Eastern European socialism became the idea that big ideas, rather than spontaneous orders, could contribute to progress.

The practical result of this has been, since no one has come up with a version of a spontaneous order other than the market, that leaving it to the market to arrange things and determine priorities, has everywhere increasingly become the order of the day. In particular, we should note that the attraction of this market order is that, among other things, rather than being shaped and directed by any particular big ideas, the market order responds to and incorporates the ideas, knowledges and preferences of all the individuals who make it up. Thus, as socialist parties, under labels like 'market socialism' or 'new realism', accept the necessity and the inevitability of the market order and the rules of the fair play idea of justice on which it depends, the recognition that this form of order, and this form of justice constitute only one possible version of order and justice looks increasingly anachronistic. If there really are no alternatives to the market capitalist order and Rule of Law justice, the revelation that their power over us, as this book has argued, largely resides in the fact that they close off alternative ways of seeing ceases to be revealing. We will return to this issue but, at this stage, it is important to recognise that the practical political critique of planned and social economic orders coming from the political right, tends to link up with the intellectual critique of modernity, post-modernism, to which we now turn, though this generally comes from the left, in that they both tend to lead back to the market.

The core sentiment of post-modernism in its many forms, the doubt of reason, has in a sense been present since the birth of the modern faith in reason in the enlightenment in the form of the recognition that, as we have noted, knowledge can be both a liberation and the form of domination; this being the dialectic of the enlightenment. What post-modernists assert, contrary to the defenders of modernity, is that the key to distinguishing liberating and dominating forms of reason and knowledge, in the form of some idea of truth, is simply not available, and that in consequence all the distinctions, such as those between appearance and reality, false and true consciousness, surface and depth, perceived interests and real interests, primary and secondary realities, etc, on which ideology critique ultimately depends, are revealed as merely rhetorical devices, which help to persuade, rather than as distinctions which can be rationally defended (for one critical account of post-modernism, see Norris, 1993).

The ways in which this doubt of reason have been expressed have been very numerous, ranging from Lyotard's grand announcement of the 'end of grand narratives' to simple demonstrations of the way knowledges operate as forms of power in particular situations (Lyotard, 1984). Particularly influential in recent years has been the approach usually called deconstructionism, which originated as a form of literary textual criticism but has increasingly been used to analyse texts like those of philosophy, sociology and more recently law, which make claims to truth. From one perspective, deconstructionism can be seen as pushing the idea of the relativism of truth one stage further than social constructionism. Thus, if one sees social constructionism, as developed, for example, by Berger and Luckmann, as a way of recognising the dependence of 'truth' on its social context (that is to say, demonstrating the social contingency of truth), deconstructionism, in seeking to give recognition to the dependence of all truth claims on the text in which they appear, aims to demonstrate the textual contingency of truth. This can be interpreted as meaning that there is no neutral language of truth which represents reality as it is, in the sense of making statements that correspond with reality, or rather that the idea of truth as that which corresponds with reality is impossible. Indeed, some would argue that the very distinction between reality and representation, fact and fiction is meaningless, thereby revealing the commonsense idea of truth as a correct statement about the world as itself a fiction, and also thereby suggesting that law is no more or less a translation or interpretation of reality than any other way of talking.

While many of these assertions are grossly overstated what they have engendered in the academic and intellectual world is an extreme suspicion about big ideas making claims to truth, such as those deriving from the tradition of ideology critique developed in this book. Furthermore, the relativism to which post-modernism leads tends to create on the left the paralysing paranoic fear I mentioned earlier, that they might be just replacing one dominating ideology for another. This effectively allows the market reality to prevail, and it is against this stark fact that we have to evaluate the contribution of big ideas today.

Conclusion

How, then, at the millennium are we to view big ideas, and in particular those developed in this book? Are we to view them simply as the remnants of a misplaced idealism and confidence that has some how managed to slip through from an earlier or more optimistic age? Or are we to see their modern day defenders in an all together more heroic light, as those who are keeping alive a vision in the face of an evermore demanding and monolithic reality? Clearly, to this big question there is no simple answer; indeed, one of the central arguments in this conclusion is that while there is a crucial, though not necessarily the hitherto peculiarly privileged, role for pursuing big questions, the events and developments of recent year should make us deeply suspicious of big, and particularly universalist, answers.

The reason why it is critical to continue to pose big questions like 'what is law?' or 'what is justice?' or 'what is the public interest?', while being deeply suspicious of big answers, is because such questions oppose what seems the most dominating power in peoples lives today, the realities of the market, which for most constitute the very facts of life. Big questions and big ideas oppose the market precisely because they open up vision, and the market stands fundamentally and irreconcilably opposed to vision. Whether one talks in terms of spontaneous orders, supply and demand, the forces of competition or responding to price signals, the most primal instinct that the market expresses is that the future should be determined by what happens, rather than by what is envisioned or planned in advance. Of course, socialists have sometimes given vision a bad name because the particular version of it adopted by most but not all of them (that of state socialism) arguably didn't work out. We should, however, not conclude from that that vision was a mistake, but rather that vision in the form of imposing a single big right answer was the mistake.

We should also note that the market not only, as it were on principle, stands against envisioning the future in advance but, in a whole host of more specific ways, it stands opposed to thinking big. For example, Adam Smith's famous argument that the pursuit of individual interests, 'as if by an invisible hand', will serve the public interest, becomes a positive argument against trying to answer the question of what is in the public interest. More immediately, it can be argued that, as the market mentality penetrates into more and more areas of life, and as access to the law and the services of a good song-dueller becomes increasingly just a matter of money, justice becomes just another commodity to be measured by its price, and law is reduced to merely being a collection of legal services. As this happens, and as law's empire is reduced to being that of a franchise of legal services, the big questions as to what law is and what justice itself is are simply dissolved away as irrelevant.

Many, and not just those on the political right, will see this dissolution or fragmentation of the big questions as positively liberating, and as freeing people to respond to small and more manageable issues like particular instances of wrong and injustice, or to engage in particular, and relatively narrow areas of research, without having to worry that they have got all the big theory, right. That this has happened is reflected not only in the narrowed focus of academic research agendas, which have increasingly retreated to the safety of disciplinary boundaries, but more importantly in the frequently noted worldwide move away from traditional political parties, with their broadly embracing agendas, in favour of single issue political groups and campaigns such as environmental pressure groups, and campaigns against particular pieces of legislation. This, many see as the new and post-modern form of politics.

The problem with this more fragmented approach is that, even though a few post-modernists may have announced the end of truth and of modernity, and proclaimed the impossibility of endeavours like those of Marx to uncover a coherent 'reality' behind the appearances of the capitalist, or indeed any, system, no one in the 'real' world seems to be listening. Thus, capitalism continues to operate in practice very much in the tradition of modernity as a coherent system, which means that generally, but not always, it will continue to defeat in the end the gains that fragmented research and single issue politics may temporarily make. In short, in our view to avoid the big questions in the belief that it is better to concentrate on the immediate and the particular is not only to adopt precisely the thinking small which the market encourages, but to forget the fact the market idea itself is a big idea, something that tends to be forgotten precisely because the market is so big and so ubiquitous it becomes almost invisible.

If the world wide triumph of the market in recent years is then for us the reason why we must continue to ask big questions, then the failure of state socialism is the reason why we should resist big answers. Going back to, perhaps, the central big idea of this book, that of the social construction of reality, the key essential message that idea was used to convey was the possibility of resisting the official knowledge of reality, of which the Rule of Law in our market capitalist society, which now of course means virtually the whole world, is such a central part. The problem is what to do with that possibility or, to put it crudely, with what knowledge do we replace the official knowledge if you consider such knowledge to be deficient, because it reflects the interests of some and not others. If one has a strong theory of ideology, as in certain versions of Marxism, with which to distinguish between true and false representations of reality, the answer is that one simply aims to ensure that the true knowledge of reality becomes the official version of reality. This is something perhaps which only has to be stated, at least against the background of 20th century history (Gulag Archipelagos and all), for the dangers to be obvious. Indeed, a recognition of such dangers is one of the main factors that leads to support for the liberal New Right answer, most forcibly argued by Hayek, namely, that of replacing centralised official knowledge with an arrangement which allows the maximum play for individual knowledges. This is, for Hayek, who believes that the greatest resource of a society is found in the separate knowledges of its members, the essential condition of freedom. It is also the basis of Hayek's central argument for the market, which is simply that, to a greater extent than any other system, the market enables individual knowledges to be used to the benefit of all.

Thus, while one response to the recognition of the knowledge/power problem, that arises from social constructionism, is to seek a strong theory of reality such as that offered by Marxism, at the other extreme, the response is to encourage the development and utilisation of individual knowledges by facilitating the market. If one takes seriously the deepening of that power/knowledge problem in post-modernism, for example, in the deconstructionist assertion that truth is merely the construct of language games, this seems to eliminate the strong theory of reality alternative, which is why most writers who would identify themselves as post-modernists, usually end up, more or less passively, supporting the small ideas, fragmented knowledges market solution.

However, the recognition that we are dominated by the knowledges we do not question cannot be used to defend the market order. For, although such an order does both resist centralised official knowledges, and gives a pivotal role to the utilisation of separate individual knowledges, it does so, as Hayek makes abundantly clear, only on condition that we passively and without question, submit to the moral and legal order of the market, because this is the order which has spontaneously evolved as a means of coordinating the actions of separate individuals. Thus, the condition of allowing for many knowledges, is that we accept that the knowledge tacitly embodied in the market, remains itself beyond question.

This is simply unacceptable, not only because of the implicit authoritarianism of this supposedly 'liberal' solution, but also because it ignores the fact that most of the socialist criticisms of market capitalism are no less correct just because attempts to establish a socialist alternative may have failed. In short, the failure of socialism only reveals market capitalism as successful in eliminating the opposition and not as right, and success is not a sufficient reason for putting the market order beyond question.

Hilary Wainwright, in a recent book (1994), written in response to the recognition that as state socialism has been swept away in Eastern Europe Hayek's ideas in particular have swept in, argues for an interesting socialist interpretation of Hayek's criticism of centralised official knowledge. Thus, she argues that while Hayek is right in resisting such centralised official knowledges, and in particular expert knowledges which claim to know best, which no doubt accounts for his popularity in Eastern Europe, he is wrong in identifying decentralised knowledges with the knowledge of individuals, because he makes 'the mistake of treating knowledge as an individual attribute, rather than as a social product' (1994, p 57).

Against this, Wainwright argues for a democratisation of knowledge, based on both a desire to give greater significance to individual understandings of the world, and a recognition that such understandings arise only in social processes. In a similar vein, one of us has argued elsewhere that Hayek totally ignores the part of argument, discussion, and conversation between people, as a source of knowledge and understanding (Thomson, 1991). Where this argument leads is to something of a third way between on the one hand knowledges, such as Marxist socialism, making universal truth claims, and on the other hand the fragmentation of individual knowledges characteristic of the market. That third way is to be found in the social knowledges, such as that of justice or the common interest, that arise when people, bringing their own particular experiences to bear, actively cooperate and communicate in response to the common problems of living together. While such knowledges can be described as socially constructed, they differ from Berger and Luckmann's socially constructed knowledges, which are essentially passively received knowledges, in that they actively involve people in consciously constructing their own knowledges for themselves. Indeed, it can be argued that, given the impossibility of universals, the most we can do in evaluating social knowledges is to discriminate in favour of those in the construction of which people have been active, as opposed to those which have been imposed.

Thus, given that people's experiences, as men and women, as black or white, as third world or first world citizen differ greatly, not to mention a whole host of more individualised differences, such knowledges will always be more or less local, and more or less restricted to particular groups, communities or contexts. Indeed, such social knowledge pluralism seems to be what the post-modern critique of modernity not only obliges us to accept, but in the form of differences, teaches us to value. What prevents it leading to a complete knowledge relativism is the application of the democratic criterion of people being involved in the construction of their own knowledges. Take, for example, the idea or knowledge of justice. While a modernist understanding of justice is essentially a search for a set of universal formulae to capture it, we would argue against this. We must resist the temptation to define justice for all, as opposed to allowing the many different views and voices of justice to emerge, as people define and discover for themselves, through communication, what justice means.

Both the liberal idea of justice as fair play, and the idea of social justice as fair shares, suffer from the same weakness, namely that they are insufficiently democratic. Thus, we would resist on this ground any assumption that social justice is in any sense more real or valid than any other interpretation of justice. In particular, we would suggest that the attempt to impose, or even to identify from the top, anything like a unitary idea of social justice, as opposed to creating the conditions under which people will find it necessary to engage in justice talk, and thereby create their own knowledges of justice, seems to create just the same problems that this book has sought to expose in relation to the Rule of Law idea of justice; namely, that it closes off other possibilities.

In conclusion, then, we would suggest that, in order to resist the world closure that all dominant forms of knowledge threaten to realise, it is critical that we continue to struggle with the big questions of the sort that have been the concern of this book, otherwise there is a very real possibility that the market knowledge of the world, which as we have suggested stands opposed to attempts to think big, will constitute such an irresistible reality as to create, at least for the time being, in Fukuyama's overworked phrase, the end of history

(Fukuyama, 1992). On the other hand, the lesson to be drawn from recent political and intellectual developments is that big answers, particularly those making claims to universality, are both intellectually unavailable and politically dangerous. Thus, we have suggested that between being dominated by universal answers, and being dominated by the fragmented knowledges of the market, there is a third way based on the recognition that the production of knowledge can be a collective and social process in a stronger and more active sense than Berger and Luckmann consider. In many groups and movements today, such as those of women, the disabled and those concerned with the environment we can perhaps see the beginnings of a new way in which people can be actively involved in their own knowledges together.

Most crucially, we would argue that people can, and in our socially constructing view should, be positively involved in creating their own knowledges of what justice means, not in the enlightenment sense of discovering the truth to encode it, but in the simple sense of creating ideas of justice to give ethical expression to what living together means in different particular circumstances. Thus, while the 'big' idea of social justice on which this book has relied is a vital idea to challenge the dominion of Rule of Law justice, there is no good reason for giving any one version of justice priority in advance. Indeed, we would argue more generally that we need to escape from seeing as central the dichotomy between the individual and the social, which dichotomy, among other things, leads to an increasingly sterile liberal versus communitarian debate.

While Justice is *the* critical idea for law, while endlessly posing the 'what is Justice?' question, we must resist the temptation of thinking we know what justice is. In finding ways of talking against the dominant conception of justice, that of the Rule of Law, this book has sought to keep open the question of 'what is Justice?', in the sense not only of insisting that we never stop asking it of law, but also in the sense of denying we can ever answer it.

Bibliography

Adams, P, *Odious Debts*, 1991, London: Earthscan

Anderson, K, 'Secular eschatologies and class interests', in Gustafson, C and Juviler, P, *Religion and Human Rights: Competing Claims?*, 1998, New York: ME Sharpe

Anderson, M, *Approaches to the History of the Western Family 1500–1914*, 1980, London: Macmillan

Arnot, M and Usborne, C (eds), *Gender and Crime in Modern Europe*, 1999, London: UCL

Atiyah, P, *Law and Modern Society*, 1983, Oxford: OUP

Auden, WH, 'Law is the law', in *Collected Shorter Poems*, 1966, London: Faber

Baker, J, *Arguing for Equality*, 1987, London: Verso

Bankowski, Z and Mungham, G, *Images of Law*, 1976, London: Routledge and Kegan Paul

Banton, M, *Roles*, 1965, London: Tavistock

Barber, B, *Jihad v McWorld: How Globalism and Tribalism are Reshaping the World*, 1995, New York: Ballantine

Barnett, H, *Sourcebook on Feminist Jurisprudence*, 1997, London: Cavendish Publishing

Barnett, H, *Introduction to Feminist Jurisprudence*, 1998, London: Cavendish Publishing

Barratt Brown, M, *Africa's Choices: After Thirty Years of the World Bank*, 1995, London: Penguin

Barrett, M and McIntosh, M, 'The family wage: some problems for socialists and feminists' (1980) 11 Capital and Class 51

Bauman, Z, 'Living without an alternative' (1992) 62 Political Quarterly 1

Beard, M, *Women as Force in History*, 1964, New York: Macmillan

Bentham, J, *Introduction to the Principles of Morals and Legislation*, 1879, Oxford: Clarendon

Berger, P, *Invitation to Sociology*, 1966, London: Penguin

Berger, P, *The Capitalist Revolution*, 1987, Aldershot: Gower

Berger, P and Luckmann, T, *The Social Construction of Reality*, 1967, Buckingham: Open University

Berman, H, *Law and Revolution*, 1983, Cambridge, MA: Harvard UP

Beveridge Report, Cmnd 6404, 1942, London: HMSO

Blackstone, W, *Commentaries on the Laws of England*, 1765–69, London: Dawsons

Bohannan, P, *Justice and Judgment among the Tiv*, 1957, London: OUP

Bonnerjea, B, 'Reminiscences of a Cheyenne Indian' (1935) Journal de la Société des Americanistes 27

Bottomley, A (ed), *Feminist Perspectives on the Foundational Subjects of Law*, 1996, London: Cavendish Publishing

Box, S, *Deviance, Reality and Society*, 2nd edn, 1981, London: Holt, Rinehart and Winston

Box, S, *Power, Crime and Mystification*, 1983, London: Tavistock

Branford, S and Kucinski, B, *The Debt Squads*, 1988, London: Zed

Britannica, The Encyclopaedia, 9th edn, 1875–89, Edinburgh: Adam and Charles Black

Brody, H, *Maps and Dreams*, 1981, London: Penguin

Brody, H, *The People's Land*, 1975, London: Penguin

Bromley, P, *Family Law*, 5th edn, 1976, London: Butterworths

Bronte, C, *Jane Eyre*, 1966, London: Penguin

Brown, G and Wright, T (eds), *Values Visions and Voices: An Anthology of Socialism*, 1995, Edinburgh: Mainstream

Brownjohn, A, 'Common sense', in McGough, R (ed), *Strictly Private: An Anthology of Poetry*, 1988, London: Penguin

Bunyan, J, Pilgrim's Progress, 1928, London: Noel Douglas

Chomsky, N, *On Power and Ideology*, 1987, Boston: South End

Chomsky, N, *Powers and Prospects: Reflections on Human Nature and the Social Order*, 1996, London: Pluto

Chomsky, N, *Profit Over People: Neoliberalism and Global Order*, 1999, New York: Seven Stories

Chomsky, N, *World Orders, Old and New*, 1994, London: Pluto

Chomsky, N, *Year 501: The Conquest Continues*, 1993, London: Verso

Clastres, P, *Society Against the State*, 1977, Oxford: Blackwells

Clifford, J and Marcus, G, *Writing Culture*, 1986, Berkeley, California: California UP

Conaghan, J and Mansell, W, *The Wrongs of Tort*, 2nd edn, 1999, London: Pluto

Coote, B, *The Trade Trap: Poverty and the Global Commodity Markets*, 2nd edn, 1996, Oxford: Oxfam

Cross, G, *Time and Money: The Making of Consumer Culture*, 1993, London: Routledge

Davidson, B, *The Black Man's Burden: Africa and the Curse of the Nation-State*, 1992, London: James Currey

Davidson, B, *The Search for Africa*, 1994, London: James Currey

Davies, M, *Delimiting the Law: 'Postmodernism' and the Politics of Law*, 1996, London: Pluto

Diamond, S, 'The Rule of Law versus the order of custom' (1971) 38 Social Research 42

Dicey, AV, *The Law of the Constitution (1885)*, 8th edn, 1927, London: Macmillan

Dickens, C, *Bleak House*, 1976, London: Penguin

Dickens, C, *Little Dorritt*, 1976, London: Penguin

Dickens, C, *Our Mutual Friend*, 1976, London: Penguin

Douzinas, C and Goodrich, P, *Politics, Postmodernity and Critical Legal Studies*, 1994, London: Routledge

Ekins, P *et al*, *Wealth Beyond Measure: An Atlas of New Economics*, 1992, London: Gaia

Elson, D and Pearson, R, 'Nimble fingers make light work: an analysis of women's employment in Third World export manufacturing' (1981) 7 Feminist Rev 87

Engels, F, *The Origin of the Family, Private Property and the State*, 1972, London: Lawrence & Wishart

Evans Pritchard, E, *The Nuer*, 1940, Oxford: Clarendon

Evans Pritchard, E, *Witchcraft, Oracles and Magic Among the Azande*, 1976, Oxford: Clarendon

Falk, R, 'The Haiti intervention: a dangerous precedent for the United Nations' (1995) 36 Harvard International LJ 341

Foucault, M, *Discipline and Punish: The Birth of the Prison*, 1980, London: Allen Lane

Fox, R, *Kinship and Marriage*, 1967, London: Penguin

Franck, T, *Fairness in International Law and Institutions*, 1995, Oxford: Clarendon

Franck, T, 'The emerging right to democratic governance' (1992) 86 The American Journal of International Law 46

Fredman, S, *Women and the Law*, 1997, Oxford: Clarendon

Fukuyama, F, *The End of History and the Last Man*, 1992, London: Hamish Hamilton

Fukuyama, F, *The Great Disruption: Human Nature and the Reconstruction of Social Order*, 1999, London: Profile

Fukuyama, F, *Trust: The Social Virtues and the Creation of Prosperity*, 1995, London: Hamish Hamilton

Galbraith, JK, *The Culture of Contentment*, 1992, New York: Houghton Mifflin

George, S, *A Fate Worse than Debt*, 1988, London: Penguin

George, S, *Debt Boomerang: How Third World Debt Harms us All*, 1992, London: Pluto

Gibbs, J, 'The Kpelle moot: a therapeutic model for the informal settlement of disputes', in Bohannan, P (ed), *Law and Warfare*, 1967, Garden City, New York: The Natural History Press

Goffmann, E, *Asylums*, 1968, London: Penguin

Golding, W, *Lord of the Flies*, 1964, New York: GP Putman

Goodale, J, *Tiwi Wives*, 1971, Seattle: Washington UP

Gorz, A, *Critique of Economic Reason*, 1989, London: Verso

Gray, K, *Elements of Land Law*, 1987, London: Butterworths

Graycar, R, *The Hidden Gender of Law*, 1990, Annandale, NSW: Federation

Greene, G, *The Third Man*, 1984, London: Faber

Grigg-Spall, I and Ireland, P (eds), *The Critical Lawyer's Handbook*, 1992, London: Pluto

Hair, P, *Before the Bawdy Court*, 1972, London: Elek

Hampton, C (ed), *A Radical Reader*, 1984, London: Penguin

Harris, M, *Cows, Pigs, Wars and Witches*, 1977, London: Fontana

Harrison, JFC, *The Common People*, 1984, London: Fontana

Harvey, D, *The Condition of Postmodernity*, 1989, Oxford: Blackwells

Hayek, F, *The Constitution of Liberty*, 1960, London: Routledge and Kegan Paul

Hayek, F, *Law, Legislation and Liberty*, Vol 1, *Rules and Order*, 1973, London: Routledge and Kegan Paul

Hayek, F, *Law Legislation and Liberty*, Vol 2, *The Mirage of Social Justice*, 1976, London: Routledge and Kegan Paul

Hayek, F, *The Road to Serfdom*, 1976, London: Routledge and Kegan Paul

Heitlinger, A, *Women and State Socialism*, 1979, London: Macmillan

Heller, J, *Catch 22*, 1962, London: Cape

Helmholz, R, *Marriage Litigation in England*, 1974, Cambridge: CUP

Hill, C, *Liberty Against the Law: Some 17th Century Controversies*, 1996, London: Allen Lane

Hindess, B, *Freedom, Equality, and the Market*, 1987, London: Tavistock

Hoebel, EA, *The Law of Primitive Man*, 1967, Cambridge, MA: Harvard UP

Holder, J (ed), *The Impact of Environmental Law in the United Kingdom*, 1997, Chichester: John Wiley

Human Development Report 1998, 1998, Oxford: OUP

Humphries, J, 'Protective legislation, the capitalist state and working class men: the case of the 1842 Mines Regulation Act' (1981) 7 Feminist Rev 1

Hunt, A and Wickham, G, *Foucault and Law*, 1994, London: Pluto

Ignatieff, M, 'Human rights: the midlife crisis' (1999) 46(9) New York Rev of Books 58

Ireland, P, 'Stakeholding in the global casino' (1997) 24 JLS 276

Illich, I, *Education*, 1971, New York: Syracuse UP

Jackson, J, *The Formation and Annulment of Marriage*, 1969, London: Butterworths

Johnson, D, 'Judicial regulation and administrative control: customary law and the Nuer' (1986) 27 Journal of African History 59

Kafka, F, *The Trial*, 1976, London: Secker and Warburg

Kahn, P, *The Cultural Study of Law*, 1999, Chicago, IL: Chicago UP

Kenny, C, 'Wife selling in England' (1929) 45 LQR 45

Kuhn, A and Wolpe, A, *Feminism and Materialism*, 1978, London: Routledge and Kegan Paul

Kuper, A, *The Invention of Primitive Society*, 1988, London: Routledge

Laing, RD, *The Politics of Experience*, 1967, London: Penguin

Laing, R and Esterson, A, *Sanity, Madness and the Family*, 1971, London: Penguin

Landes, D, *The Wealth and Poverty of Nations*, 1998, London: Little, Brown

Lawrence, P, *Road Belong Cargo*, 1964, Manchester: Manchester UP

Lazonick, W, 'The subjection of labour to capitalism: the rise of the capitalist system' (1978) 10 Rev of Radical Political Economics 1

Lee, R and Devore, I (eds), *Man the Hunter*, 1968, Chicago, IL: Aldine

Levi-Strauss, C, *The Elementary Structure of Kinship*, 1969, London: Eyre and Spottiswoode

Levi-Strauss, C, 'The family', in Shapiro H (ed), *Man Culture and Society*, 1971, London: OUP

Lewis, J, *Women in England 1870–1950*, 1984, Brighton: Wheatsheaf

Lewis, J, *Women in Britain since 1945*, 1992, Oxford: Blackwells

Lewis, N, *The Missionaries*, 1988, London: Secker and Warburg

Lim, H, 'Message from a rarely visited island: duress and lack of consent in marriage' (1996) 4 FLS 195

Llewellyn, K and Hoebel, E, *The Cheyenne Way*, 1941, Oklahoma City: Oklahoma UP

Lowe, R and Shaw, W, *Travellers: Voices of the New Age Nomads*, 1993, London: Fourth Estate

Lukes, S, *Power: A Radical View*, 1974, London: Macmillan

Luther, M, 'Table Talk', quoted in *Not in God's Image,* O'Faolain, J and Martines, L, 1973, London: Fontana

Luttwak, E, *Turbo-Capitalism: Winners and Losers in the Global Economy,* 1999, London: Orion Business

Lyotard, J, *The Postmodern Condition,* 1984, Manchester: Manchester UP

Macintyre, A, *After Virtue,* 2nd edn, 1985, London: Duckworth

Mackintosh, M, 'The sexual division of labour and the subordination of women', in Young, K, Walkowitz, C and McCullagh, R (eds), *Of Marriage and the Market,* 1981, London: CSE

Macpherson, CB, 'The meaning of property', in *Property: Mainstream and Critical Positions,* 1978, Oxford: Blackwells

Macpherson, CB, *The Political Theory of Possessive Individualism,* 1962, Oxford: OUP

Mair, L, *Marriage,* 1971, London: Penguin

Malinowski, B, *Crime and Custom in Savage Society,* 1926, London: Routledge and Kegan Paul

Malinowski, B, 'Parenthood – the basis of social structure', in Calverton, B and Schmalhausen, S (eds), *The New Generation,* 1930, New York: McCauley

Mannheim, K, *Ideology and Utopia,* 1936, London: Routledge and Kegan Paul

Mansell, W, 'Legal aspects of international debt' (1991) 18 JLS 381

Mansell, W and Scott, J, 'Why bother about a right to development' (1994) 21 JLS 171

Marcuse, H, *The Aesthetic Dimension: Towards A Critique Of Marxist Aesthetics,* 1970, London: Macmillan

Marx, K, 'Economic and philosophical manuscripts', in Collett, L, *Introduction to Marx: Early Writing,* 1975, London: Penguin

Marx, K, *Economic and Philosophical Manuscripts of 1844,* 1977, London: Progress

Maybury-Lewis, D, *Millennium: Tribal Wisdom and the Modern World,* 1992, New York: Viking

Menefee, S, 'A halter round her neck' (1978) New Society 181

Merrills, J, *International Dispute Settlement,* 3rd edn, 1998, Cambridge: CUP

Miller, L, *Global Order: Values and Power in International Politics,* 2nd edn, 1990, Boulder: Westview

Millman, G, *Around the World on a Trillion Dollars a Day: How Rebel Currency Traders Destroy Banks and Defy Governments,* 1995, London: Bantam

Monbiot, G, *No Man's Land,* 1994, London: Macmillan

Moore, S, *Law as Process,* 1978, Boston: Routledge and Kegan Paul

Moynihan, D, *On the Law of Nations,* 1990, Cambridge, MA: Harvard UP

Moynihan, D, *Secrecy: The American Experience,* 1998, New Haven: Yale UP

Mullan, B (ed), *RD Laing: Creative Destroyer,* 1997, London: Cassell

Murphy, C, *The Word According to Eve,* 1998, Harmondsworth: Penguin

Nicholson, D, 'Telling tales: gender discrimination, gender construction and battered women who kill' (1995) 3 FLS 185

Norris, C, *The Truth About Postmodernism*, 1993, Oxford: Blackwells

O'Donovan, K, 'Marriage: a sacred or profane love machine?' (1993) 1 FLS 75

O'Donovan, K, *Sexual Divisions in the Law*, 1985, London: Weidenfeld and Nicholson

O'Faolain, J and Martines, L, *Not in God's Image*, 1973, London: Fontana

Okin, S, *Justice, Gender and the Family*, 1989, New York: Basic

Ottenberg, S, 'Ibo oracles and intergroup relationships' (1958) 14 South Western Journal of Anthropology 295

Owen, A, *The Darkened Room*, 1989, London: Virago

Panitch, L and Leys, C (eds), *Global Capitalism Versus Democracy*, 1999, Suffolk: Merlin

Parkin, F, *Class Inequality and Political Order*, 1972, London: Paladin

Pascal, B, *Pensées Sur la Réligion et Sur Quelques Autres Sujets*, 1867, Paris: Garnier

Pashukanis, E, *Law and Marxism*, 1978, London: Ink Links

Pateman, C, *The Sexual Contract*, 1988, Cambridge: Polity

Pirsig, R, *Zen and the Art of Motorcycle Maintenance*, 1974, London: Bodley Head

Pollock, F and Maitland, F, *The History of English Law*, 1911, Cambridge: CUP

Popper, K, *The Open Society and its Enemies*, 1945, 1, London: Routledge and Kegan Paul

Popper, K, 'Against the sociology of knowledge', 1945, 2, in Miller, D (ed), *Popper Selections*, 1985, Princeton: Princeton UP

Proudhon, PJ, *What is Property?*, 1970, New York: Dover

Qureshi, A, *The World Trade Organisation*, 1996, Manchester: Manchester UP

Ramelson, M, *The Petticoat Rebellion*, 1967, London: Lawrence & Wishart

Reich, C, *Opposing the System*, 1995, London: Little, Brown

Rich, PB, *Race and Empire in British Politics*, 1986, Cambridge: CUP

Roberts, S, *Order and Dispute*, 1979, London: Penguin

Rosenhan, D, 'On being sane in insane places' (1973) Science 250

Rushdie, S, *Satanic Verses*, 1988, London: Viking

Sachs, A and Hoff Wilson, J, *Sexism and the Law*, 1978, Oxford: Martin Robertson

Sachs, W (ed), *The Development Dictionary: A Guide to Knowledge as Power*, 1992, London: Zed

Said, E, *Culture and Imperialism*, 1993, London: Chatto and Windus

Sayers, S, *Marxism and Human Nature*, 1998, London: Routledge

Schneir, M (ed), *The Vintage Book of Historical Feminism*, 1996, London: Vintage

Scott, J, *Development Dilemmas in the European Community*, 1995, Buckingham: Open University

Schiebinger, L, *Nature's Body*, 1993, Boston: Beacon

Seabrook, J, *The Myth of the Market*, 1990, Bideford: Green

Selznick, P, *The Moral Commonwealth*, 1992, Berkeley, California: California UP

Shaw, M (ed), *Man Does, Woman Is*, 1995, London: Faber and Faber

Simon, D, 'Master and servant', in Saville, J (ed), *Democracy and the Labour Movement*, 1954, London: Lawrence & Wishart

Simpson, S and Stone, J, *Cases and Readings in Law and Society*, Vols I–III, 1948, St Paul: West

Smart, C, *Feminism and the Power of Law*, 1989, London: Routledge

Smart, C (ed), *Regulating Womanhood*, 1992, London: Routledge

Smith, G, *The Last Years of the Monroe Doctrine*, 1994, New York: Hill and Wang

Solomon, R, *Money on the Move: The Revolution in International Finance since 1980*, 1999, Princeton: Princeton UP

Stenton, D, *The English Woman in History*, 1957, London: Allen and Unwin

Stetson, D, *Family Law and Women in England: A Woman's Issue*, 1982, Westport: Greenwood

Stone, L, *The Family, Sex and Marriage in England 1500–1800*, 1977, London: Weidenfeld and Nicholson

Stone, L, *Road to Divorce: England 1530–1987*, 1990, Oxford: OUP

Stone, L, *Uncertain Unions: Marriage in England 1660–1753*, 1992, Oxford: OUP

Strange, S, *Mad Money*, 1998, Manchester: Manchester UP

Stretton, T, *Women Waging Law in Elizabethan England*, 1998, Cambridge: CUP

Sturgess (Judge), 'Sayings of the week' (1928) *The Observer*, 22 July

Swift, J, *Gulliver's Travels*, 1959, Oxford: Blackwells

Szasz, R, *The Manufacture of Madness*, 1970, New York: Harper and Row

Tomasevski, K, *Development Aid and Human Rights Revisited*, 1993, London: Pinter

Thompson, EP, *The Poverty of Theory*, 1978, London: Merlin

Thompson, EP, 'Time, work discipline and industrial capitalism' (1967) 38 Past and Present 56

Thompson, EP, *Whigs and Hunters*, 1977, London: Penguin

Thompson, EP, *Writing by Candlelight*, 1980, London: Merlin

Thomson, A, 'Taking the right seriously: the case of FA Hayek', in Fitzpatrick, P, *Dangerous Supplements*, 1991, London: Pluto

Tomlinson, J, *Cultural Imperialism*, 1991, London: Pinter

Trainer, T, *Developed to Death*, 1989, London: Green Print

Tressell, R, *The Ragged Trousered Philanthropist*, 1965, St Alban's: Panther

Turnbull, C, *The Forest People*, 1984, London: Triad/Paladin

Unger, R, *Law in Modern Society*, 1976, New York: Free Press

United Nations Development Programme, *Human Development Report*, 1993, New York: OUP

Wade, E and Bradley, A, *Constitutional and Administrative Law*, 10th edn, 1984, London: Longman

Wainwright, H, *Arguments for a New Left*, 1994, Oxford: Blackwells

Watson, A, *The Limits of Independence: Relations Between States in the Modern World*, 1997, London: Routledge

Weart, S, *Never at War: Why Democracies Will Not Fight One Another*, 1998, New Haven: Yale UP

Weber, M, *The Protestant Ethic and the Spirit of Capitalism*, 1984, London: Allen and Unwin

Williams, M, 'Medico legal stories of female insanity' (1998) 6 FLS 3

Winfield, C, 'Factual sources for two episodes in *The Mayor of Casterbridge*', in *Nineteenth Century Fiction* Vol 25, 1970, Berkeley, California: California UP

World Bank, *World Bank Debt Tables 1989/90 First Supplement (1989)*, 1989, Washington DC: World Bank

World Bank, *World Debt Tables 1993/94*, 1993, Washington DC: World Bank

World Bank, *World Development Report: Infrastructure for Development*, 1994, New York: OUP

World Guide: An Alternative Reference to the Countries of Our Planet, 1999, Oxford: New Internationalist Publications

Wright, S, 'Patriarchal feminism and the law of the father' (1993) 1 FLS 115

Zinn, H, *A People's History of the United States*, 1980, London: Longman

Ziolkowski, T, *The Mirror of Justice: Literary Reflections of Legal Crises*, 1997, Princeton: Princeton UP